Second Edition

SALES MANAGER'S DESK BOOK

Gene Garofalo

PRENTICE HALL
Paramus, New Jersey 07652

Library of Congress Cataloging-in-Publication Data

Garofalo, Gene.
Sales manager's desk book / Gene Garofalo. — 2nd ed.
p. cm.
Includes bibliographical references.
ISBN 0-13-244625-1 (cloth)
1. Sales management—Handbooks, manuals, etc. I. Title.
HF5438.4.G37 1996 96-16098
658.8'1—dc20 CIP

Printed in the United States of America

10 9 8 7 6 5 4

For the "guys," Evan and Joshua. Come and play with Grandpa, guys.

ISBN 0-13-244625-1

PRENTICE HALL
Paramus, NJ 07652

On the World Wide Web at http://www.phdirect.com

Prentice-Hall International (UK) Limited, *London*
Prentice-Hall of Australia Pty. Limited, *Sydney*
Prentice-Hall Canada Inc., *Toronto*
Prentice-Hall Hispanoamericana, S.A., *Mexico*
Prentice-Hall of India Private Limited, *New Delhi*
Prentice-Hall of Japan, Inc., *Tokyo*
Simon & Schuster Asia Pte. Ltd., *Singapore*
Editora Prentice-Hall do Brasil, Ltda., *Rio de Janeiro*

CONTENTS

Foreword xxxi

CHAPTER 1
HOW TO HANDLE A MANAGERIAL ASSIGNMENT
1

Thinking Like a Manager 1
How to Be a Leader 1
A Short Definition of Management 2
The Best Way to Spend Management Time 2
Methods of Leadership 3
Management by Intimidation 4
Ten Characteristics Salespeople Love in Their Sales Managers 4
Developing a Sense of Style 5
Meeting New Staff Members 5
Group Meetings 6

Meeting the Staff One-on-One 6
The Manager's Personnel List 7
Conducting Staff Interviews with Good Performers 8
Conducting Staff Interviews with Nonquota Performers 8
Allowing the Staff to Interview the Manager 8
Points to Cover in Individual Meeting with Staff Members 9
Action Plans 10
The Gap 10
How to Analyze Last Year's Sales 10
How to Fill the Gap 11
What to Do When the Territory Salesperson Won't Commit to Goals 13
The Importance of Performance Reviews 14
How to Deal with Sales Problems 14
The Teamwork Concept in Sales 14
Where the Teamwork Concept Fail 15
Why It's Important to Build a Sense of Common Purpose 15
Six Steps to a Sense of Common Purpose 16
The Four Tried-and-True Motivators 16
Traits That Identify Management Potential 17
How to Establish Good Communication Links 17
Eight Steps to the Ideal Communication System 19

CHAPTER 2
HOW TO SET SALES PERFORMANCE STANDARDS
21

Evaluating Action Plans 21
The Value of the Review Process 21
Review Techniques 22
14 Points to Cover in a Review Meeting 22
Other Items on a Review Agenda 23
Three Forms to Help Salespeople Get Organized 23
What the Manager Gets Out of a Review Meeting 24

The Five Benefits of the Review Process 24
Management Preparation for Review Meetings 29
Review Questions That Pin Down the Evasive 29
Review of Remote Sales Personnel 30
Following Up the Review 30
The Sales Force's Attitude Toward Review Sessions 31
How to Make the Review Session a Positive Experience 31
How to Get Staff Members to Provide Accurate Information 32
When Reviews Aren't Necessary 32
How to Adjust Sales Targets 32
What to Do When Sales Targets Are Not on Schedule 33
What to Do About Noncorrectable Problems 33
When It's Time to Tell Top Management That Objectives Can't Be Met 34
When Not to Go to Management About Target Problems 34
A Summary of the Sales Review Process in 12 Easy Stages 34

Chapter 3 Your Company's Organizational and Political Structure 36

Why It's Important for the Manager to Understand the Organizational Structure in His or Her Company 36
The Definition of an Organization Chart 36
Two Typical Organization Charts 37
Getting Inside the Boxes on Organization Charts 37
The Facts and Fancies of Organization Charts 38
Sales Managers' Concerns About Organizational Structure 39
How to Cut Across Organizational Lines of Authority 39
A Quick-and-Easy Guide to Organizational Structure 40
The Organization of Sales and Marketing 41
Reengineering and Sales Management 42
The Fundamental Differences Between Sales and Marketing 42

Field Sales Reporting Structures 42
The Chain-of-Command Concept 43
The Importance of Loyalty 43
How to Regard Your Relationship with Your Boss 44
The Rewards for Loyalty 44
How to Work with the People in the Home Office 44
A Seven-Point List That Will Make Any Field Manager a Home Office Darling 45
A Short Course in Office Politics 46
What Office Skirmishes Are All About 46
How Office Politics Affects the Ambitious Sales Manager 47
What to Do If the Boss Is Out of Favor 47
Downsizing: Eight Signs That Suggest It's Time for a Sales Manager to Start Sending Out Resumés 48
A Summary of Company Politics 50

CHAPTER 4 HOW TO BUILD A REPORTING SYSTEM THAT WORKS 51

Why Salespeople Don't Like to Fill Out Reports 51
Why Management Needs Reports 51
The Secret to Setting Up a Successful Reporting System 52
Why Reports Should Be Reviewed Periodically 52
What Kinds of Reports Are Absolutely Necessary 53
Two Vital Sales Historical Records 53
The Sales Itinerary Sheet 56
Why the Sales Itinerary Sheet Is Vital to the Manager 56
The Infamous Call Report: Why Salespeople Hate It 57
Three Kinds of Call Reports 57
The Detailed Report 58
The Summary Report 60
The Narrative Report 60
How to Design Your Own Call Report 63

How to Read a Call Report: Ten Things the Manager Can Learn 63
The Kinds of Sales Reports That Should Be Most Carefully Read 63
How to Ensure That Sales Reports Will Be Turned In on Time 65
Three Ways to Handle Late Report Die-Hards 66
How Call Reports Benefit Salespeople 67
How to Use Call Reports as a Reeducation Tool 68
How to Use Call Reports to Unmask the Nonworking Salesperson 68
Why the Nonworking Salesperson May Be Difficult to Spot 69
Four Call Report Clues to the Nonworker 69
Ten More Ways to Detect the Nonworker 70
What to Do About Nonworkers Once You Find Them Out 71
When Call Reports Should Be Verified 72
Six Signs That Point to a Phony Call Report 72
How to Verify Call Report Entries 73
When Checking Up, Leave Room for Doubt 74
The Difference Between the Lazy and the Nonworking Salesperson 74
Chapter Summary 74

CHAPTER 5
HOW TO FIND AND HIRE SALESPEOPLE WHO CAN SELL
75

When It May Be Time to Add New Salespeople 75
How to Pick the Right Moment to Add to a Sales Staff 75
Five Specific Signs That Will Help Convince Senior Management That More Staff Is Needed 76
The Seven Points to Cover on a Sales Personnel Requisition 77
Why Recruiting Is the Toughest Job a Sales Manager Has 78
The Difficulty of Judging Sales Talent 80
Why Sales Talent Can't Be Measured 80

Why Hiring Mistakes Are Expensive 80
How to Lower the Odds of Making a Hiring Mistake 81
Where to Find Qualified Sales Talent 81
Why the Sales Talent Search Should Begin at Home 81
How to Use Professional Connections to Find Sales Talent 82
How to Find Sales Talent Through Referrals 82
When Looking for Sales Talent Don't Forget About Retreads 83
Prospecting for Free 83
Prospecting on the Internet 83
Other Free or Low-Cost Possibilities for a Sales Talent Search 83
The Kind of Talent Search a Sales Manager Shouldn't Make 84
How to Find Sales Talent by Spending Money 84
How to Find Sales Talent by Advertising for It 85
How to Write a Sales-Help-Wanted Ad 85
Use Proven Ads When They're Available 86
The Eight Specifics That Should Be Included in a Sales-Help-Wanted Ad 86
A Sample Sales-Help-Wanted Ad That Gets Results 87
The Kind of Responses That Can Be Expected from a Sales-Help-Wanted Ad 88
Six Tips to Help Sort Through Resumés to Find Qualified Applicants 88
How to Decipher Résumé Language 89
How to Reduce the Applicants to a Manageable Number 91
How to Screen Applicants: Ten Things to Look For 91
Why First Impressions Don't Mean Everything 92
How to Match the Applicant to the Opportunity 92
What Information the Manager Wants to Get Across at Initial Interviews 92
What Information the Manager Wants to Obtain from Initial Interviews 93
The Worst Hiring Mistake a Sales Manager Can Make 93
Eight Clues to Help Uncover a Job Hopper 94
How to Conduct Follow-up Interviews with Job Candidates 94

Three Questions Managers Should Ask Themselves About Job Candidates 95
Rating Job Candidates on Intangible Factors 95
The Most Desirable Trait a Prospective Salesperson Can Have 96
"Tiebreakers" When It's Difficult to Choose Between Job Applicants 96
Getting Senior Management Approval Before Selecting Job Candidates 96
How to Make the Job Offer 97
Why Background Investigations Are Necessary 97
Background Investigation Courtesy 97
Three Basic Questions to Ask on a Background Check 98
One Question That Shouldn't Be Asked on a Background Check 99
How to Find Out What a Previous Employer Really Thinks About a Job Candidate 99
The Probing Questions to Ask About a Job Candidate 100
The One Essential Question That Must Be Asked About a Job Applicant 100
Using Other Resources to Check on Job Applicants 100
The Legal Implications of a Formal Offer 101
Nine Points to Include in an Offer Letter 101
Three Sample Job Offer Letters 102
Chapter Summary 104

CHAPTER 6 HOW TO ESTABLISH COMPENSATION PLANS 105

The Difficulty of Developing Good Sales Compensation Plans 105
The Four Basic Objectives of a Sales Compensation Plan 105
Four Secondary Objectives of a Sales Compensation Plan 106
Six Things Salespeople Like to See in Compensation Plans 107
Management and Staff's Common Compensation Goals 107

How Overmanaging Gets in the Way of Establishing Equitable Compensation Plans 108
Using Incentive Compensation 108
The Questions Regarding Compensation and Motivation 108
The Six Most Common Sales Compensation Arrangements 109
Straight Commission 109
Straight Salary 110
Draw Against Commission 110
Salary Plus Commission 111
Salary Plus Bonus 111
Salary Plus Commission Plus Draw 111
Other Types of Compensation Plans 112
Sales Managers' Compensation 112
The Manager with a Territory 113
The Key to Picking a Sales Compensation Plan for Your Company 113
The Biggest Mistake Managers Make When Developing Compensation Plans 113
Compensation Plan Objectives Summary 114
House Accounts: Why They're Usually a Bad Idea 114
Five Reasons Why a House Account Is Sometimes Necessary 115
One Bad Reason to Establish a House Account 115
Why House Accounts Should Be Examined Regularly 116
Field Management Responsibility for House Accounts 116
How to Compensate a Salesperson for a House Account 116
The Reasons for Sales Contests 117
12 Rules to Follow When Setting Up Sales Contests 117
Sales Contest Prizes 118
Merchandise and Trip Prizes 119
Five Tips on How to Get the Most Value for the Sales Promotion Dollar 119
Three Ways to Keep Sales Rolling In After the Contest Is Over 120
Why Managers Make the Mistake of Trying to Do Everything Themselves 120
Motivating the Manager to Manage 121

The Mistake Many Companies Make When Promoting to Management 121
The Four Basic Rules That Will Motivate Managers to Manage 122
A Chapter Summary of Sales Compensation Plan Objectives 122

CHAPTER 7 HOW TO CONTROL SALES EXPENSES 124

Typical Sales Management Attitudes Toward Expenses 124
Why Budget Preparation Is Not a Pleasant Task 124
Why Expense Controls Are Necessary 125
Six Items That Go into a Typical Sales Branch Operating Budget 125
How Budgets Are Prepared and Calculated: A Typical Worksheet 126
The Importance of Accurately Forecasting Costs 126
Why Expense Forecasts Help Senior Management 126
The Sales Manager's Function as a Controller and Why It's Important 128
The Branch, District, or Regional Office as a Profit Center 128
When the Home Office Prepares the Field Operating Budget 129
How to Prepare a Field Operating Budget 129
The Best Budget a Manager Can Develop 130
Eight Questions to Ask When Starting to Prepare a Budget 130
Why the Sales Staff Should Prepare Their Own Budgets 131
Give Staff Members Budget Guidelines 131
One Expense Item That's Always Under a Manager's Direct Control 132
How to Control Travel Expenses 132
The Surefire Method to Control Expenses 132
Controlling Expenses Through Allowances 132
Paying Expenses on a Discretionary Basis 133
Complete Expense Reimbursement 133
Why Reimbursement Systems Must Be Controlled 134

The Expense Report Form as a Control Tool 134
Two Sample Expense Report Forms 134
How to Handle the Salesperson Who Is Chronically Late Turning In Expense Reports 137
The Ten Typical Items on a Travel-and-Entertainment Expense Report 137
Five Specific Steps Toward Expense Control 138
Expense Control Through Per Diem 139
How to Control Expenses by Exception 139
Ten Signs That Point to a Phony Expense Claim 139
How to Verify Individual Expense Items 140
Charting Mileage Expense Claims 141
Verifying Travel Itineraries 141
Checking Up on Actual Amounts Spent 141
How to Handle the Bogus Expense Claim 142
What to Do About the Company's Big Spender 143
Using a Bonus Plan to Control Expenses: Sample Scales 143
Four Warning Signs That Indicate Expenses May Be Out of Control 144
Six Steps for Getting an Out-of-Control Budget Back on Track 144
Expense Control: A Key to Promotion 145
Chapter Summary 145

CHAPTER 8
HOW TO MAKE UP NEXT YEAR'S SALES FORECAST
146

What a Sales Forecast Is 146
Why Forecasts Are Vital 146
The Problem of Forecasting a Full Year in Advance 147
The Three Classical Methods of Forecasting 147
The Easiest Way to Forecast 147
How to Use Historical Data as a Basis for a Sales Forecast 148
The Benefits of a Historical Chart 150
Using Variable Data to Fine-tune a Sales Forecast: A List of Six Common Variables 150

What Data Not to Include in a Sales Forecast 151
The Role of Art in Forecasting 151
How to Use Sales Staff Members to Help Prepare Accurate Forecasts 152
Why the Field Sales Force Is the Best Source for Accurate Forecasts 153
Using National Accounts as a Forecasting Barometer 153
Instructing the Field Sales Force in How to Make a Forecast: A Forecasting Chart 153
Why Field Forecasting Charts Measure More Than Business Potential 154
Avoiding Blue-Sky Forecasts 154
Avoiding Pessimistic Forecasts 154
Comparing Forecast Data 156
What to Do When Forecasts Don't Agree 156
Adjusting Forecasts 157
The Give-and-Take of Forecast Meetings 157
Using Networking to Make Sales Forecasts: The Delphi Method 158
The Most Critical Factor in Forecasting 158
Ten Actions to Take During a Sales Drought 159
What to Do When a Forecast Is off the Mark 160
Why Midyear Corrections Are Sometimes Necessary 160
How to Sell Senior Management That a Midyear Correction Is Necessary 161
How to Make a Midyear Forecast 161
An Important Tip About Midyear Corrections 162
What Managers Can Do When They Have No Input into Their Sales Targets 162
How to Raise an Objection to an Unreasonable Sales Forecast 163
What to Do When Objections over Quota Assignments Are Ignored 164
How to Negotiate Goals with Senior Management 164
What to Do When the Sales Staff Says Next Year's Sales Goals Can't Be Met 165

Answering Objections to Quota Assignments 165
What to Do When a Salesperson Can Prove That a Quota Assignment Is Too High 166
The Last Word on Forecasts and Quota Assignments 166

CHAPTER 9
HOW TO SET UP BRANCH, DISTRICT, AND REGIONAL OFFICES
167

The Argument Against Office Space for Sales Representatives 167
Seven Reasons Why Branch Office Space Becomes Necessary 167
Shared Facilities: A Popular New Approach to the Sales Office Space Problem 168
What Shared Facilities Offer 169
When Shared Facilities Are the Best Solution to the Sales Office Space Problem 169
The Ten Signs That Tell the Manager Exactly When a Branch Office Is Necessary 169
Ten Questions That Help the Manager Establish a Branch Office Location 170
Getting Help to Acquire Field Office Space 171
Using a Commercial Real Estate Agent 171
How to Calculate the Costs for Office Space 172
Additional Office Costs 172
Lessor Concessions 172
How to Negotiate a Good Office Lease 173
The Legalities of the Commercial Office Lease Form 173
The Mechanics of Running a Field Sales Office 177
Seven Things That Must Be Done Before a New Sales Office Is Opened 177
The Physical Move into a New Sales Office 180
Smoothing Out the Details 181
Chapter Summary 181

Chapter 10
Communications Technology and the Sales Manager
182

The Changing Dynamics of the Field Sales Force 182
Electronic Communications 101 183
Why On-line Communications Between Customer and Supplier Means Less Control for the Account Salesperson 186
The End of the Weekly Sales Meeting? 187
Should Salespeople Come into the Office? 188
Three Advantages of Outside Salespeople Working Out of Their Homes 188
Three Disadvantages of Outside Salespeople Working Out of Their Homes 189
Nine Things to Consider When Furnishing an In-Home Office 190
The "Soft" Costs of Too Much Equipment 192
The Overriding Consideration When Selecting Equipment for Reps Who Will Be Working Out of Their Homes 192
Establishing a Database 192
What Goes into a Database 193
Seven Places to Obtain a Database If You Don't Have One 194
Six Ways to Create Your Own Database 195
Four Suggestions for Selling by Fax Machine 196
The Internet 196
Access to the Internet 198
Soliciting on the Internet 198
Electronic Bulletin Boards 198
The World Wide Web 199
The Difference Between the Web and Bulletin Boards 199
Electronic Catalogs 200
How to Start Marketing on the Internet: Eight Things to Know 200
The Information Superhighway 201
Home Shopping Networks 201
Chapter Summary 202

Chapter 11
How to Develop a Sales-Training Program
203

The Value of Sales Training 203
The Manager's Responsibility Toward Sales Training 203
The Ten Reasons Why Continuous Sales Training Is Necessary 204
Why Managers Should Begin Training Programs with Themselves 205
Formalized Training Programs 206
What to Expect from a Formalized Training Program 206
What Managers Teach During Sales Training Courses and Where They Teach It 207
The Classroom 207
How to Present Sales-Training Material 207
The Least Successful Teaching Techniques 207
How to Get Students Involved in the Course Material 208
Using Case Studies as a Teaching Tool 208
Using Competitive Spirit to Make Classroom Work Challenging 208
Role-playing as an Overrated Teaching Tool 208
Six Topics That Should Be Included in a Basic Sales-Training Class 209
The Length of Classroom Training 210
Scheduling Multiple Training Sessions 210
Why Classroom Training Is Never Enough 210
Field Training: Five Reasons Why Managers Shouldn't Put Raw Recruits with Old Pros 211
Who Has the Primary Responsibility for Field Training? 211
Three Things Not to Do as a Field Trainer 212
The Proper Way to Conduct Field Training 212
The Field Trainer as a Coach 213
Joint Calls 213
Why "Rescuing" Is a Bad Idea 213

Using Questions as a Training Tool: Ten Prompting Questions That Help a Sales Trainee Plan a Sales Call 214
How to Handle a Sales Call with a Sales Trainee: Three Things to Remember 215
A Manager's 14-Point Checklist to Help Critique a Trainee's Sales Call 215
After the Call Is Over 216
Eight Prompting Questions That Help a Trainee Plot Call Strategy 216
How to Handle the Critiquing Session: Using the Observation/Question Technique 218
Why It's Important Not to Be Overly Critical 219
Five Ways to Suggest Actions Needed for a Trainee's Improvement 219
Four Suggestions on Reinforcing Good Habits 220
The Six Stages in Selling and Buying Cycles 221
Ways to Relieve Pressure During a Field Training Session 222
How to End a Day's Field Training Session 222
Training Programs for Veteran Salespeople 222
Rules When Retraining Old Pros 223
How to Retrain the Old Pro Who Has Gone Stale 223
Three Easy Training Pills for the Old Pro to Swallow 223
Field Training the Veteran Salesperson 224
Setting Training Objectives for Veterans: Sample Dialogues That Won't Bruise Egos 225
Using a Sales Trainee to Retrain an Old Pro 225
Going Back to Basics: The Ultimate Training Tool for Veterans and Rookies Alike 225
The Status of Sales Training in Many Small Companies 225
How a Small Company Can Set Up and Run an Effective Sales-Training Program 226
Seminars 226
The Sales Evangelists 226
How to Check Out a Seminar 227
Subscribing to Sales Journals and Bulletins 227
Using Local Educational Facilities as a Training Tool 227
The Sales Manager as an Educator 227
The Two "Nevers" in Sales Training 228

Chapter 12
How to Motivate Sales Personnel
229

What Motivation Is All About 229
Some Questions on the Need for Motivation 230
Compensation and Fear as Motivators 230
Why Motivating People Is a Difficult Problem 231
Using Motivational Techniques Based on Human Nature 231
One Assumption to Make When Developing Motivation Programs 231
The Manager's Job as Motivator 232
18 Things, Other Than Money, That Motivate People to Perform Better 232
The Manager's Attitude as Motivator 236
Sales Contests: A Quick-Fix for Slow Sales 236
Contest Time Periods 236
Contest Objectives 236
Simple Sales Contests 237
The Most Common Type of Sales Contest 237
Merchandise Prizes 238
Publicizing the Contest Results 238
Contests Focused on Profit 238
Team Sales Contests 238
How to Get the Most Dollar Value Out of a Contest 239
How to Keep Sales Coming in After the Contest Is Over 239
How to Use the Promise of Promotion as a Motivational Tool 240
Assessing Promotion Possibilities 240
When a Good Salesperson Isn't Management Material 241
Holding Back a Promotion 241
What to Do When There Are Two Good Management Candidates 241
What to Do When There Are Few Opportunities for Promotion 242
Why It's Wrong to Give False Hopes About Promotion Opportunities 242
How Managers Can Motivate Themselves 242

The First Step in Self-motivation 243
Selecting Different Kinds of Goals 243
Motivation Through Personnel Improvement 243
Motivation Through Competition 244
Motivation Through Wielding Influence 244
A Summary on Self-motivation 244

CHAPTER 13 HOW TO RUN A SALES MEETING 245

The Essential Ingredient in Every Sales Meeting 245
The Seven Common Reasons for Calling a Sales Meeting 245
Know the True Cost of a Sales Meeting 246
How to Determine the Kind of Meeting You Want to Hold 246
Why the Kind of Meeting Determines Its Structure 247
The Small Office Meeting 247
The Negative Implications of an Office Meeting 247
The Advantages of Moving Meetings Out of the Office 248
Calling the Larger Meeting 248
Six Advantages to Planning a Meeting Far in Advance 248
Site Selection for Sales Meetings 249
Travel Arrangements 249
Hotel Accommodations 250
A Short List of Meeting Requirements 250
Inspecting the Site of the Meeting 250
Meeting-Room Size 251
Scheduling 251
How to Arrange the Seating 251
Sound Systems and Other Meeting Props 252
Four Questions to Ask Yourself When Developing a Meeting's Agenda 253
A Typical Meeting Agenda 253

Five Reasons Why It's Important to Use Different Speakers at a Meeting 255
Breaking Up a Sales Meeting into Specialized Sessions 255
Sales Meetings Evening Sessions 256
Scheduling the Meeting's Breaks 256
Private Meetings 256
Food and Beverage Service 257
Using the Hotel's Catering and Convention Services 257
Some Details That Can Make for a Successful Meeting 258
How to Address a Meeting 258
13 Tips on Speaking Before an Audience 259
Why Meetings Don't Run on Schedule 260
Four Tricks for Keeping a Meeting on Schedule 260
The Teleconference 261
Five Instances When Teleconferences Are Appropriate 262
13 Tips for Making a Teleconference a Success 262
Some Final Thoughts on Sales Meetings 264

CHAPTER 14
HOW TO RUN TRADE SHOWS AND CONVENTIONS
265

Brief History of Trade Shows 265
Making a Big Splash at a Trade Show 265
Why Managers Must Prepare for Trade Show Management 266
Eight Typical Costs Associated with Trade Shows 266
Why Companies Exhibit at Trade Shows: The Return on Money Spent 268
Seven More Reasons Why Companies Participate in Trade Shows 268
The Economy of Trade Shows 269
The Key to a Successful Trade Show 270
The 22 Planning Steps Necessary to Make Trade Show Participation a Success 270

Preparing Sales Reps for Trade Shows 274
The 11 "Musts" for Sales Personnel Working a Trade Show Booth 274
Leads: The "Product" of a Trade Show 276
The Ten Essential Points to Cover in a Trade Show Lead Card 276
A Sample Lead Form 277
The Importance of an Immediate Review of Lead Cards 278
Distributing Trade Show Leads 278
A Sample Trade Show Follow-up Letter 278
Postshow Strategy 279
The Trade Show Payoff 280
A Summary on Trade Shows 280

CHAPTER 15
HOW TO DEAL WITH SUBPAR PERFORMERS
281

Sales Performance Is Easy to Measure 281
The Ten Early-Warning Signs of Poor Performance 281
What to Do with a Classic Nonperformer 284
Classic Nonperformance Is Rare; Subpar Performance Isn't 284
How to Begin Changing Poor Performance 284
Every Manager's Four Primary Responsibilities Regarding the Performance of Staff Members 284
Why Managers Can't Complain About Poor Performance 285
The First Rule in Dealing with Subpar Performers 285
Setting Higher Expectations: The Gateway to Improved Performance 285
Raising Potential 286
How to Get More Output from Salespeople 286
How to Encourage Staff Members to Set Higher Standards for Themselves 286
A Sample Dialogue with a Salesperson on a Performance Issue 287
What the Dialogue Demonstrated 288

Setting Incremental Goals: A Nine-Step Program 288
Spending Time Improving Performance Where It Will Show the Best Results 289
A Five-Step Program That Will Improve Staff Performance by 25 Percent 290
Burnout 290
Why Performances Fall Off 290
Confronting Subpar Performers 291
Eliminating Probable Causes for Subpar Performance 291
Treading on Dangerous Ground: Intruding into the Private Life of an Employee to Determine Causes for Subpar Performance 291
Some Less Obvious Reasons for Burnout 292
Some Quick-Fix Solutions for Burnout 292
Going Back to Basics: A Six-Step Solution to Burnout 293
The Cure for Sales Lethargy 294
What Actions Not to Take When Faced with Subpar Performance 294
What to Do When Disappointed in Results 294
When Termination Is Necessary 295
The Legal Side of Termination 295
Putting an Employee on Probation 295
How to Handle an Employee Termination 296
A Sample Termination Letter 296
Chapter Summary 300

CHAPTER 16 HOW TO SELL THROUGH DEALERS, DISTRIBUTORS, AND MANUFACTURERS 301

Three Different Distributing Systems 301
Why Indirect Marketing Channels Are Important 301

The Advantages of Direct Marketing 302
The Disadvantages of Direct Marketing 302
Marketing Trends 302
The Advantages of Using Indirect-Marketing Channels 302
The Disadvantages of Using Indirect-Marketing Channels 303
How Dealers Function 303
How Dealers Sell 304
Product Exclusivity and Dealers 304
The Objectives When Selling Products Through a Dealer Organization 304
One Big Problem with Selling Through Dealers 305
Required Sales Support for a Dealer Network 305
Ten Characteristics That Make for a Good Dealer 305
Where to Find Good Dealers 306
How to Recruit Good Dealers 307
The Irresistible Enticement for a Dealer 307
Good Profit Margins Never Scare Dealers Away 308
Dealer Attitudes Toward Price Cutting 308
Establishing Sales Prices 308
Product and Profitability: The Real Keys to a Good Dealer Network 309
A Ten-Point Program Designed to Attract Dealers and Establish a Good Dealer Network 309
A Sample Dealer Agreement 311
How Distributors Function 312
The Changing Role of Distributors 312
Why Manufacturers Need Distributors 312
How Distributors Sell 313
How to Attract a Good Distributor: Four Requirements 313
Are Distributors Really Useful? 313
How Manufacturers' Representatives Function 314
The Profile for a Manufacturer's Rep 314

How Manufacturers' Reps Are Compensated 314
The Advantages of Using a Repping Outfit 315
The Disadvantages of Using a Repping Outfit 315
Mixing Reps with Direct Salespeople 316
Five Ways to Find Good Manufacturers' Reps 316
Chapter Summary 317

Chapter 17
Shifting Sales Channels and the Phenomenon of Mass Distribution
318

Definition of a Sales Channel 318
Why Sales Channels Are Important 319
Using Multiple Channels to Distribute Products 319
Ten Typical Sales Channels 320
The Six Basic Rules for Moving Product into Any Channel 322
Shifting Distribution Channels 323
The Impact of Channel Realignment on Suppliers 324
11 Warning Signs to Determine If Your Sales Channels Are in Trouble 324
Four Reasons Why Sales Channels Fail 326
Distributors' New Muscle 327
How Distribution Giants Function 327
Distribution Niches 328
How to Sell to the New National Distributors: A Ten-Point Program 329
Are the New Distribution Channels Set in Concrete? 331
The Reaction Against Mass-Merchant Distributors 332
Chapter Summary 332

Chapter 18
How to Use Advertising Effectively
333

Local Advertising 333
The Local Advertising World 333
Advertising to Satisfy Demand 334
The First Management Consideration About Advertising 334
Six Questions Managers Must Ask Before Developing an Advertising Program 334
The Big Question of the Advertising Budget 335
Three Ways of Calculating an Advertising Budget 335
How the Calculations Work 336
The Problem with Using a Percentage of Sales to Develop an Ad Budget 336
When Using a Percentage of Anticipated Sales for Budget Preparation Works to the Advantage of the Manager 336
Other Kinds of Ad Budget Calculations 336
How to Develop an Ad Budget That Top Management Won't Shoot Down 337
A Sample Advertising Budget 337
Where Advertising Money Is Best Spent: Advertising Media 337
Newspapers and Magazines 339
The Advantages of Newspaper Advertising 340
The Disadvantages of Newspaper Advertising 340
The Cost of Newspaper Advertising 340
Positioning a Newspaper Advertisement 341
Designing a Newspaper Ad 341
Five Design Tips That Help a Newspaper Ad Look Professional 342
Repetition: The Key to a Successful Newspaper Ad Campaign 342
The Advantages of Magazine Advertising 343

The Disadvantages of Magazine Advertising 343
Magazine Ad Preparation 343
Magazine Advertising Costs 344
Yellow Pages Advertising 344
What a Yellow Pages Ad Should Accomplish 344
The Four Kinds of Yellow Pages Ads 344
Buying Ads in the Yellow Pages 345
Seven Tips on Designing a Yellow Pages Ad 345
What to Do When the Phone Rings 346
Radio: Back from the Dead 346
Why Advertisers Like Radio 346
Five Decisions That Must Be Made When Buying Radio Time 347
The Strength of Radio 347
Radio's Disadvantages 348
How to Use Radio 348
Buying Radio Time 348
Ten Tips for Writing Radio Scripts 349
The Advantages of Television Advertising 350
The Disadvantages of Television Advertising 350
Television Advertising Alternatives 351
The Advantages of Direct-Mail Advertising 351
The Disadvantages of Direct-Mail Advertising 351
Five Situations When Direct Mail Can Be Effective 352
How to Conduct a Direct-Mail Campaign: Obtaining the Mailing List 352
The Three Parts of a Direct-Mail Package 353
Seven Tips on Writing a Direct-Mail Piece 353
The Value of the Product Brochure 354
The Direct-Mail Response Form 354
Two Ways to Increase Direct-Mail Response 354
Cutting Direct-Mail Costs 355

Cooperative Advertising: What It Is 355
The Advantages of Cooperative Advertising 355
The Disadvantage of Cooperative Advertising 355
The Internet and the World Wide Web 356
Chapter Summary 356

Chapter 19
Benefits of Sales Force Automation
357

A "Gift" from Technology 357
What Sales Force Automation Is Not 358
An Explanation of Sales Force Automation 358
A List of 16 Popular Sales Force Automation Programs 358
A Typical Sales Automation Application 360
Eight Advantages of a Typical Sales Automation Application 361
Five Benefits of Sales Automation 362
Territory Balancing 362
A Possible Fly in the Territory-Optimization Ointment 366
Why Sales Force Automation Is Possible 367
How Not to Install Sales Automation Systems 367
The First Ten Baby Steps Toward Installing a Sales Force Automation System 368
Sales Force Automation and the Customer 369
Review of the Six Sales Force Automation Benefits 371
Six Disadvantages of Sales Force Automation 372
Can You Put a Number on Sales Force Automation Benefits? 373
15 Things Needed to Implement a Sales Force Automation System 373
A Final Caution on Sales Force Automation 375
Chapter Summary 376

Chapter 20
Managing for the Future
377

The Question That Stays with Managers Throughout Their Careers 377

The 11 Yardsticks That Determine If a Manager Is Ready for Another Promotion 378

Waiting for the Right Opportunity 379

The Problem of Doing Too Good a Job 379

The Importance of Grooming a Successor 380

When to Begin Training a Successor 380

How to Evaluate Staff Members as Potential Candidates for Promotion 380

Eight Characteristics That Identify the Potential Manager 381

How to Groom Someone for Management 381

Make Sure the Management Candidate Is Willing 382

Bringing Along a Management Candidate Slowly 382

Avoiding the Appearance of Favoritism 383

Using Competition for a Managerial Position to Improve Overall Performance 383

"Advertising" the Candidate for Management 383

Management Candidates Reflect on Their Sponsors 384

Polishing Leadership Skills in Management Candidates 384

Confiding in a Management Candidate 385

Embracing Change 385

What Else Managers Need to Know to Advance to Senior Management 385

Chapter 21
How to Survive the Very First Managerial Assignment
387

Why Salespeople Are Promoted to Management 387
The Entry Fee into Management 387
Four Similarities Between Running a Territory and Managing an Area 388
The Ten Major Responsibilities of a Sales Manager 388
The Dirty Dozen: 12 Common Mistakes New Managers Make 390
Other Management Responsibilities 391
The Phenomenon of Being Promoted in Place 391
Five Advantages of Being Promoted in Place 392
Three Disadvantages of Being Promoted in Place 392
How to Handle an In-Place Promotion: Five Actions to Take 393
Five Things Not to Do When Promoted in Place 394
Training for the New Manager 394
11 Tips for Handling People 395
Six Tips on Working with Senior Management 396
A Final Word for the New Manager 396

Chapter 22
How to Make Ethics and Integrity Valuable Sales Tools
398

Why an Ethical Code of Conduct Is Necessary 398
How to Establish Trust 399
The Ethical Standards Sales Managers Should Set for Themselves: A 14-Point Program 399

How to Train Salespeople to Conduct Themselves Ethically 401
11 Benefits of a Strong Ethical Code 401
A Sales Manager's Personal Code of Business Conduct 402
A Dozen Ethical Rules Applicable to Any Salesperson in Any Company 403
Eight Specific Sales Benefits from a Strong Ethical Code 404
Candor as a Sales Management Tool 405
The Internal Benefits of Candor 406
The Candor Litmus Test: Practicing to Be Forthright 406
Confronting Problems Head-on: How to React When Things Go Wrong 407
Seven Reasons Why Knocking the Competition Doesn't Work 408
What to Do When the Boss Orders the Sales Manager to Engage in Unethical Behavior 409
A Sample Ethics Test 410
A Final Word on Ethics 410

INDEX
411

Foreword

The first edition of the *Sales Manager's Desk Book* was intended to be a practical guide to the common problems that face sales managers every day. Based on the book's success, managers did find within its pages valuable answers to the nuts-and-bolts questions related to running a sales operation. Things have changed, however, in the six years since the *Desk Book* was published. Nowhere has change been more dramatic or significant than in the sphere of sales and sales management.

Corporate America has "reengineered," or "downsized," or "rightsized," depending upon the spin doctors' choice of euphemisms when they hand out the pink slips. New and vigorous sales channels have surged upon the business world with the force of a tidal wave, a wave that has swept away old, comfortable relationships and connections. Personal computers and sales automation offer sales managers new control tools through access to better and more current information. Advanced communications systems make closer interaction between supplier and customer possible and at the same time force managers to rethink the typical sales force structure. For example, if on-line communication between field sales force and home office is practical, does the manager-and-crew weekly sales meeting still make sense?

The first *Desk Book* promised information on "a thousand practical things every sales manager needs to know." All that material is still here: how to run a branch office, how to organize and run a sales meeting, how to make an accurate sales forecast, how to spot a phony expense claim, how to set up a sales-training program, how to run a trade show, how to design reports, how to develop compensation plans that keep salespeople motivated. These tasks, and countless more, are still a fundamental part of the sales manager's responsibility.

This revised edition addresses the changes to the sales manager's role and duties by adding four completely new chapters covering the previously mentioned phenomena of shifting sales channels, sales automation, and advanced communication techniques. There's even a chapter on ethics, more important than ever, since downsizing forever changed the relationship between employer and employee. Information in the existing chapters has been updated to reflect new circumstances.

In the simpler past of 1989 there were a few thousand things every sales manager needed to know. The ensuing years have added a few thousand more. They're all here, the old, time-validated sales management functions, and the new realities, at the manager's fingertips, in easy-to-use, easy-to-find reference form.

Chapter One
How to Handle a Managerial Assignment

Thinking Like a Manager

Managers must acquire different attitudes than those they had as territory salespeople. It's important to learn how to delegate responsibility even if the managers can do the job better themselves. As one manager put it, "A manager doesn't do it; he or she sees that it's done." Any manager who is working 10- or 12-hour days and is still always overloaded has this problem because he or she doesn't trust staff members to do the jobs they're paid to do.

How to Be a Leader

Are you a leader or a boss? If you're not sure what category you fall under, there are some telltale signs. Bosses shout orders. Leaders give direction. Bosses are always right. Leaders are willing to admit that others may have good ideas. Bosses bully their people. Leaders motivate. Bosses intimidate. Leaders educate. A British merchant, H.

Gordon Selfridge, nicely defined the differences between a boss and a leader. He said:

- The boss drives his men, the leader coaches them.
- The boss depends upon authority, the leader on good-will.
- The boss inspires fear, the leader enthusiasm.
- The boss says "I," the leader "we."
- The boss fixes the blame for the breakdown; the leader fixes the breakdown.
- The boss says, "go"; the leader says, "let's go."

If you always remember to lead instead of bossing, you're well on your way to becoming a successful manager.

A Short Definition of Management

Forget about the textbook definitions. Management, all management, is the endeavor to control time, money, and/or people. The sales manager gets a crack at handling all three. Time and money control fall under the category of administrative management. That includes budgets, policies, procedures, and generally running the operation. People management includes hiring, training, coaching, setting goals, motivating, counseling, and even firing when necessary.

The Best Way to Spend Management Time

True leadership is a rare commodity, and rare commodities always command top price in the market. Managers are paid according to how well their people do. Their performance is the result of the performance of the people who report to them. Spend time improving staff members and improve as a manager. So the first rule of good sales management is *Spend at least 75 percent of all your time working with people and less than 25 percent of your time on adminis-*

trative details. (If the company had wanted a paper shuffler they probably would have hired someone else for the job.)

METHODS OF LEADERSHIP

How managers lead is largely a matter of personal style. There's more than one right way to do it. The following are some of the more popular methods of leadership:

Through example. The manager who leads in this manner works harder than anyone else in the office. He or she knows the most about the product line, can give the best demonstrations, and possesses excellent closing skills. Example has always been a successful leadership technique. People respond to managers they know are willing to pay the price for success.

Through encouragement. These managers genuinely take pleasure when their people succeed. They have no jealousy, they glory in the triumph of others, and they always have something positive to say. These managers stimulate and inspire the people who work for them. They are popular and successful leaders.

Through teaching and technical expertise. These managers know exactly how the job must be done, and they don't mind sharing the information with members of their sales team. They are the problem solvers. They teach their people selling skills. They know all the applications for the product and invent new ones. They have the respect of customers. The salespeople who work for one of these teachers are well-equipped to face whatever comes next in their careers.

Through motivation. These managers encourage their people to improve themselves, to work harder and smarter. They are the goal setters, they dangle carrots, they groom people for promotion. Often those who motivate produce the best results year after year.

Through determination. Some managers are never discouraged by temporary setbacks. They don't seek out excuses or scapegoats. These managers know darned well that they're going to get the job done. They prevail in good times and bad.

Many sales managers use a combination of these styles. They'll all work if the manager who uses them is sincere.

Management by Intimidation

One popular management style was deliberately omitted from the above list. It is management by intimidation. Some managers attempt to get results by bullying and browbeating the people who report to them. The people who use this style aren't leading at all, they're trailing behind and snapping at the heels of those they're supposed to be guiding.

Ten Characteristics Salespeople Love in Their Sales Managers

Some sales managers enjoy the complete devotion and loyalty of their sales teams. Their directions are followed willingly. Good salespeople don't often leave the team for greener pastures. The manager is respected (as opposed to just being liked). What builds this kind of loyalty? The following characteristics will build a devoted crew:

1. *The manager treats everyone on the staff fairly.* Not everyone is necessarily treated the same way, because people react differently, but everyone on the team is confident that he or she is getting a fair shake.
2. *The manager is accessible and a good listener.* The legitimate concerns and problems of the sales crew are heard and addressed.
3. *The manager recognizes achievement and uses praise when a salesperson does something praiseworthy.*
4. *The manager is loyal to sales team members.* Sales team members are defended to senior management and other company departments.

5. *The manager runs interference for sales team members when interacting with other company management and departments.* The manager gets orders expedited, argues with credit concerning raising the limits for certain customers, obtaining special pricing for big deals, and so forth.
6. *The manager makes sure every salesperson gets proper credit for accomplishments.* For example, the manager sends notes acknowledging achievement by team members to senior management.
7. *The manager spends most of his or her time in the field and assists salespeople in closing important business.*
8. *The manager knows the company policies and procedures, the industry, the product line, the pricing schedules, and so forth, better than any member of the sales crew.* He or she is a wonderful source of information.
9. *The manager has developed a positive working atmosphere.* Working for this manager is enjoyable.
10. *The manager is a good coach and teacher.* Lessons are taught to improve the skills and earning power of sales team members.

Developing a Sense of Style

Successful managers have a clear sense of purpose. They know where they're going. That's the main reason others are prepared to follow. The job of a manager is to act as a pathfinder, to search out the best trail that will get staff members to the desired destination with the least amount of difficulty.

Meeting New Staff Members

Most managers don't have the luxury of handpicking every member of their staffs. Some are assigned, others are transferred, and so forth. Whenever managers are given a managerial assignment in a different geographical area, they inherit every member of the sales staff. They get the good, the bad, and all those in between. Even though they may have the benefit of some evaluation from an immediate supervisor or predecessor, it's important to conduct early interviews with new staff members to learn something about them and what can be expected. Staff members will also want to know what they can expect from the new manager.

Group Meetings

The best way for a manager to get acquainted with new staff members is to set up both group and individual meetings.

The group meeting's objectives are:

1. For the manager to introduce him- or herself
2. To announce the specific objectives set for the area
3. To meet the members of the staff

The meeting should be kept short. *Avoid making major changes at introductory meetings.* Don't announce new, complicated reporting procedures. This is not the time to introduce a different compensation plan that may affect everyone's income. Don't hint at a shakeup. It's enough to let staff members know that there's a new regime. There's no need to suggest that there's going to be a new form of government.

The manager shouldn't expect to learn much about the staff members during these early group meetings. They're likely to be tight-lipped and judgmental, more anxious to find out something about the new manager than to reveal anything about themselves.

Meeting the Staff One-on-One

Individual meetings with staff members will be more productive in learning more about them. Adapt an open-minded attitude about the person being interviewed even though there may be some information on file about his or her reputation. Don't be pompous, overbearing, or dictatorial. These attitudes are self-defeating. Here are some of the things to look for:

1. Is the person capable? Does it appear as if the person has the ability to get the job done? Evaluate the person in terms of the manager's total area responsibility. Can assigned objectives be met with this person on the team?

2. Is the person willing? Does the person appear open to suggestions and willing to work to accomplish common goals?

3. Is the person a team player? Can this person be counted on to work with the manager and the other people in the office? (Don't discard someone just because he or she has a lone-wolf personality. Some are excellent performers. However, don't bother trying to sell the team concept to the lone wolf. Just make sure that he or she profits most when the entire area achieves assigned goals.)

4. Does the person know the produce line, the applications, the competition, the territory, and the customer base? This information is important so that the manager can determine how much training and assistance is needed for each member of the staff.

5. What motivates this person? Is it money? Recognition? The desire for promotion? Praise? The approval of peers?

6. Is the person honest and truthful? Is the manager going to have to check on every word this person says? Will it be necessary to verify expense accounts, confirm call reports, and so forth?

The Manager's Personnel List

The manager should make a mental or written list of the attributes, traits, and shortcomings of each staff member in order to develop a clearer picture of the work that needs to be done in the personnel area. Who, if anyone, needs to be replaced? Where are the weak links? Where are the points of strength that can become building blocks? What kind of training is needed? What's the best way to motivate each person? What help must the manager provide to improve performance? What help does the manager need from the home office to improve the staff?

Conducting Staff Interviews with Good Performers

During meetings with staff members, go over every individual's past sales records. Don't play "gotcha!" Ask them to come prepared for this discussion. If the person has proven to be a consistent quota performer, give praise. (Praise has always been one of the most effective motivators.) Offer help if weak spots are detected, but go lightly on offering unsolicited advice with good performers. Batting coaches never interfere with a swing, no matter how awkward, if the player is making good contact with the ball.

Conducting Staff Interviews with Nonquota Performers

When interviewing staff members whose performance has been disappointing, ask for an explanation of the reasons. (There will be plenty.) Make the request in a nonthreatening way. The purpose of the interview is to find out what's wrong so it can be fixed. No matter what the reasons given, ask the person to develop a plan that will put him or her at 100 percent of quota. Offer help to formulate such a plan, but make sure the person understands that it is his or her responsibility to make the plan work. Make it clear that everything possible will be done to help him or her achieve the goals set for the territory. *Setting expectations is the most effective way to take charge as a manager.* Make people accountable for attaining the goals set for them.

Allowing the Staff to Interview the Manager

During the first private meetings with staff members the manager is not the only one making an evaluation. The people being interviewed will be interviewing the new boss. They want to learn something about their new leader. Encourage this reverse interview.

Learn how to field and respond to implied questions. If a salesperson "jokingly" mentions the difficulty of getting call reports in on time, state your position on necessary paperwork. If another hints about a raise, discuss the salary review procedure and the kind of performance expected to warrant raises and promotions.

Anything the manager reveals to one person will soon be known by everyone on the staff. When enough private interviews have been conducted, the manager will have, in effect, established the policies and procedures of the local operation without committing anything to paper. *Note:* The company's policies and procedures should always be a matter of written record. However, a manager may choose not to write down everything that relates to personal management style.

Points to Cover in Individual Meetings with Staff Members

In conversations with staff members, be sure to cover the company's objectives for the upcoming year. An explanation of broad objectives helps give staff members perspective about their specific roles. Be candid about any problems facing the company that may make objectives difficult to reach. Candor is usually disarming because it is so infrequently used in the manager–salesperson relationship. The manager who employs it will quickly develop a reputation as a "straight-shooter."

Ask for suggestions on how goals can be met. If the suggestions are any good, try them out. *Be sure to give proper credit for the idea.* Recognizing, implementing, and rewarding ideas is the surest way to nurture creativity.

Ask about problems the salespeople perceive that may prevent goals from being reached. Expect to be deluged with advance alibis, but also expect to get valuable input on the legitimate obstacles in the path. Some of the problems may be handled with a quick fix. Others must be dealt with through careful planning. Still others are beyond the manager's control. Work on the first two sets of problems and ignore the things that can't be helped.

Action Plans

Action plans are the details by which this year's sales objectives are met. It's usually a good idea to have staff members develop the action plans for their respective territories. Most of them will need help with this project. That help should come from the area manager.

Territory action plans start with two givens. They are

1. Last year's actual sales figures for the territory.
2. The quota the company has assigned to the territory for this coming year.

The Gap

Most companies want to expand, so it's likely that this year's quota is larger than last year's results. The difference, the required increase in sales volume, is called "the Gap." This year's big question, both for the individual territories and the total area of responsibility, is how does the gap get filled? Where is the extra business going to come from?

How to Analyze Last Year's Sales

Inspect the following chart (Exhibit 1–1). On the left-hand side it lists last year's sales volume by month, the customers who produced that volume, and the dollar amount of each customer's order. On the right-hand side it lists the orders anticipated from those customers this year. When making such a chart, don't list customers who are shaky. However, do include any expected increases in business from old customers. The difference between the business that there's a reasonable assurance of getting this year and the new quota assignment is the gap that needs to be filled.

EXHIBIT 1–1

LAST YEAR'S SALES		*THIS YEAR'S PROJECTION*	
Month			
January		*January*	
Customer	*Amount*	*Customer*	*Amount*
Dynamic Ind.	$4,250	Dynamic Ind.	$4,000
Costello Prod.	$1,300		
City Purchasing	$3,725	Tree-Top Farms	$3,500
Tree-Top Farms	$2,696	Phillips Parts	$5,000
Phillips Parts	$5,284	Star Manufact.	$5,200
Star Manufact.	$4,008		
Financial Press	$2,425	Dombey & Sons	$2,300
Stadium Supply	$ 813	Chalkboard, Inc.	$3,000
Dombey & Sons	$1,866	Lacey Co.*	$1,500
Chalkboard, Inc.	$3,525		
Actual Sales Last January	$29,892	Projected Sales from Existing Customer	$24,500

This year's January projection	—	$32,500
Anticipated orders from existing customers	—	$24,500
Gap that must be filled by new business	—	$ 8,000
Repeat exercise for all months to obtain year.		

*Lacey Company is an existing customer who did not order last January, but is expected to place an order this January.

HOW TO FILL THE GAP

Learning what the gap is gives the manager a handle on the job that needs to be done. In the example shown, the salesperson had a gap of $8,000 for the month of January. That means $8,000 in new business must come from somewhere. Now, it's up to the territory representative, with the manager's help, to develop a plan to meet that gap. This segment of the plan can also be charted (Exhibit 1–2). In the example, the average sale for the company is worth $2,700. That means the salesperson must make three additional sales in January to meet the $8,000 gap.

Exhibit 1–2
Call Plan for January

PARAMETERS (BASED ON HISTORICAL RECORD)
20 calls = 1 demo. 2 demos = 1 proposal.
5 proposals = 3 sales.

January Requirements

200	calls
10	demos
5	proposals
3	sales

These numbers can be intimidating until they are broken down to a daily work schedule.

First Week

Monday	—	12 calls
Tuesday	—	12 calls
Wednesday	—	12 calls
Thursday	—	8 calls, 1 demo
Friday	—	8 calls, 1 demo

Second Week

Monday	—	12 calls
Tuesday	—	12 calls
Wednesday	—	8 calls, 1 proposal
Thursday	—	6 calls, 2 demos
Friday	—	12 calls

Third Week

Monday	—	12 calls
Tuesday	—	6 calls, 2 demos

Wednesday	—	8 calls, 1 proposal
Thursday	—	6 calls, 2 demos
Friday	—	8 calls, 1 sale
Fourth Week		
Monday	—	8 calls, 1 proposal
Tuesday	—	12 calls
Wednesday	—	8 calls, 1 proposal
Thursday	—	6 calls, 2 demos
Friday	—	8 calls, 1 sale
Fifth Week (two days)		
8 calls	—	1 proposal
8 calls	—	1 sale

It's surprising how sales results can be tied to numbers, and sales yield to effort. The needed result can be reduced to so many personal calls, so many proposals, and so many demos. Using the figures available, insist that the territory salesperson work out the plan of attack. This helps the person reach the conclusion that company-set objectives are reachable.

What to Do When the Territory Salesperson Won't Commit to Goals

What happens if the salesperson claims the job can't be done, that the goals set by management are not achievable? It's the manager's job to show the salesperson *how* the goals can be reached. If the target seems high in the manager's eyes, perhaps extra assistance can be offered in the form of a direct-mail campaign to prospects in the salesperson's territory. Maybe the manager can work directly with the salesperson for a specified period of time. *Make commitments to provide needed help in exchange for commitments from the salesperson to do the job required.*

The Importance of Performance Reviews

The manager should ask the salesperson to sign the completed territory action plan as a commitment to making it work. This action plan becomes the basis upon which to monitor objectives against actual performance. This measurement is a primary management responsibility. *Good managers continually review the performance of their people to determine if plans are on track.*

How to Deal with Sales Problems

Managers should never ignore the problems that staff members bring to them. If they say the competition is too tough or the company's pricing too high, don't dismiss these complaints as being simple alibis. If there are roadblocks in the way of achieving objectives, the manager wants to know about them, and the farther in advance, the better. Of course, the alibis will have to be sorted out. (A few salespeople will use any opportunity to set up excuses for anticipated failure.) Among the alibis will be matters of real concern to staff members. They should also be of concern to the manager no matter how trivial they appear. The problems mentioned are early-warning systems of the obstacles that must be overcome to achieve sales objectives. By acknowledging and addressing these problems, the manager develops a reputation as a problem solver, someone staff members can come to in time of trouble.

The Teamwork Concept in Sales

"Teamwork" is a term so popular in business today it has become a cliché. Sales managers are fond of using analogies comparing their salespeople to football, basketball, and baseball squads. It's an attractive concept. In sports everyone pulls together to achieve victory. Shouldn't the same sort of spirit work in sales?

Like most analogies, the comparison of a sales team to a sports squad is partially true, but far from perfect. The true part is that when the company wins by producing more sales and profits, the salespeople usually win through larger incomes and increased chances for promotion. The imperfect part is that the interests of the company and the company's employees, while similar, are not identical. The manager who tries to "sell" it that way soon gets a reputation for being insincere.

Where the Teamwork Concept Fails

Salespeople have never been considered a part of management or labor, but rather a species apart. For the most part, they are independent contractors (no matter what the method of compensation) measured and paid on the basis of results. How can these independent spirits be persuaded to behave as members of a team? On a team one member may be asked to "give himself up," that is, sacrifice a chance for personal glory to give the team a better chance to win. Try that idea out on a member of the sales staff. Better yet, don't bother. No self-respecting salesperson willingly gives up a better territory or prime account just because it may be in the company's best interests. The manager may force such a change, but don't ask the salesperson to agree because it's for the betterment of the team.

Why It's Important to Build a Sense of Common Purpose

If the team concept has its drawbacks, what's the best way to build a sense of common purpose? What is the adhesive that binds a sales staff together? It is the age-old glue of common interest. Team spirit is built by making staff members believe that the manager is always looking out for their best interests just as long as they're looking out for the company's best interests. Validate that belief by becoming the guardian of their rights, by fighting for everything they have coming, by recognizing their successes, by recommending them for raises and promotions, by praising them to top management. The manager keeps promises—all promises.

All members of the sales team should feel that they'll participate in any local triumphs and be rewarded accordingly. In a sales group, team spirit is nothing more than thinly disguised private enterprise augmented by mutual trust. The manager who works it right provides the atmosphere of trust while staff members provide the energy and enterprise.

Six Steps to a Sense of Common Purpose

Here's a step-by-step program that can build a sales version for team spirit (common purpose) within a sales group:

1. The salespeople, every one of them, must believe that when the company benefits they will benefit. They must believe that when the area's operation wins, they will win.

2. Organize friendly contests with winners, but without scapegoats, if certain objectives are met.

3. Intramural competition is healthy, but never set one salesperson against another. Praising Jane for doing a great job last month is okay. Asking Bill why he can't perform the way Jane did is not. Bill may hope that Jane will fail next month so the heat will be off. That kind of feeling doesn't build team spirit, common purpose, or anything else constructive.

4. Encourage members of the sales team to work together. Ask them to assist one another, to balance strengths and weaknesses.

5. Spending time together is the surest way to build a sense of camaraderie. Hold celebrations when objectives are reached. Participate in award ceremonies. Invite everyone, including spouses, to special dinners. Have an office picnic!

6. Make sure the home office is informed of any outstanding performance by a member of the sales team. Make sure the person knows that the home office has been informed.

The Four Tried-and-True Motivators

There are four motivators that have been used to build a sense of common purpose since there have been sales teams. These motivators are

1. Financial reward when goals are achieved
2. Recognition for accomplishment
3. Generous praise for a job well done
4. A genuine opportunity for promotion for those who deserve it

That's a pretty simple list. Use these motivators instead of trying to instill a false "college spirit" in sales team members. They'll respect a manager for it.

Traits That Identify Management Potential

There are several traits that help identify good management material. These traits are:

1. *Leadership.* This quality is fairly easy to spot. Who among their peers do the staff members look up to?
2. *Ability to take direction as well as give it.* The army requires officer cadets to take a good many orders before they're allowed to give any.
3. *Maturity.* This is an attitude, not a record of physical years. The mature person is steady, doesn't panic, can be counted on in any emergency.
4. *Organization.* Some salespeople can get by without being organized. The sales manager cannot.
5. *Cooperation.* The potential manager has learned how to cooperate with others in the company. He or she fights battles outside the company—against the competition.

How to Establish Good Communication Links

The dictionary defines "communications" as "the act of transmitting information." This definition is incomplete. The best communication system is a two-way station that is able to receive information as well as send it out. That means becoming a good listener. Managers can't pass along directions from top management unless they thoroughly understand what needs to be done.

The ability to receive information is very important to any management level. Consider the local area to be like a military outpost in a war zone. As the military commander, it's the manager's job to receive orders that come down from headquarters and pass these orders along to the troops. The manager also gathers information from the front lines (receiving information again) and passes it up the chain of command.

Which is more important, receiving or transmitting? Obviously, both share equal status. The manager should set up a sales communication system that will do both. See Exhibit 1–3 for a diagram of the ideal communication system.

Exhibit 1–3
Sales Communication System

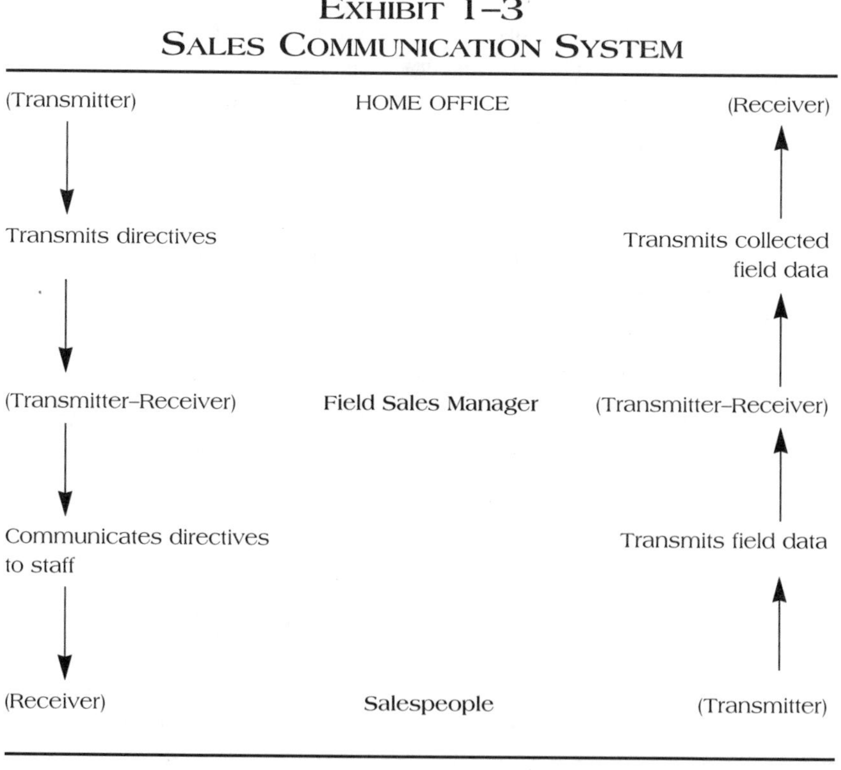

Eight Steps to the Ideal Communication System

In the ideal communication system, the manager is set up as a receiver–transmitter–receiver. Here's how to achieve that objective:

1. When there is a direction from top management, understand it thoroughly before you pass it along. Know what needs to be done, the time frame for completion, and the means that can be used to get it done.

2. Ask for clarification on anything not understood. Senior managers would rather spend a few extra minutes explaining something in more detail than send someone speeding in the wrong direction.

3. Understand the reasons behind the directions. Those who understand *why* are in a better position to suggest ways *how*.

4. Managers who disagree with directions should state their objections plainly. The company isn't paying anyone to be a rubber stamp. If the objection is heard but dismissed, proceed with the plan determined to make it work.

5. Don't get into the career-squelching habit of questioning every direction that comes along. (Managers who want to know how top management feels about this habit should think about their own reactions when a salesperson quarrels with every new program.)

6. When the manager thoroughly understands top management's directions and purpose, this information should be passed along to staff members in clear language that can't be misinterpreted. Ask for feedback to make sure that directions are understood. If time commitments are needed, put them in writing. Get agreement and signoffs from staff members on project completion dates.

7. Set up a reporting system that provides interim progress bulletins. It's important for the manager to know if everything is running on schedule.

8. Periodically report back to superiors on the plan's progress. Make sure the reports are accurate. If things are off-schedule, say so.

Never sugarcoat bad news. To quote former secretary of state Henry Kissinger. "What must be revealed eventually should be revealed immediately."

Putting this two-way communication system in place will earn any manager the reputation of a great communicator. The system is based on the simple precept of making sure that you understand what others mean when they speak and making sure that others understand what you mean when you speak.

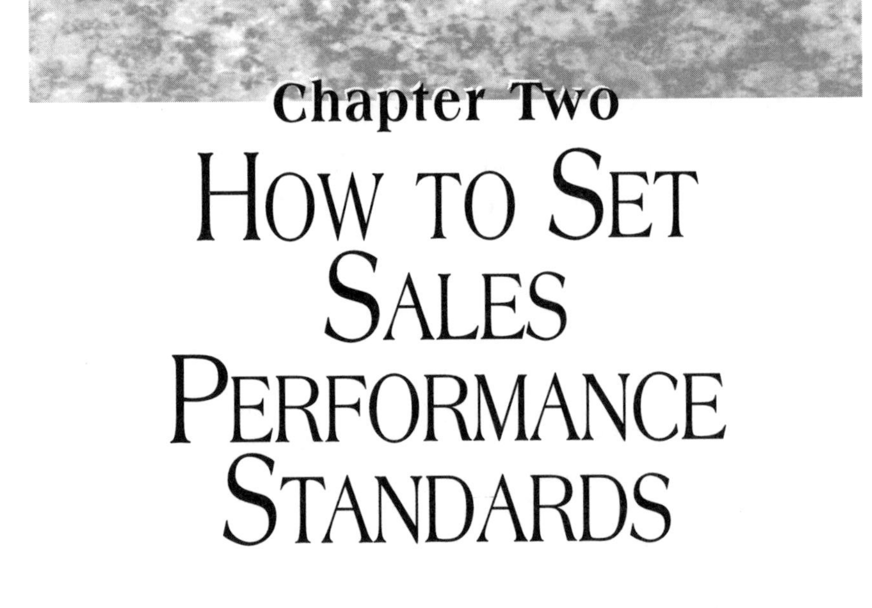

Chapter Two

How to Set Sales Performance Standards

Evaluating Action Plans

How can managers be sure that those elegant action plans, painstakingly developed by staff members with manager's help, will work? An even bigger question is how can managers be sure that staff members will actually work their plans? It's one thing to plan 40 calls a week. It's another to go out and actually make those calls. How can managers know if programs are on schedule, if forecasts will be met, or if goals will be reached? These things can't be known unless there's a continual examination of what has been done and a comparison of the actual results with what had been planned.

The Value of the Review Process

One of the key elements of management is making sure that staff members are really carrying out their commitments to the manager, to the company, and to themselves. This checkup procedure is called the review process. It means *follow up, follow up,* and *follow up.*

Continually reviewing the performance of each staff member is the only way to ensure that agreed-upon goals are being met. Reviews are a time for honest appraisal of the sales situation in each territory. They are best handled in person and are vital for any sales manager who wants to be in charge of the results in his or her area.

Review Techniques

The essence of the review is to pay attention to the details of the action plans that have been developed. Managers and staff members have carefully drafted step-by-step procedures to reach the goals that were set. They review attempts to determine if each of these steps is being fulfilled.

Conducting a review means arranging for at least one direct meeting per month with each salesperson on staff. Let the person know that he or she is expected to come prepared to discuss what was accomplished in the territory last month and what can be expected this month. (On short-term action plans, the direct meetings may be more frequent.) It's far more detailed than a discussion on the number of sales that were made. That information is important, but the manager is now trying to determine if long-range objectives are on target.

Managers should consider themselves like a reporter trying to get to the heart of a story. The reporter asks, Who? What? Why? When? and Where? These same questions are used to get to the heart of the salesperson's story, the story of what's happening in the territory.

14 Points to Cover in a Review Meeting

Tell each salesperson what is to be covered. Make sure that each comes prepared to discuss the following specific points:

1. How many calls were made during the period.
2. The names of the customers and prospects contacted.
3. The results of those calls.
4. The business, or orders, that can be anticipated as a result of those calls.

5. The dollar value of those orders
6. When the orders will be obtained
7. The products or services that will be ordered
8. The orders or customers that were lost
9. The reason those prospects got away
10. The status of prospects or customers that couldn't be closed this month
11. What tasks were left undone
12. Where the person stands in relation to the action plan
13. If the person is below target, what action is planned to get back on track
14. What specific assistance or guidance the salesperson can expect from the manager

When those questions are satisfactorily answered, start the procedure all over again relating to what will happen in the coming month. When a salesperson has been through a few of these review meetings there'll be little attempt to "snow" the manager.

Other Items on a Review Agenda

During a review the manager will also want to discuss the number of demos and proposals that were made, the prospects who have been dangling for a time but can't seem to be closed, and the salesperson's "feel" for achieving yearly objectives. The discussion on all points should be as frank as possible. If the manager is disappointed by a lack of results, the review meeting is a place to express that disappointment.

Three Forms to Help Salespeople Get Organized

Initially, the salespeople may not come prepared for review meetings unless they are given clear guidelines on what to expect. This expectation can best be communicated by asking each salesperson to fill out the following forms:

1. A travel schedule for the forthcoming month (Exhibit 2–1)
2. A forecast of business that will be closed this month (Exhibit 2–2)
3. A summary of last month's results (Exhibit 2–3)

The completion of these forms almost forces some organization on the salesperson.

What the Manager Gets Out of a Review Meeting

The review session helps the manager keep on top of the job by telling him or her where the area stands in relation to the goals that must be reached. It also informs the manager about the staff's real commitment to the job, their work habits, and their skill levels.

The Five Benefits of the Review Process

1. The monthly review will almost automatically increase the amount of sales activity going on in the individual territories. Salespeople won't want to come to review meetings unprepared or with a poor record of calls and accomplishments.

2. The quality of activity will also improve. The manager is now questioning why certain things were done. This will cause the salespeople to think out their actions. They'll begin to work smarter.

3. Close monitoring helps the manager gain control of the action plan. There are no more end-of-month unpleasant surprises.

4. Once salespeople realize the review process will be a standard procedure, they'll come prepared for questions. The intelligence from the field will be more accurate.

Exhibit 2–1
Monthly Calendar/Travel Schedule

DSM ________ Days in Territory ________ Office Days ________ Month of ________ District ________

SUNDAY	MONDAY	TUESDAY	WEDNESDAY	THURSDAY	FRIDAY	SATURDAY

Due last day of previous month. Indicate close of business, holidays, shows, office days, vacations, and days out of territory. List all scheduled appointments by dealer and location.

EXHIBIT 2–2
30-DAY GOAL FORECAST

(Units and Revenue)

Salesperson ______________ District ______________ Month of ____________ Date Submitted ________

Annual Quota ____________ YTD Results ____________ Remaining Quota ____________ Months Remaining ____________ Adjusted Target ____________

Acount (N/E)	Product A	Product B	Product C	Product D	Product E	Product F	Access.	Supplies	Total Units	Total Revenue	YTD Units	YTD Total Revenue
TOTALS												

Due last day of previous month. Indicate both unit and revenue forecast by model.

Exhibit 2–3
Regional Summary Report

Month of: ______________

Sales Summary

Salesperson	Model	Prod. A	Prod. B	Prod. C.	Prod. D	Prod. E.	Prod. F		Access.	Supplies	Other
	Units										
	Revenue										
	Units										
	Revenue										
	Units										
	Revenue										
	Units										
	Revenue										
	Units										
	Revenue										
	Units										
	Revenue										

		Total Activities Completed					
		Initial Contact	Quality	Presentation	Product Demo.	Contract Close	Initial Order
TOTALS							

Here's an easy way for managers to chart sales projections against actual sales:

EXHIBIT 2–4
CHARTING SALES PROJECTIONS

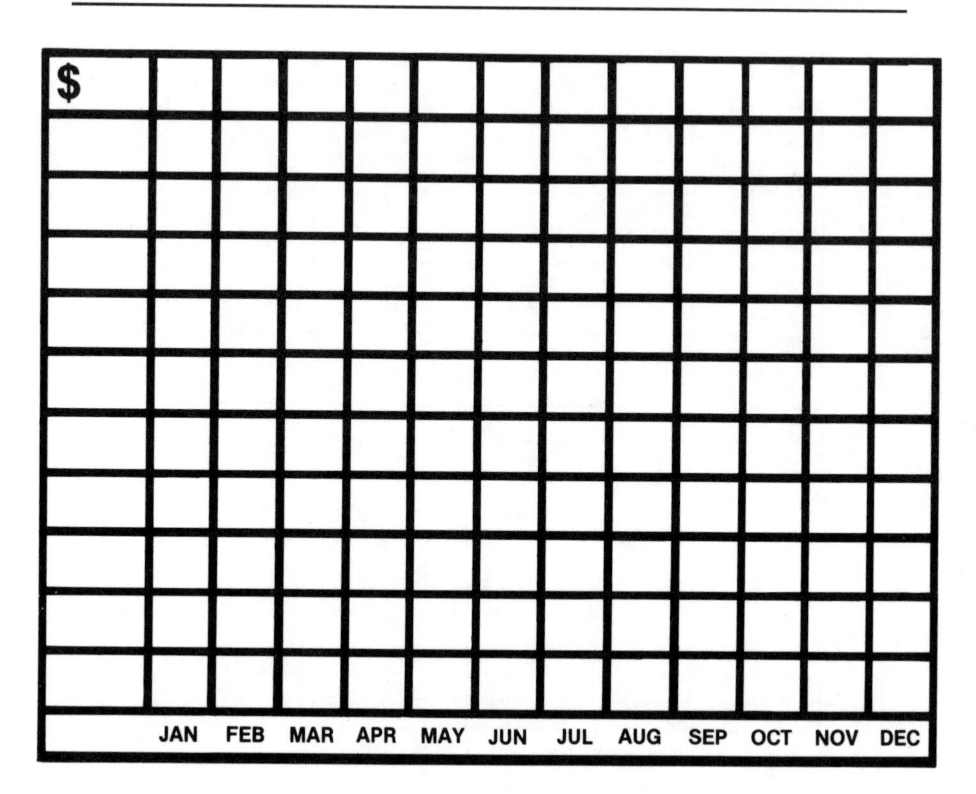

In the first column, under the $ sign, put the monthly projection in ten equal segments. If the sales quota is $60,000 a month, the bottom box would show $6,000, the next $12,000, and so on, until the top box showed the total projection of $60,000. When sales are made during the month, just draw a bar with a pen or pencil for the total value of the orders received. The manager knows exactly what remains to be done to meet quota. The chart also provides good insight into seasonal fluctuations because the entire year is shown at a glance. Obviously, such a chart can be kept for every person on the sales team.

5. There'll be no more management after-the-fact. There'll be no need to put out forest fires because the fires will be recognized almost before they are kindled. The problems will be smaller because there will be enough time to make necessary adjustments.

Management Preparation for Review Meetings

The sales force aren't the only ones who must prepare for monthly review meetings. The manager must do homework in reviewing staff member's past month's activity, pinpointing problem areas and making plans for needed improvements.

Review Questions That Pin Down the Evasive

Many salespeople are masters at evasive tactics. The manager must counter this evasiveness with specific questions that pin down responses. Make the questions quantitative if possible. Here's how an interrogation might work when questioning a salesperson about a call to a specific prospect.

"When did you see the Acme Company?"

"Who did you speak with over there?"

"Does this person have the authority to sign the order?"

"Will others be involved in the decision?"

"What products did you discuss?"

"What are they using now?"

"What was their reaction to the discussion?"

"Are they considering any of our competitors?"

"Did you make a demo? For whom?"

"Does our product solve their problem?"

"What's their time frame for a decision?"

"Have you given them a proposal? When?"

"Do they like our proposition?"

"Do they have the budget for the project?"

"What's the size of the potential order?"

"When will it close?"

"What could hold it up?"

"Is there anything I can do to help?"

Review of Remote Sales Personnel

In many instances it is not practical for managers to conduct face-to-face reviews with their sales team members. Some salespeople may be located in territories far from the manager's base of operation. Many companies are employing "outbound" sales forces, that is, personnel who work out of their homes and come to the office infrequently. In these circumstances, the review can be conducted by telephone, giving the salesperson advance notice that it will occur. Make sure that both of you have allotted enough time to make the review process thorough.

Don't reduce the review to an examination of call reports or data gathered electronically. The interplay between manager and salesperson is important.

Following Up the Review

The answers to these questions, and others like them, tell the manager if the salesperson being interviewed is on top of the account. Ask specific questions and don't settle for vague answers. Of course, some of the answers may be incomplete or reflect actions that are still undone. For example, the salesperson may say that a demo is scheduled within the next two weeks. Make a notation on a follow-up sheet. At the next review session, ask about the demo and the results.

The Sales Force's Attitude Toward Review Sessions

In-depth questioning that forces salespeople to be candid and pins them down may not be greeted with enthusiasm. The veteran staff members in particular may object to what they regard as a "grilling." Those with poor sales records and the alibi artists will surely find the practice offensive.

How to Make the Review Session a Positive Experience

The review session can be sold to staff members if presented properly. Most staff members will understand that the purpose is to improve their performance. The review attempts to put each account in a spotlight—look at it critically and without emotion. The review pinpoints not only the status of each account, but also which accounts need more time and which represent time poorly spent.

Reviews are meant to improve the performance of the entire area by improving individual performance. By improving individual performance they improve individual income. Here are two pointers on review sessions:

1. Make sure the sessions are a true dialog between two people trying to achieve a common objective. They'll fail if the manager turns them into an I-speak–you-listen kind of meeting.
2. If the salesperson claims there is a problem, volunteer to help solve it. Always offer to help close a deal, work with the plant to get a special delivery schedule, and so forth.

How to Get Staff Members to Provide Accurate Information

(Making up sales forecasts will be the subject of a separate chapter. This section is limited to the forecast in relationship to the review process.)

Encourage staff members to make accurate forecasts by confirming every line item on the forecast. How sure are they that a particular prospect will sign on the dotted line? Could the decision be delayed? Have all the competitive factors been considered? Is the prospect truly sold? Is there an element inside the prospect company that has reservations about the proposal? What's the fallback plan if the prospect doesn't sign as anticipated?

When Reviews Aren't Necessary

The necessity for frequent reviews diminishes once the salespeople learn that the intent is to drive them toward a more professional approach to selling. When a staff member begins to have all the right answers at every review session, try lengthening the time period between reviews. There's no greater flattery than this kind of trust.

How to Adjust Sales Targets

Sales would be a much easier profession if all plans performed exactly on schedule and all forecasts came in at 100 percent. (Maybe not. The field would get overcrowded.) That ideal may occur in some alternative universe, but in this one things go awry. Part of management's responsibility is to recognize when goals are not being met. Some reasons for missing targets are under the manager's control and some are not. Put things back on track when possible and report back to higher levels when it appear as if corrections won't make up for anticipated shortfalls.

What to Do When Sales Targets Are Not on Schedule

When a schedule is not being met, the first thing to do is to find out why. In many cases it's because the details of the action plan are not being fulfilled. For example, the targets for one salesperson may have been to make 25 calls a week. In the review session, the call report reveals that the salesperson is achieving only 15 calls a week. That's a shortfall of 40 percent of projection. If the salesperson's production is also down by 40 percent, the reason is plain.

The next step would be to determine *why* the salesperson has not been able to meet the call objective. Perhaps the person does not plan well and needs help in route scheduling. Perhaps too much time is spent socializing on each call. Perhaps the person is not sufficiently committed to making the necessary sacrifices. Perhaps too much time is spent on paperwork or in the office. (Perhaps there's been too much paperwork assigned.) These problems are revealed through the review process. Whatever the situation, once the problem has been pinpointed the first step has been taken toward getting the program back on track. (In the case of insufficient commitment by a staff member, it may be necessary to make a personnel change. It's still a problem that can be corrected.)

What to Do About Noncorrectable Problems

Some problems are not correctable in the short term. The salesperson may have lost a big account that represents a third of the territory's total sales volume. Forgetting for the moment the subject of assessing blame for the loss, the manager is still faced with a decrease in sales volume until the customer can be replaced. (Perhaps the one big customer will be replaced by 20 medium-sized customers, but this project takes time.) In this instance, the forecast needs to be corrected to reflect a lower volume of anticipated business.

When It's Time to Tell Top Management That Objectives Can't Be Met

When the manager knows for certain that circumstance or business conditions, or even plain incompetence, mean that objectives can't be met, the corrections won't help, then the manager must bite the bullet and inform the senior managers in the reporting structure. To quote Henry Kissinger a second time, "What must be revealed eventually must be revealed immediately." Top management needs the information just as badly as do local area managers. If area figures are not going to be accomplished, then necessary corrections must be made to the company forecast.

When Not to Go to Management About Target Problems

Never go to upper management with a claim that targets can't be met until absolutely sure that corrective measures won't resolve the problem. They may decide to put someone else in place to make the corrections. Always do the best job possible to meet all company objectives, and report fast when something insurmountable gets in the way. Managers who behave in this way develop a reputation for reliability that carries them high on the management ladder.

A Summary of the Sales Review Process in 12 Easy Stages

1. Review sessions can keep the manager informed on staff members' progress in meeting their territorial objectives. It's the easiest way for the manager to determine if area objectives will be met.
2. Review sessions are most productive when salespeople come to them fully prepared. Preparation is in the form of complet-

ed reports on what has been accomplished during the period under review.

3. The manager must also prepare for the review session. The manager should understand the details of every territory's operation.
4. During the review the manager should ask specific questions and not settle for vague answers.
5. The quickest way to melt any "snow job" is to match actual territory performance against the forecast of what was promised.
6. The manager never takes forecasts on faith.
7. The review process is an early-warning system. It helps the manager design corrective action when goals aren't being met.
8. When corrections won't work, the manager takes the bad news to senior management as soon as possible.
9. Reviews, questioning, and following up all demonstrate professionalism. These procedures show that the manager is dedicated to making goals.
10. Reviews can be a teaching tool. The manager who asks tough questions of staff members forces them to ask tough questions of themselves.
11. Plans aren't pie-in-the-sky dreams. The performance standards are set toward reaching defined goals.
12. Reviews demonstrate dedication. The manager who uses them gains the reputation of being completely in charge of the operation.

Chapter Three
Your Company's Organizational and Political Structure

Why It's Important for the Manager to Understand the Organizational Structure in His or Her Company

The perceptive manager soon learns that things don't happen by themselves. Nature abhors a vacuum, and so does business. The manager needs able salespeople in the field, good leadership from above, and an efficient home office administrative team to get the job done. That's why it's so important to pay attention to the organizational setup of your company. To really understand the game, you've got to know who the players are and what positions they play.

The Definition of an Organization Chart

The company's organization chart is the scorecard that will guide you. What are organization charts? They are diagrams that show the division of responsibilities within a company. They show who's at the top and who reports to whom. Most charts are made up of little boxes with job titles inside. The higher the box, the grander the title.

Two Typical Organization Charts

Here are two typical organization charts (Exhibits 3–1 and 3–2).

There's no such thing as a standard organization chart, though many are very similar. When you start your own company, you can design any kind of reporting structure you like.

Exhibit 3–1

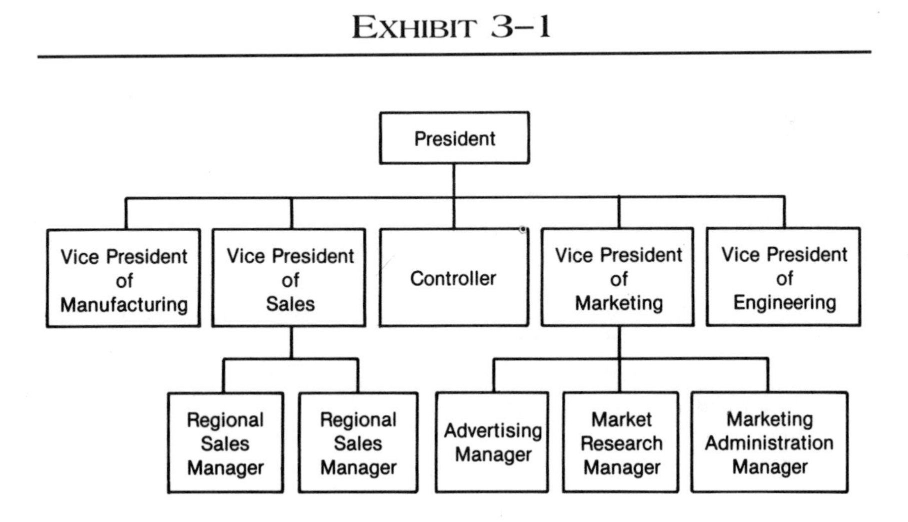

Getting Inside the Boxes on Organization Charts

The charts are line drawings on paper. The titles inside the boxes don't mean anything until they're tied to real people. In your company, in every company, individuals with real personalities, with prejudices, strengths, weaknesses, and a host of human idiosyncrasies, represent those titles. There is no such thing as a "treasur-

EXHIBIT 3–2

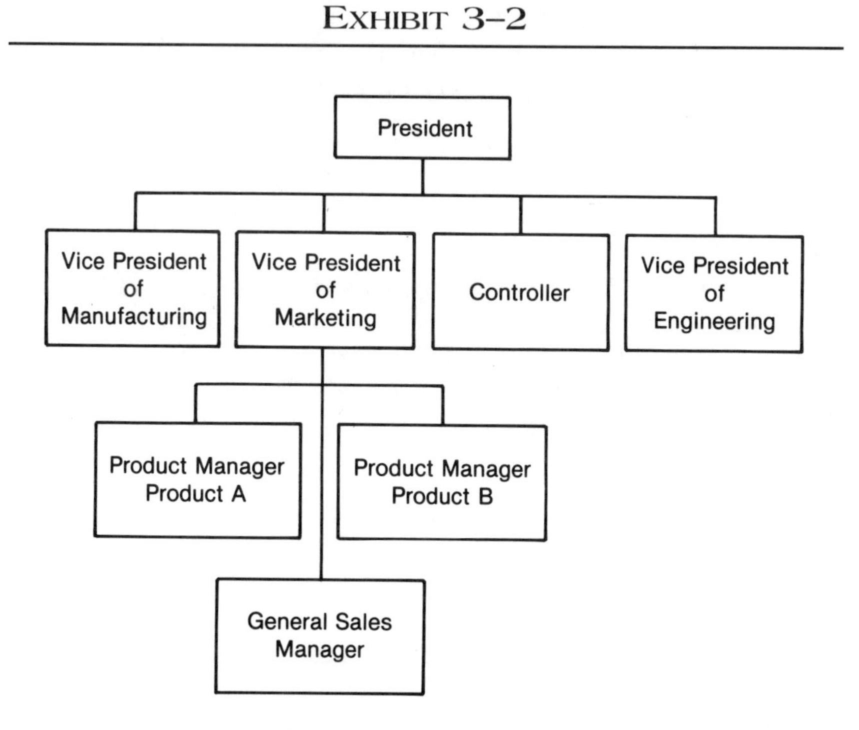

er." There's only Sam Adams, the tight-fisted miser who squeezes a nickel until the buffalo bellows in pain.

The first rule of organizational behavior is to be aware that you're dealing with personalities and not just job titles.

THE FACTS AND FANCIES OF ORGANIZATION CHARTS

Every chart is part fact and part wishful thinking. According to the charts, the tasks that need to be done are assigned to those best qualified to do them. That's the theory anyway. In actual business practice you'll find that some people are more qualified than others. There are a few special individuals inside every company who make things happen. These are the people you want on your side. Your company may have a controller who can cut through the red tape no matter what department has done the snarling. Doesn't it make sense to develop a cooperative relationship with this individual?

Sales Managers' Concerns About Organizational Structure

The sales manager must be concerned about company organizational structure because it helps him or her do the job. The field manager is in weekly, and sometimes daily, contact with the home office. Many different departments and job levels are contacted, such as the credit department, the order entry people, the customer support group, the shipping department, the service group, and so forth. The field manager is likely to be in less frequent, but steady, contact with manufacturing, product development, advertising, and many other company home office groups.

This contact is necessary to make sure that the manager's area customers are properly serviced. Most field managers scramble near the end of the month to ensure a decent showing. They pull all the strings they can yank to get orders out the door and invoiced. They find themselves in the position of persuading, cajoling, pleading, maybe even threatening—if they can get away with it—to get priority shipments.

How to Cut Across Organizational Lines of Authority

At times every manager finds it necessary to cut across organizational lines to get something done. It's important for these managers to know exactly what they're doing and who they're talking to. They could make the wrong demand of the wrong person and lose much more than the priority treatment they sought. The manager should exercise courtesy and diplomacy when speaking to people in other departments. They should be particularly polite to the line employees who are responsible for getting things moving.

Sometimes corporate survival depends on understanding the authority level and explosion point of the person on the other end of the telephone (or memo). Don't expect to be forgiven for rudeness on the grounds of enthusiasm toward your job. If you don't want to tread on the wrong piggies, learn the organizational and *power* structure inside your company.

A Quick-and-Easy Guide to Organizational Structure

Here's a quick reference guide to fairly common organizational makeups.

Let's begin with a typical organization chart for a manufacturing company, keying on those areas that most affect a field sales manager (Exhibit 3–3). Everyone in the company reports to some-

Exhibit 3–3

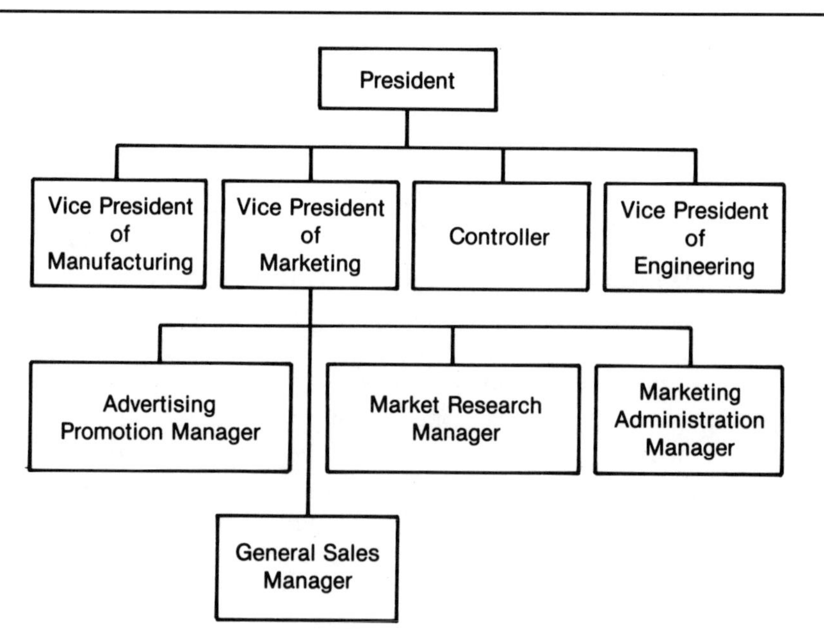

one who eventually reports to the president. That's a given in almost every company. (Incidentally, the president reports to the chairman of the board and the board of directors. No one gets a free ride unless it's a privately held company owned by one individual.) Just below the president, apparently on equal footing with one another, are the company controller, the V.P. of marketing, the V.P. of engineering, and the V.P. of manufacturing.

These positions are apparently equal, but in every company some department heads wield more influence than others because of strong personalities, company orientation, relationships, precedence, and so forth. That topic will be discussed more fully in the section on company politics.

The Organization of Sales and Marketing

We'll focus on the V.P. of marketing, because in many companies this person controls the destiny of field salespeople and field sales managers. Reporting to the vice-president of marketing are the advertising manager, administrative manager, and so forth. These people are support types who are responsible for providing the field sales force with all that good stuff like brochures, training manuals, advertising pieces, and so forth. They don't have deadlines and usually aren't as deadline-oriented as most field salespeople. Many organizations also have product managers on staff, the tunnel-vision people who are responsible for the care and feeding of a single product or product line.

Also reporting to the V.P. of marketing is the general sales manager. If you're a branch, district, or regional sales manager in a big company, chances are that the sales manager is the highest level communication contact you have in the company except in unusual circumstances. That's because the sales manager is more directly concerned with day-to-day sales while the V.P. of marketing is absorbed with advance planning (also known as taking care of the "Big Picture").

Reengineering and Sales Management

The philosophy behind reengineering is to eliminate middle layers of management and give more decision-making responsibility authority to employees on the firing line. As it applies to sales, the territory salesperson is given access to more information, perhaps via a mobile computing device, and allowed more latitude in making decisions concerning the customer.

Does reengineering mean less control for the sales manager? Perhaps in overseeing day-to-day nitty-gritty details it does. With the petty decisions out of the way, however, the manager can now spend more time on and give more attention to legitimate management tasks.

The Fundamental Differences Between Sales and Marketing

As a general rule, the marketing job is considered more cerebral and the sales manager's role more rough-and-tumble. In some organizations the head of sales has a position equal to the top marketing job. This is an enlightened attitude. Without today's sales, tomorrow's marketing ideas are irrelevant.

Field Sales Reporting Structures

In almost all organizations, branch, district, and regional managers report up the line that leads to the general or national sales manager. If you're the branch manager the salespeople who work out of your branch report to you. You, in turn, report to the district or regional manager, who controls many branches. The regional managers report directly to the general sales manager.

The bigger the company the more this division of responsibility is necessary to control the sales operation. It allows senior managers to get a sense of what's going on in the field without talking to or reading the reports of every single person on the sales force.

In essence, the branch managers summarize the data for their areas; the district and/or regional managers summarize the sales data of all the branches they oversee. The national sales manager reads these summaries of summaries.

The Chain-of-Command Concept

Most companies revere and venerate this chain-of-command concept. Line managers are supposed to report up the line in the manner described. If a manager has had a request turned down by the person directly above, it's considered bad manners, and worse politics, to polish the proposal and take it up the line. Going over the boss's head is counterproductive to career aspirations. No matter how persuasive the case, no matter how important the circumstance, this action won't be appreciated.

While it's not okay for the field manager to bypass the boss, it's considered acceptable for the boss to bypass the field manager. (Although the best senior managers won't do it.) Occasionally a senior manager will telephone or otherwise contact one of the field reps directly to get needed information quickly. The manager must not feel that he or she is being superseded. The boss may have needed information in a hurry. When field managers get to the top, they can ignore organizational protocol too.

The Importance of Loyalty

Every manager should give complete loyalty to the person in the slot above. Loyalty is one of the most important attributes any manager can bring to the job. It's the one thing a leader can't do without. If managers want loyalty from the people who report to them, they should give it to their superiors. Managers who want to advance their careers never disparage their superiors to staff members or to senior management. Neither group will appreciate this kind of backbiting. If nothing else, it's poor judgment because word will certainly get back to the boss eventually. It's perfectly acceptable to quarrel privately over a decision or direction, but when the discussion is finished, the disagreement should be left in the room.

True loyalty means more than refraining from making derogatory remarks. The loyal manager gives enthusiastic support to the programs superiors have developed. The loyal manager repays the confidence shown him or her by demonstrating confidence in the company programs.

How to Regard Your Relationship with Your Boss

Take advantage of the field management experience that your boss has to offer. Accept guidance and advice. Don't sulk over a criticism, because it was probably meant to improve you. You could do worse than to consider your boss a surrogate parent with the parent's usual ability to both reward and punish. The path to your next promotion is through your superior's approval of your performance. "Attitude" is one of the character traits considered most important.

The Rewards for Loyalty

Is there a reward for loyalty? Perhaps you're lucky enough to be working for a boss who's headed higher. Ride the rocket! Many managers take their loyal people with them as they ascend in the organization.

How to Work with the People in the Home Office

When speaking with company executives in the home office, remember that each of them has a "franchise." The surest way to irritate them is to interfere with the operation of this franchise. The credit manager won't appreciate pressure to override a credit decision just because you wanted to get an order shipped out this month. It would be better to work with the credit manager to find ways to get the customer's past-due account current.

Some departments are more powerful than others. You'll soon find out which department wields the whip in your company. (Here's a quick hint: It's the department with the veto power over other departments' programs.)

When dealing with home office personnel at every level, assume that everyone is acting in good faith, if not efficiently. The shipping department didn't deliberately send out your last order via the wrong carrier. Perhaps your directions weren't clear. If you get a reputation as a constant complainer the people at the home office or plant can literally wreck your career. Deliberate sabotage isn't necessary. All that's needed is to ignore all those priority requests you make. So respect the fact that the people in the home office are trying to do the best job they can.

A Seven-Point List That Will Make Any Field Manager a Home Office Darling

Here's a short list that will make you a home office favorite:

1. Make your requests politely.
2. Don't make every call a "the bomb is going off in 30 seconds" emergency. This gets stale.
3. On any special requests give full instructions.
4. Follow up verbal requests with written memos.
5. Call and thank people when you get the special handling you asked for. Send memos to their superiors.
6. Delay at least 48 hours before sending memos complaining about poor handling. Then throw the memos away.
7. Spend a few seconds recognizing that the voice on the other end of the line belongs to a person.

If you do all these things, your rush-rush jobs will be treated in a rush-rush fashion.

A Short Course in Office Politics

"Man is a political animal," said the Greek philosopher Aristotle, back in the third century B.C. Things haven't changed much in the past 2,300 years. Maneuvering, backbiting, and elbowing for position are still favorite pastimes. Not in your company you say? As long as people are competing for promotions, power, and the prestige corner office, they will play company politics.

The battles are waged with self-serving memos, secret agendas, and power alliances. The skirmishes are not always between individuals. Entire departments may be feuding with one another. You can almost see the barbed wire strung as you move from one part of the office building to another.

In some companies, organizational structure encourages internal maneuvering. For example, executive compensation is often based on the number of people supervised. The more people in the department, the bigger the paycheck for the person running it. This gives the executive a real incentive to collect bodies. If the executive can manage to take over a department headed by a rival, he brings home a bigger paycheck and consolidates his power base.

What Office Skirmishes Are All About

Rivalries often develop because individuals and departments within companies have common "public relations" goals. These goals are

- To claim glory for the things that go right.
- To avoid blame for the things that go wrong.

If the company enjoys a banner year, who gets most of the credit, the sales department, who got the orders in the front door, or manufacturing, who shipped the goods out the back? When the torrent of red ink threatens to cut another Grand Canyon through the company parking lot, who's to blame, the sales department, who can't obtain signed orders at pistol point, or manufacturing, who jacked up the cost of goods so high it gave buyers vertigo?

The battle rages endlessly. The stakes are promotions, raises, power, and control. The credit department feels salespeople demand irresponsible credit limits. Service thinks manufacturing has allowed quality to deteriorate. Manufacturing *knows* that service is nitpicking.

How Office Politics Affects the Ambitious Sales Manager

Does office politics mean anything to the ambitious sales manager? Field managers are lucky to be a long way from the front lines (the home office). They usually can keep their distance from home office disputes if they choose to. Sometimes the home office manager is forced to choose sides.

Whatever the case it's important for managers to know the political situation in their companies. The best tactic is not to become involved in any intramural battles. However, it is necessary to understand them. For example, managers should learn just how much clout their bosses have. Is the boss a rising comet or a burned-out meteorite? The manager's direct superior's place in the company pecking order determines what he or she can and can't get done. The boss's power often determines just how far a manager can rise in the company.

What to Do If the Boss Is Out of Favor

If the boss appears to be losing a power struggle, the manager must still offer complete loyalty. The senior executive can still be a mentor or "rabbi" who sponsors the manager and gives advice on how to move up in the company. If a manager is stuck with a boss near retirement and deadheading for the last few years, some company showcasing may be necessary. A manager in this circumstance should get involved with projects and in-house presentations where skills, enthusiasm, and personality can be viewed by other senior executives. The manager should reach out, establish recognition among other managers and departments within the company.

Still, one of the biggest problems a manager can face is reporting to a person who is out of favor. The superior's predicament could easily become the manager's predicament.

A weak or unpopular supervisor is not an easy dilemma to resolve. Loyalty must be maintained. A subordinate who is disloyal is regarded as shifty and unreliable, regardless of the circumstances. However, if a superior is supported in losing battles, the manager who fought alongside becomes tainted. In some cases when senior managers are fired, their subordinates are dismissed along with them.

The best tactic for the manager faced with this situation is to build a network of friends and allies outside his or her immediate line of authority. Relationships are established with others, but there is never an effort to make the out-of-favor boss look bad. This kind of behavior would cause the manager to be regarded as untrustworthy. The senior manager probably still has the authority to fire people. A show of disloyalty could result in dismissal. Never forget that a senior manager in trouble may still possess a powerful network of friends inside the company. Some survive their wounds and eventually triumph.

Downsizing: Eight Signs That Suggest It's Time for a Sales Manager to Start Sending Out Résumés

The sales department isn't immune from the corporate rush to reduce the workforce. Downsizing is a fact of organizational life. Who survives after the smoke clears is as much a matter of positioning as anything else. Is your job safe? Here are some signs that suggest when sales managers may be vulnerable even if they're knocking quota for a loop:

1. Salespeople aren't asking for the manager's help anymore. The sales process has become so complicated that bringing in the sales manager for one call won't matter, or he or she isn't particu-

larly effective. Either way, the field sales force has ceased to regard the sales manager as a resource to be tapped.

2. Sales channels are changing. If the sales manager is tied to dying channels, he or she may not be able to shift quickly enough to the new avenues.

3. The word "reengineering" is frequently whispered in the corporate hallways. Reengineering is a gentle way of saying "we are determined to cut out the fat." Are you adding a layer of blubber to the corporate waistline?

4. Sales training, marketing support, and other goodies are being reduced. A "Night of the Long Knives" may not be far behind.

5. There's too much on the manager's plate. The manager has become responsible for paper shuffling and cranking out so many different reports that there's no time left to spend in the field with reps and customers.

6. Line salespeople are given more authority. If salespeople are given the authority to make decisions previously made by the sales manager, why is that manager needed? (You can bet senior management is asking that question.)

7. Mergers, consolidation, and channel realignment in the industry have led to larger but fewer customers. Okay, the deals are bigger, but there aren't so many of them. With fewer customers, fewer salespeople *and managers* are needed to service them.

8. New systems are installed that put field reps on-line with the corporate office. If salespeople can tap into the system to get inventory information, customer data, pricing updates, and so forth, from their laptops, the sales manager's role as an information source is limited.

What these signs suggest is that the role of the sales manager in that particular organization is changing. Technology is forcing much of that change, aided by a strong push from senior management. There is no way an individual sales manager can resist this force. The best strategy is to remain valuable to the company.

A Summary of Company Politics

Company politics are a fact of corporate life. Field managers are partially shielded from office manipulations, but home office people are not. No one is entirely immune. The best "pacifist" policy is to do the job the best way possible. The manager should always give complete loyalty to the person in the slot above. A good rule of thumb is to always act in the company's best interest. One defense against being on the wrong side in a company squabble is superperformance. A solid record of meeting or exceeding quota assignments is as strong a political statement as any sales manager can make.

Chapter Four

How to Build a Reporting System That Works

Why Salespeople Don't Like to Fill Out Reports

One of the most aggravating tasks any sales manager faces is getting staff members to turn in timely, accurate reports. Most salespeople are not detailed-oriented, and they resent the time and thought necessary to keep up with paperwork requirements. It doesn't matter what kind of reports they are—call reports, sales projections, sales summary sheets, customer activity reports, expense reports, and so forth—salespeople object to them all. Salespeople don't like to complete these reports because they're time-consuming, they take up valuable selling time, and some of the reports are complicated to complete. Most of all, reports are not liked because they pin the salesperson down, making him or her fully accountable for time and effort spent.

Why Management Needs Reports

There's a price that must be paid for organization. Timely reports are the basis of the company's intelligence system. Management cannot make informed decisions without knowledge about what's going on in the field. That knowledge must come through the activity of the field sales force. The way the knowledge is transmitted is through the reporting structure the company has set up. The reports are like weather balloons sent into the atmosphere to report on the current weather and to detect changes that could mean rain or a long dry spell. Instead of changes in atmospheric conditions, sales reports send back data on current market conditions and are sensitive to high and low pressure areas in the selling environment.

The Secret to Setting Up a Successful Reporting System

There's no question that accurate sales information is absolutely vital, but managers setting up reporting systems for their areas should remember their own distaste for paperwork when they ran territories.

Many of the complaints about paperwork requirements can be avoided by keeping the system as simple as possible. Some paperwork is absolutely necessary, but an excess of reports will prove to be a handicap, slowing down both the manager and staff members in a paper treadmill. Managers should design reports that will get the field information needed to effectively run operations, but they shouldn't insist on one more scrap of data than is absolutely vital. They should resist the temptation to obtain information that would be "nice to know." All the reporting forms in the system and those being considered should be examined with a critical eye. The primary criterion is whether the information is really necessary. Just as important is if the information is being effectively used. Many managers demand reports that never get read.

Why Reports Should Be Reviewed Periodically

About every six months reporting systems and forms should be reviewed. Are they telling the manager the things that are necessary?

Are staff members spending valuable time filling out forms just so they can be filed? Is the manager sending information up the line that is being yawned over? Are copies being distributed to disinterested parties? (The plain paper copier, more than any other device, has contributed to the dissemination of information to people who don't want it, can't use it, yet feel compelled to keep it and so file it unread. The filing cabinet industry owes a debt of gratitude to Xerox.)

What Kinds of Reports Are Absolutely Necessary

Managers should design reports that provide the kind of information that is vital to the sales operation: reports that will tell the managers what they want to know when they want to know it. The best way to develop this kind of system is by eliminating all extraneous reports. If it's not being used, it should be discarded. It's difficult enough to get staff members to file the essential reports on time.

Two Vital Sales Historical Records

The first files that should be established are a historical record and a customer profile sheet. Historical records are profiles of customers and prospects within every salesperson's territory. A basic profile sheet should contain such data as the customer name, his or her address and phone number, key contracts, number of employees, products purchased from your company, dollar volumes, and so forth. Exhibit 4–1 depicts a sample customer or prospect profile sheet.

These profile sheets should not be developed by the manager alone, but through the contribution and participation of the salesperson responsible for the account or prospect. This is a good time to discuss the potential for each account and the best plan to achieve that potential.

Exhibit 4–1
Customer or Prospect Profile

SALESPERSON________TERRITORY #_______DATE___

ACCOUNT NAME ______________________________

EXISTING CUSTOMER? __________________________

STREET ADDRESS ____________________________

CITY & STATE _______________________________

PHONE NUMBER _____________________________

KEY CONTACTS: TITLE:

____________________ ____________________

____________________ ____________________

____________________ ____________________

ANNUAL REVENUES________NO. OF EMPLOYEES______

NO. OF LOCATIONS________TYPE OF BUSINESS_______

CREDIT RATING ______________________________

ORDERS LAST FISCAL PERIOD $_________

PRODUCTS PURCHASED ________ _________ _______

ORDERS ESTIMATED THIS FISCAL PERIOD $__________

PRODUCTS_________ __________ ________________

COMPETITIVE EQUIPMENT USED __________________

COMMENTS___________________________________

____

____

____

The salesperson should carry a similar but slightly different profile sheet when working in the territory. This profile sheet should include entry spaces to record calls made on that specific prospect or customer. Space for the salesperson to write in individual comments is also valuable. Exhibit 4–2 shows a sample salesperson's customer profile sheet.

Exhibit 4–2
Salesperson's Customer Account Record

Name ______________________________
Address/Location ______________________________
Telephone No. ______________________________
Company Products Installed ______________ Contact ______________

Sales

Model		Prod. A	Prod. B	Prod. C	Prod. D	Prod. E	Prod. F	Access.	Supplies	Other	TOTAL
1st QTR.											
2nd QTR.											
3rd QTR.											
4th QTR.											
TOTAL											

Action

ID ________ ________ ________ ________
Sales Call ________ ________ ________ ________
Product Presented ________ ________ ________ ________
Demo ________ ________ ________ ________
Signed Agreement ________ ________ ________ ________
Install ________ ________ ________ ________

The Sales Itinerary Sheet

All managers want the salespeople who report to them to make effective use of their time through good advance planning. Unfortunately, many salespeople like to "play it by ear," floating like thistles on a breeze to wherever opportunity and whim take them. One of the ways to use reporting to force salespeople to do adequate advance planning is through the itinerary sheet, which can be prepared on either a weekly or monthly basis. An itinerary plan is nothing more than a calendar on which the salesperson writes down where he or she plans to be every day. This calendar is completed and filed with the manager in advance of the period to be worked. An example of a typical monthly itinerary plan is shown in Exhibit 4–3.

Why the Sales Itinerary Sheet Is Vital to the Manager

Itinerary sheets give managers an opportunity to review how their salespeople plan to spend their time. If one is making too many calls on old customers and not enough time prospecting for new ones, the manager has a chance to recommend changes in the schedule *before* the time period has passed. Managers are not always working with after-the-fact information. They must spend time in the field with staff members. Going over the itinerary plans helps them decide what days or weeks they want to spend with which salesperson to make the most efficient use of time. The itinerary sheets can be compared with sales call reports to see how effective sales personnel are in carrying out their plans. Another use of the itinerary sheet is to make comparisons with sales projections. Do the accounts the salesperson plans to call on during the period coincide with the orders projected? If not, how does the salesperson hope to close those orders?

Exhibit 4–3
Sales Itinerary

Salesperson_________________________ Territory #_________
Week of__________Days in Territory_____ Office Days____

Date	Time	Company	Purpose

The Infamous Call Report: Why Salespeople Hate It

The average salesperson has the same reaction to the required weekly call report that Dracula had to garlic and the Wolfman had to wolfbane—they shrink from these abominations. The information requested on call reports seems simple enough: Where did you go?

Who did you see? What did you sell? There's no question that the answers to these questions are absolutely vital to management. Call reports are fingers on the pulse of the business. But salespeople are not known to be detailed-minded. Most have never liked the call report, and it's doubtful that they ever will. That doesn't mean that sales managers don't need call reports from their sales teams in order to fulfill all of the responsibilities of their management roles.

Three Kinds of Call Reports

The Detailed Report

Call reports that take ten minutes a day to fill out can be designed, or ones can be developed that require a laborious two hours. Managers may be satisfied with a word or two comment after each call, or they may demand a two-page essay. The first thing to decide when designing a call report is its purpose. What kind of information is the manager seeking to obtain? Will he or she be using the call report as a kind of field warden, keeping track of salespeople, making sure that they're out there the full working day carrying the company's flag? If so, and many call reports are used for this purpose, the kind of report that's wanted is one that lists every call, the time the call was made, who was seen, and what was said. There should be a space to note phone versus in-person calls. For a thorough check, the mileage between calls could be included. A sample of a detailed call report is illustrated in Exhibit 4–4.

Managers know better than anyone else if this kind of "paper surveillance" is necessary. The detailed report does provide much detail about what staff members are doing every day. The reports are easy to check for veracity because they're hard to fudge. The problem is that they take time to fill out—and, more important, time for the manager to read. If the field sales force is large, much valuable management time will be taken up wading through these kinds of call reports. Sometimes significant information can get lost because of the sheer volume of stuff to be read. They can be useful for very young or inexperienced sales forces because the manager can determine how time was spent and counsel team members on

EXHIBIT 4–4
DETAILED CALL REPORT

DATE	ACCOUNT	PERSON CONTACTED	TIME CALL STARTED	TYPE OF CALL	RESULT

Weekly Summary

Calls made ____________________

Number of demos ____________________

Number of surveys ____________________

Number of proposals ____________________

Number of sales ____________________

Dollar value of sales ____________________

Call Types

A—Cold call

B—Survey

C—Demo

D—Proposal

E—Call back

F—Close

how to spend it more wisely. Managers who require this kind of sales report from experienced sales professionals can expect some kind of protest.

The Summary Report

The next sales report shown (Exhibit 4–5) is used by the manager who isn't interested in nonsignificant calls. This manager doesn't want to know about the number of times the salesperson walked into an office, but didn't get to talk to anyone about the company's product. The sheer number of calls isn't important, the quality of the calls is. A basic assumption is made by the manager, mainly that the salesperson is out there working. Trying is important to this manager, but it isn't as important as succeeding. Calls by themselves don't mean anything. This manager's interested in a summary of results. How many surveys were scheduled? How many demos were arranged? How many contracts were signed? The manager who relies on this kind of form doesn't need or want an hour-by-hour report on the whereabouts of his people. Results tell who's doing the job.

Because this call report gives information to the manager in summary form it's easier and less time-consuming to read. Trends are easier to spot. Potential problem areas are more apparent. The manager finds it's easier to get a picture of what's happening throughout the area. This manager is able to spend time managing and guiding, not being a warden who needs to verify the whereabouts of his people. This kind of call report is used by managers who have veteran sales forces and/or trust their people to be working.

The Narrative Report

A third kind of sales report (Exhibit 4–6) is favored by the manager who wants data in narrative form, with specific areas of information or checklists to be covered. This kind of report is useful in major-account or big-ticket sales activities that take several months, or more, to complete. Major account sales are often an up-the-ladder

Exhibit 4–5
Summary Weekly Call Report

	Contact	Surveys	Demos	Sales (Amount)
MONDAY	________	________	________	________
	________	________	________	________
	________	________	________	________
	________	________	________	________
	________	________	________	________
TUESDAY	________	________	________	________
	________	________	________	________
	________	________	________	________
	________	________	________	________
	________	________	________	________
WEDNESDAY	________	________	________	________
	________	________	________	________
	________	________	________	________
	________	________	________	________
	________	________	________	________
THURSDAY	________	________	________	________
	________	________	________	________
	________	________	________	________
	________	________	________	________
	________	________	________	________
FRIDAY	________	________	________	________
	________	________	________	________
	________	________	________	________
	________	________	________	________
	________	________	________	________
TOTALS	________	________	________	________

Exhibit 4–6
Narrative Checklist Call Report

Date____________

ACCOUNT____

INDIVIDUAL CONTACTED ______________________TITLE____________

OTHERS PRESENT______________________________________

STAGE OF NEGOTIATION (CHECK OFF IF COMPLETED):

Agreement on survey	_________
Survey completed	_________
Present survey results	_________
Review possible "advocates" from prospect company	_________
Select advocate	_________
Present solution	_________
Get agreement on benefits of solution	_________
Discuss solution with prospect's affected departments	_________
Demonstrate system	_________
Visit existing installation	_________
Trial-run proposal	_________
Fine-tune proposal	_________
Get agreement on costs	_________
Formal proposal	_________
Close sale	_________
Is program on schedule?	

COMMENTS:

____

____

____

____

process, and the measurement of interim success depends on what rung of the ladder the salesperson is perched upon. Surveys, demonstrations, agendas, getting agreement from various departments within the prospect's company, proposals, negotiations—all can chew up a lot of time, with hesitations, stutter-steps, and backsliding along the way. That's why the checklist is important. Those using the narrative sales report form may make only a few sales calls weekly. The rest of the time is spent in preparation. An entire team of people may be used to close one prospect, with the team leader preparing the report. The sales manager reading this form to check the progress of the project is often a major account manager or the general sales manager.

How to Design Your Own Call Report

These are only three kinds of call reports. There are hundreds of others—and, as stated earlier, a call report can be custom-designed for any kind of sales activity. The critical questions to be addressed when designing a call report for your operation are as follows:

1. What information do you need to know concerning your sales area to effectively manage the operation?
2. What summary information are you required to pass on to senior management?
3. How can you make it simple and painless for field salespeople to provide this information?
4. How can you make it easy for management to read and interpret the information you send them?

If you keep these questions in mind when laying out a report form, if you avoid asking for unnecessary data, you will develop a sales report that your people won't mind filling out and that you won't have trouble reading.

How to Read a Call Report: Ten Things the Manager Can Learn

Once the form is designed, how does the manager gather information from it? When sales managers go over call reports they've finally bullied their people into completing, what are the things to look for? Where's the gold that's to be mined out of the report? Where are the rich veins? Where the shovel is placed depends on what the manager wants to learn from the report. Here's a fairly standard checklist of the things most managers look for:

1. How many sales were made by the salesperson during the period reported, and what dollar volume did those orders produce? Sales is still a results-oriented game. Many a sin can be washed clean by a dynamite month. Remember the old joke? Question: How do you shut up your sales manager? Answer: You stuff his mouth with orders.

2. How many calls were made during the period? Many managers strongly believe that data on failed calls is important because each failure brings the salesperson closer to the successful call. However, those who stress quantity should remember another old sales joke: Manager: "How many calls did you make today?" Salesperson: "Forty-five. I'd have made more, but some wiseguy asked me what I was selling." You may require a list of total calls made, or perhaps just significant calls will do. Either way, your people aren't going to sell anything unless they're out in front of prospects and customers.

3. What's the ratio between calls on existing customers and calls on prospects? The manager needs this information to determine if some members of the sales team have become too comfortable, calling only the people they know. Calling on prospects, facing rejection daily, is a painful process—but business won't grow unless there is a constant influx of new customers.

4. Does the company product require more than a one-call close? If so, how many preliminary steps such as surveys, demos, proposals, and so forth, has the sales person completed during the reporting period? Does the ratio of total calls to the completion of these preliminary steps seem in line with what the other successful salespeople on the team are accomplishing?

5. Check the names and titles of the persons seen. Does it appear as if the salesperson is getting to the decision makers? The manager needs this data to make sure that some members of the team aren't spinning their wheels—making their quota of calls but not reaching the right people.

6. Check for a repetition of calls on a single prospect or customer. If such a repetition exists, the manager may wish to call the salesperson in for an explanation. Perhaps it's the sign of a problem account, and the salesperson is there frequently trying to put out a fire, or maybe the salesperson is spending time where he or she feels comfortable.

7. Check the salesperson's projections against actual sales for the period. Is this salesperson making accurate forecasts? Enthusiasm is terrific, but it must be based on realism.

8. If a manager is concerned about a particular salesperson's ability to "work smart," then the geography of the territory should be reviewed, overlaid against where the calls are being made. Is the salesperson running from one end of the territory to the other to complete two sales calls? If so, perhaps some help on planning is needed.

9. Compare total calls, surveys, demos, proposals, and so forth, on this report with those of the most successful salespeople. Are the ratios similar?

10. *Read the commentary section of the report,* if the salesperson has provided any remarks. These few sentences of narrative can help identify many different things such as the salesperson's frame of mind, comments on competitive activity, potential problems in the territory, and so forth. Most salespeople don't like to spend more time than necessary filling out these reports. If they take the effort to scribble out a few sentences when they aren't required to, you can bet that they consider the matter significant.

The Kinds of Sales Reports That Should Be Most Carefully Read

Of course, the manager won't want to look for each of those items on every report that is read. Most sales managers will want to spend more time on the reports of their marginal or problem people than they will on their top performers. When they do this they'll be putting into practice, perhaps without knowing it, the theory of *management by exception,* which is a fancy way of saying, "Pay attention to those things that are going wrong."

How to Ensure That Sales Reports Will Be Turned In on Time

When there's a short, snappy call report in use that tells the manager what he wants to know and when he wants to know it, when it gives him the basis for the information that top management needs and takes only seconds to complete—but some salespeople are still consistently late turning it in—what can the manager do next? A few salespeople will send the reports in only after repeated reminders, demands, perhaps even threats. What action can the manager take? The manager needs the information the call reports contain when it is hot, freshly popped out of the field oven. That's when the data is of peak value, when it can still be acted on. Besides, senior management won't accept the explanation that the field reports were late coming in when they want your summary data. They won't tolerate delays.

There are actions the manager can take, short of dismissal, that will prompt those staff members who are always tardy with their sales reports (they may be among the best performers) to be on time in the future. One of the simplest steps you can take is to tie the call report form to expense account approval. The manager should let the sales team know that any weekly expense account form that comes in without a call report attached will sit in a desk drawer, unapproved, until the call report arrives. Once the salespeople understand that their expense money will be delayed until they've complied with reporting requirements, most will suddenly discover that they have the time to fill out the reports after all.

Three Ways to Handle Late Report Die-Hards

Of course some salespeople are so apathetic toward paperwork that even their expense accounts don't get done for months at a time. Every so often a bulging envelope arrives from these paperwork phobics containing enough expense statements to start a roaring bonfire. For these individuals other measures to get timely call reports are required. Expense account procedures are treated in another chapter.

One system to ensure compliance with call-reporting procedures by salespeople who are always late is to ask them to be in the office on the afternoon of the day the call report is due. Those who don't have the reports completed can sit at their desks until they are done. This procedure eats into valuable selling time, and the salespeople realize it. They won't like it, but they're not behaving as responsible adults, so treating them like children is deserved.

Still another method is to make the prompt filing of sales reports one of the conditions in awarding bonuses and prizes for local sales contests. Obviously, no manager wants to make the call report the focus of any sales contest, but it can be one of the factors. Anyone with a spectacular month that will mean a substantial bonus isn't going to throw it away because he or she is too lazy to fill out a few forms.

A third system is to hold private meetings with those individuals who are always tardy with reports. Most have ambitions and aspirations beyond their current positions. They want to be managers someday. Tell them that the managers' jobs they aspire to require a heavy commitment to paperwork. When it's promotion time, one of the things that will weigh heavily in the decision of who gets the step up is how well the person is organized. A sign of self-organization is the ability to handle paperwork.

How Call Reports Benefit Salespeople

One of the things managers should stress to all members of their sales team is that the call report is a tool that they as well as managers can use. It provides valuable information to the salespeople who complete them. They're reminded about where they've been, who they've seen, and what they've accomplished.

They can see where they've been successful and where they've wasted valuable selling time. The historical record of the report gives them the information they need to reinforce their successes and to eliminate their failures. Encourage salespeople to read their own reports every week and review the past month's reports periodically.

How to Use Call Reports as a Reeducation Tool

When a salesperson is having a bad month, pull out several old reports from times when things were going great. What was happening then that is not happening now? What successful strategy was being employed then that has since been forgotten? What new, poor work habit has been learned? When a baseball player loses his rhythm, teams now refer to old films or television tapes to discover the differences in style, the bad habits that have been picked up. Call reports are the salesperson's old tapes, the replays on the past. A philosopher named Santayana said, "Those who cannot remember the past are condemned to repeat it." Well, those who record the past can profit by it.

How to Use Call Reports to Unmask the Nonworking Salesperson

One problem that all sales managers occasionally face is salespeople who just aren't working. These salespeople may look like winners. They may be articulate, have impressive work histories, know the product line, have likable personalities, dress well, and tell a convincing story on the number of orders they're going to bring in *next* month. They'd be perfect if it weren't for this one tiny flaw: They're not out there day after day working their butts off to do the job. They're at the race track or the golf course or the movie matinee or the beauty parlor (there are many more women in sales jobs these days), but they're not in front of prospects and customers.

Most sales managers will go a long way with a salesperson who is busting a gut but not getting results. The person making the effort, trying his or her best, will eventually improve. All sales managers detest those people who are there for the ride, anxious to get off the minute the trolley stops. The question is how can the free riders be detected before they're taking up every seat in the trolley? Detection often isn't easy because of the nature of selling.

Why the Nonworking Salesperson May Be Difficult to Spot

One of the things that brings people into sales is the freedom this profession offers. No company can afford a supervisor to accompany every salesperson on every sales call. Some sales jobs require the salesperson to report to the office every morning and evening, but the bulk of the day is still their own, spent with no one looking over their shoulders. For some, this lack of direct supervision is a heady freedom they cannot handle. Once beyond the sight of their managers these people can't discipline themselves to make the necessary calls that will bring success. Others may have been able to cut the mustard at one time, but now they're burned out, unwilling to face the inevitable daily rejections that are an integral part of the selling game. Some realize they're not going to last long, but in desperate efforts to hang on to their salaries or draws for a few more months, or even weeks, a few will fake call reports, making up fictitious entries, and lie about their activities.

These people are obviously not currently suited for careers in sales. They don't last long because their lack of activity inevitably shows up in the sales figures. But in the interim the manager's team quota production suffers. The sales group is like a six-cylinder engine trying to pull a heavy load with only five cylinders working.

Four Call Report Clues to the Nonworker

How can the sales manager detect and weed out the nonworker earlier, before the territory that salesperson is mishandling becomes a disaster area? The longer a malingerer has the territory, the longer it will take for the next person to put it back into shape.

A close study of the call report and attention to some behavioral patterns can help identify the shirker. Here are some of the things to look for:

1. Look for call reports that list the same calls, the same customers, the same prospects, week after week. These calls have

been fabricated, but the nonworker doesn't want to invest time or energy into anything, least of all being inventive about call reports. However, the reports are usually turned in on time. The shirker has little else to do.

2. Look for reports with very few demos or surveys in proportion to the total number of calls. Most shirkers know that these specifics are easier to check up on.
3. Look for reports that carry very few names and phone numbers. The shirker doesn't want you to check up.
4. Look for *below*-average expense accounts. The malingerer doesn't want to risk exposure over a too-high expense statement. Besides, most don't have the ambition to fabricate one that would stand up to inspection.

Ten More Ways to Detect the Nonworker

A thorough review of call reports is one way to spot a salesperson who isn't working. Behavior is another clue. Some behavioral traits to keep an eye out for include:

1. Notice the salespeople on your staff who are particularly interested in your personal schedule. They want to arrange their phone calls and visits into the office for times when the manager won't be there. They want to avoid the manager at all costs, hoping that out of sight is out of mind. Most of all they want to delay questions about what's going on in their territories.

2. Notice the salespeople who always make a point of explaining in great detail exactly where they're going when they leave the office. They give this information even when it hasn't been asked for. These people are trying to give the appearance of hustle and activity.

3. Notice the people who are always negative and unenthusiastic about any new company promotion or program. Nothing new will work as far as they're concerned. That's because they've already given up.

4. Look for the people who complain that the competitors have insurmountable advantages, superior products, better prices, wonderful advertising. They're setting up advance excuses for failure.

5. Notice those salespeople who are envious of the success of others. They imply that any good performance is due to blind luck or favoritism, or a better territory, or anything other than hard work.

6. Look for the people who continually complain that the company has set goals that are unrealistic and unreachable.

7. Look for those who don't like the company's support, who whine about delivery schedules, downgrade the company's product quality, moan about the pricing structure, scream that the credit department is cutting their throats, and ridicule management.

8. Look for those who try to convince their managers that their territories are completely unworkable, desert wastelands filled with sand and scrub cactus.

9. Look for the alibi artist with a thousand and one reasons why the job can't be done, why the prospect can't be approached, why the order can't be closed.

10. Look for those who are always late for sales meetings, who come in slovenly dressed, who haven't read the bulletins, who are never in the office one more minute than they have to be, who are surly, who, in short, have given up even the pretense of trying to do the job. They are the malingerers who will drag down the performance of the entire group.

What to Do About Nonworkers Once You Find Them Out

What to do with malingerers once they are found out? The answer is evident, but not pleasant. Nonworkers should be let go and others hired who are willing to give a day's effort. A manager is better off with a raw beginner who doesn't know the first thing about getting past a secretary than the most experienced pro who's trying to fake performance. An advanced degree in marketing won't help the person who doesn't put out any effort. The manager can polish the roughest of diamonds, but quartz never becomes a rare gem. The person who won't work can't be salvaged. Last chances, final warnings, and threats only delay the inevitable, while the hemorrhage that is draining the area of sales and profits continues. Endure the temporary pain that comes from cauterizing the wound. The manager is really doing the nonworker a favor. This kind of person is obviously not going to have a successful career in sales.

When Call Reports Should Be Verified

When should the manager check up on call reports to verify them for accuracy and make sure the calls listed were actually made? Being the warden to the sales crew steals a manager's time that could be more productively used for other activities. Managers can get more accomplished by working with people they trust to be in the field every day than they can by snooping through call reports to make sure the information is accurate.

However, instances will occur when the manager suspects that a member of the sales team is not giving that 100 percent effort. Perhaps some work is being done, but the manager can sense that the activity level in that territory is not what it should be. In this instance, the call reports should be verified.

Six Signs That Point to a Phony Call Report

What are the signs that might lead you to such a suspicion? Here are some of the most common:

1. Sales in that territory have been falling steadily for the past few months. The trend downward in this one territory is contrary to what other territories are experiencing.
2. The orders that do come in are all from existing customers. No new accounts are being opened.
3. New company products are not being sold to old customers.

4. If the manager asks to accompany the salesperson while working the territory, only old contacts and existing customers are visited. The manager is never introduced to an exciting new prospect.
5. The salesperson doesn't seem familiar with his or her territory—the layout of the customer's office location or even the customers themselves.
6. As the salesperson drags the manager from customer to customer, the manager quickly recognizes that the people being met are those who are easy to see and not necessarily the decision makers.

How to Verify Call Report Entries

When several of these conditions occur, the manager may wish to verify the salesperson's call report. The easiest way to do this is to telephone several of the customers or prospects listed on the call report. Obviously the manager shouldn't make any of these verification calls unless suspicions are very strong with some evidence to back them. When calls are made, don't pick the best customers in the territory. This could be awkward for both the manager and the customer, who may feel a degree of loyalty to the salesperson.

A prospect who is frequently listed in the salesperson's call report is a good choice. Try to telephone the prospect shortly after the salesperson claimed the call was made. You may not wish to reveal that you are checking up on the salesperson, so your telephone conversation with the prospect could go something like this:

Manager: "I'm Joe Smith, Ed Brown's boss over at Consolidated. I'm following up on a call he made to your place last week. Since Ed's visit, the company has come out with an even better offer I think you should know about." (The manager goes into the rest of the sales pitch.)

This call should not arouse any suspicion on the part of the prospect. If Ed wasn't' there, the prospect is likely to say so and ask about the offer that he should have been told about.

When Checking Up, Leave Room for Doubt

Checking up on any salesperson is a distasteful chore. Managers don't like to do it because there's no way to make the job pleasant. When the manager is forced to verify, the task should be handled in a manner that won't upset the customer or the salesperson being checked out. (The manager should always allow for the possibility that suspicions may be unfounded.)

The Difference Between the Lazy and the Nonworking Salesperson

Don't equate the lazy salesperson with the person who isn't working at all. If members of the staff aren't working hard, managers should look to themselves first. Perhaps they haven't done the best motivational job they could have done. The lazy salesperson can be redeemed, the nonworker can't. The lazy person can be persuaded to try harder, the nonworker won't try at all. The manager with a lazy salesperson has a project. The manager with a nonworker has a problem that won't go away unless it's sent away. The manager saddled with a nonworker should make a change just as fast as possible.

Chapter Summary

Reports are the method through which the sales manager learns what is happening in the field. The keys to building a reporting system that works are to request from field salespeople only that information which is important and to actually spend the time to carefully examine what is reported.

One way to "encourage" salespeople to turn in reports on schedule is to hold back processing expense account claims until all required reports are submitted.

There is hope for the inept, or even lazy, salesperson through training and encouragement. The nonworker, however, is a lost cause and should be removed from the sales team as soon as possible.

Chapter Five

How to Find and Hire Salespeople Who Can Sell

When It May Be Time to Add New Salespeople

When the sales operation is stretched too thin, when the phone is ringing off the hook with customers demanding service, when there's a file cabinet full of leads that can't be handled, when the product line is sizzling hot, when quota has been doubled and entirely new product lines are being introduced, when one of the salespeople isn't working and another is behaving like a prima donna—it may be time to add to or change members of the sales team.

How to Pick the Right Moment to Add to a Sales Staff

Aside from a shortage of bodies, how do managers decide when the time is right to add a new salesperson to the sales crew? Sometimes this decision is made for them. New people are added when there's money in the budget or when senior management approves the expense. Replacing existing salespeople is easier. Approval for replacements is generally granted when a salesperson leaves or when the manager decides a change is necessary.

Five Specific Signs That Will Help Convince Senior Management That More Staff Is Needed

When managers wish to add more salespeople they must make a convincing case to their management before getting approval. When is it time to tell the boss that additional bodies are needed? Sorry, the answer is not, When everyone is very busy. The manager must present convincing arguments that support the contention that more staff is needed. Getting approval for additional bodies is similar to making any other sales pitch, except that now the manager is selling internally. The first step is to gather the information needed to write a proposal. Here are the things to look for that will tell the manager and senior management that more staff is needed:

1. Examine the geographical size of the area the staff covers. Is it physically possible for the crew to visit all the customers and prospects within the area the number of times the company has deemed necessary? Are customers and prospects being ignored because of a lack of time?

2. What are the demographics of the area? What is the business potential of the district? Is the area growing or declining? Is the potential being realized with the number of people on the staff? Could business be improved by adding a person?

3. What is the disbursement of salespeople used in other districts within the company? Is the district under review bringing in more sales with fewer people? (Some managers might want to keep it that way. The company will give this manager high marks for efficiency.) Is the area overstaffed compared with others? (If so, tear up the proposal right now.) Can the manager guarantee that more bodies will result in more volume?

4. What's the nature of the company business? Is the company selling to a stabilized or declining market? If so, the company may

wish to keep expenses down to maximize profits. In an expanding market, the addition of new people could take advantage of the growth opportunity.

5. What's the mentality of the company at this moment in time? If the company is on an economy kick and unwilling to approve additional sales personnel no matter how convincing the arguments, why should the manager be embarrassed by making the request?

If all this information has been reviewed and the decision made that an additional person or persons are needed, the manager should put in a requisition to the immediate superior. The request should be put in as much detail as possible. It should contain the following information:

The Seven Points to Cover on a Sales Personnel Requisition

1. The job title and job description of the person the manager is requesting. Job descriptions are important. They cover the areas of responsibilities for each member of the staff. If the company doesn't use job descriptions, managers should create them. This exercise will give managers a clear idea of the exact functions they want their personnel to perform. (It's always interesting to ask every person on the staff to write his or her job description. You'll get a revelation when you discover what people think their jobs entail.) A sample job description is depicted in Exhibit 5–1.

2. The area the person will cover, if the person is to be involved in outside sales.

3. The salary the manager plans to offer.

4. The other costs to the company that are anticipated (commission income, fringe benefits, travel expenses, car allowance, and so forth).

5. The benefit to the company in terms of projected increased sales.

6. Any territory realignment that bringing on a new person will require.

Exhibit 5–1

JOB DESCRIPTION

Position: Territory salesperson, Southern California	Division: Office Equipment

Summary:
Sell office staplers, paper shredders, and mail room supplies to office equipment dealers and major account end-users in Southern California territory.

Specific Responsibilities:
Cover Orange, Los Angeles, and Riverside counties. Call on dealers and important end-users. Meet quota projections. Check dealer inventory. Discuss promotions/incentives. Help train dealer sales staff. Product-train dealer. Supply dealer literature. Work with dealer on store displays and advertising. Work product shows. Enter orders and follow through with order entry system. call on major accounts. Make demos, surveys, and proposals. Report on competitive activity. Report calls and sales activity. Suggest new products.

Reporting Structure:
Report to District Sales Manager.

Knowledge, Skills, and Experience:
Requires two years college, some mechanical aptitude, good verbal and writing skills, and four years outside sales experience, preferably in office equipment industry. Experience calling on dealers mandatory. Experience calling on end-users highly desirable.

7. The anticipated start date if approval is given to go ahead.

A sample job requisition form is illustrated in Exhibit 5–2.

Why Recruiting Is the Toughest Job a Sales Manager Has

Once approval for a staff addition is obtained, the sales manager faces the hardest task of all the varied responsibilities he or she pos-

EXHIBIT 5–2
PERSONNEL REQUISITION

Date________

Job Title ____________________	Location ____________________
Department ____________________	Date Needed____________________
Reports to ____________________	____________________
Name	Title
Group/Level____________________	Salary Range ____________________
	From ______ To______

Job Description

Brief Description of Duties ____

____

____

Experience or Qualifications Needed ______________________________

____

____

Education Required ____

Justification

Is this an increase in staff?

❑ No, replacement for ____

❑ Yes, this is an increase in staff due to the following reasons:

____

____

____

sesses—job recruitment. This task is so difficult because in sales it's impossible to judge, in advance, who will succeed and who will fail. A crystal ball that revealed this information would be worth more than the gross industrial output of North and South Dakota. There aren't any hard-and-fast rules when it comes to sales ability. Experience isn't an infallible guide. The old pro with 15 years to his credit in a similar industry could fall flat on his face when moving over to a new company. Appearance and glibness don't mean everything. The Dacron-suited ex-clerk who has difficulty stringing sentences together could become the hottest salesperson your company has had the pleasure of employing in the past 20 years.

The Difficulty of Judging Sales Talent

Judging prospective sales talent is an art, not a science. It can't be reduced to a set of numbers and run on a computer. The sales "aptitude" tests that claim to lower the odds on screening applicants eliminate only the paranoid and those too stupid to see where the questions are aimed. (No, I don't think people are whispering about me behind my back. Yes, I do enjoy persuading people to accept my point of view. And, oh boy—I'd much rather be with a group of friends than alone reading a book.)

Why Sales Talent Can't Be Measured

The truth is that sales talent, like any of the artistic talents, can't be measured or defined in the simplistic terms used by the psychologist who design and peddle the aptitude tests. This is so because many different personality types can make it in sales. The clichéd sales-type personality of an extroverted, fast-talking, flashy dresser is just that, a cliché that has no relevance to reality. An introverted, thoughtful listener may possess exactly the right personality and skills for many kinds of products and selling situations.

Why Hiring Mistakes Are Expensive

Selecting a new member of the sales team, then, is a judgment call, and it's the toughest any manager will ever have to make. When someone is hired, the company risks a chunk of money on salary, expenses, and training with no guarantee that that person will succeed. Worst of all, a territory may be dreadfully mismanaged for a time before the mistake is discovered. How can such a mistake be avoided? Unfortunately, there are no guaranteed methods.

How to Lower the Odds of Making a Hiring Mistake

Managers can lower the odds of making an incorrect decision, not by relying on the results of a battery of inconclusive tests, but by using the observations and perceptions that made them successful salespeople and is making them successful managers. That's right, the first step in the selection process is to throw away the scientific theories and use intuition, experience, and educated judgment when hiring salespeople. There are indicators and signposts any manager can use that can assist this judgment, but nothing should interfere with a "feel" as to whether or not a person belongs with the company.

Where to Find Qualified Sales Talent

Good salespeople are not easy to find. Good salespeople who will fit in with a specific company are even more difficult to uncover. Where does the manager begin to look?

Why the Sales Talent Search Should Begin at Home

The first place managers should research for a new salesperson is inside their own companies. Existing employees should be considered, including those outside the sales department. There are many who would welcome a promotion to sales. They bring knowledge about the product line and the way the company operates that would take a long time to teach to an outsider. A service technician knows how the equipment operates. A marketing support rep knows how it's used. A secretary understands product benefits from years of typing out proposals.

Existing employees who have been with the firm a length of time are good choices because they are known entities. Their reliability is known, their personalities observed. Perhaps the manager has a feeling for whether they'd make it in sales. Of course, sales techniques would have to be taught and so would the discipline that brings sales success, but promoting from within gives everyone in the organization a good feeling. It offers the impression that upward mobility is possible in the company.

How to Use Professional Connections to Find Sales Talent

A second place to look is among the salespeople managers have met in a professional capacity. These could be the people who have called on the managers trying to sell their products and services. Perhaps the manager has noted a particularly good presentation. Prospects could be among people the manager has met at seminars or trade shows or even in the waiting rooms of common prospects. Perhaps one of the company suppliers or customers has remarked about a crackerjack salesperson who's been calling on him. Certainly every manager is aware of the competitive salespeople who have given him or her headaches over the years.

Whenever the manager runs into a salesperson who he or she thinks might be an asset to the company, a business card should be requested. These cards will be the basis for a file of "prospects." When new talent is needed, the manager will have a handy list—a starting point—for the search for that new salesperson or needed replacement.

How to Find Sales Talent Through Referrals

Still another source is referrals from members of the sales team. Perhaps one of them knows a good salesperson who would love to work for the company. Most salespeople won't jeopardize their own careers by recommending someone they don't consider worthy. Managers should ask their staff members to keep their eyes open for good prospective candidates.

When Looking for Sales Talent Don't Forget About Retreads

Former sales representatives for the company are still more candidates for hire. Managers should not discount a prospect because he or she has previously worked for the company, unless that person left under a cloud. Occasionally good salespeople leave because they think the grass is greener on the next hill. Personality conflicts can force a good salesperson out the door. There are a variety of other reasons that have nothing to do with performance. These retreads have the advantage of knowing both the product line and how the company operates. Often they can get up and running faster than a completely new employee.

Prospecting on the Internet

Thousands of resumés from professional salespeople are available "on-line" through the Internet. Computer-literate sales managers can browse and, hopefully, find a match made in heaven.

Prospecting for Free

Four prospect areas—current company employees, professional contacts, referrals, and ex-employees—are relatively cost-free. They can be canvassed for potential sales staff additions without spending any money on help-wanted advertising or employment agencies. The important thing to remember about sales talent prospecting is to start well ahead of time. Establish the proper files early so you're ready to begin contacting people the moment the need arises.

Other Free or Low-Cost Possibilities for a Sales Talent Search

If beginners are acceptable, other free or low-cost areas to prospect are local high school, trade school, college, and university employment services. These services are always happy to place their graduates. States' unemployment offices will also be happy to send over a steady stream of applicants. Many of them are well qualified.

The Kind of Talent Search a Sales Manager Shouldn't Make

Some sales managers take this talent search one step further. They continually conduct preliminary interviews with prospective salespeople even though they don't have current openings. They do this so they can plug someone into a spot faster if a vacancy arises. Although it works, I don't agree with this tactic because I feel it is deceptive. The act of interviewing strongly *implies* that a job opening is available. The manager is giving the people interviewed the impression that they are candidates for immediate hire. If the manager isn't wasting his own time, he's wasting the time of the people being interviewed. Constant interviewing also takes time from other sales management duties, and the parade of people in and out of the manager's office can do nothing to lift current employees' morale. (If someone is being interviewed, is it possible that someone else is being terminated?)

How to Find Sales Talent by Spending Money

If the manager has exhausted all the networking capabilities and still isn't satisfied with any of the applicants, some company money will have to be spent to find suitable candidates. The most common methods for finding new employees is through the classified sections of the newspaper or through employment agencies. The right-sized ad, if it is well written and placed in a metropolitan newspaper, will result in a blizzard of resumés. Put an employment agency on the job, if the company has agreed to pay their fee, and they'll send over an army of applicants.

How to Find Sales Talent by Advertising for It

Many advertisements for salespeople appear in the classified section of the Sunday edition of metropolitan newspapers. These ads can go on for pages and pages. Good sales talent is always in demand, and sales ability is a transferable skill. Leaving one job for another does not have the same stigma in sales as it does for other professions, so salespeople tend to migrate a bit—always drifting toward the next valley where the competition hasn't yet been discovered and in which the prospects' lips haven't learned how to shape the word "no."

The business news sections of many metropolitan papers also carry help-wanted ads. These ads are usually bigger, in impressive black borders, and sold at higher per-line rates on the theory that they are more distinctive. The rates for either the classified or a news section of the paper will vary widely from city to city. The critical factor is the number of readers the paper can deliver. Recently, a three-inch ad in the Sunday edition of the *Los Angeles Times* is $2,766.00. In the *Chicago Tribune* it is $2,300.00. In the *New York Times* it is $2,419.00.

How to Write a Sales-Help-Wanted Ad

Every Sunday section will contain page after page of advertisements for sales help. Why should an applicant respond to any particular ad? More important, how does the manager entice *qualified* applicants to answer his or her ad? The trick is to write appealing copy. Gimmicks aren't important. Managers won't get a better response by using arrows or stars in the ad or resorting to trick phrasing. Information about the position offered is *very* important. The job, the requirements, and the opportunity should be described in as much detail as possible.

Use Proven Ads When They're Available

Large companies may have standardized help-wanted ads that are developed by the personnel department. Smaller companies may save past ads with proven "pulling power." The availability of such ads can shorten the sales manager's task. If the manager must write an ad from scratch, there is certain basic information that should be included and recommended rules to follow. Here are some specifics on how to construct your ad and what information to include.

The Eight Specifics That Should Be Included in a Sales-Help-Wanted Ad

1. The general rule for writing a help-wanted ad is, Be concise, pertinent, and truthful.

2. Always advertise the job title that is available. Is the company looking for a salesperson, district manager, marketing support rep, or what?

3. List the minimum qualifications that are required. If the company won't hire anyone with less than five years' experience in the industry, put that requirement in the ad. The company will save itself many irrelevant resumés and phone calls.

4. Detail the products the individual will be selling. It isn't necessary to give the company name if a blind ad is preferred. But if the company makes copiers, then let the ad readers know that that's the kind of product they're expected to sell. Many job seekers won't respond to an ad that doesn't carry any information about product. They fear the company doing the advertising is hustling a product they're ashamed of.

5. Include a broad description of the compensation plan. Is the company offering a salary, plus commission, plus expenses? Say so in the ad. Is this a straight-commission opportunity? Let applicants know before they mail in their resumés. It's not necessary to state the exact amount of the salary or the commission structure, but the ad should provide some idea of the position's earning potential.

(Some managers make the mistake of being overly optimistic about the income opportunities in an open territory. Try to be realistic in the earnings estimates. What do people who have similar positions earn? What were the earnings of the last person who held that specific job? There's no point in claiming earnings potential at 100 percent of quota if quota hasn't been reached in that territory for the past ten years. If a falsely rosy picture of the earnings potential is suggested, the company will recruit a salesperson who doesn't trust it once the truth is learned.)

6. Don't include anything in the ad that isn't true. Don't even use the almost obligatory statement, "opportunity for advancement" unless there is a real opportunity. Managers should be honest with themselves in this regard. If the company is growing fast and adding management levels every year, then by all means put something about promotion opportunities in the ad. If the company is in a mature industry and the average salesperson slugs it out in the trenches for years waiting for the old managers to retire, then leave out "opportunity for advancement." Apply the same yardstick for everything in the ad. Is the statement true?

7. Fringe benefits are becoming an important part of compensation packages. Include some information about the company's benefits plan.

8. If a salesperson is needed quickly, the manager may wish to include the company's phone number. Some applicant screening can be done over the phone. Actual interviewing can begin a day or two earlier than if just a post office box number is listed. However, the manager should be prepared to spend the next few days fielding phone calls. Not much of anything else will get done.

A Sample Sales-Help-Wanted Ad That Gets Results

Exhibit 5–3 is a sample of a well-written sales-help-wanted advertisement. It contains all the elements discussed in the last few pages.

Exhibit 5–3
Sample Ad

District Sales Mgr. for Ariz. and Calif. Minimum 5 yrs. exp. Cosmetics Ind., prefer. to beauty salons. Sal., comm., exp., bonus, ins., car, ret. plan. Call 999-6500

The Kind of Responses That Can Be Expected from a Sales-Help-Wanted Ad

Once the ad is in the paper, wait for the résumés to arrive. Expect anywhere from several to several hundred replies depending on the opportunity outlined, the job market in the locality, the economic climate, and a variety of other factors. One of the things that may be a surprise is the number of résumés that aren't responsive to the position available. (Some hard-core job seekers must feel an urge to mass-mail their résumés to every opening listed in the paper.) If the ad asked for someone with experience selling high-tech electronic security equipment to banks, there may be a reply from a pet food salesperson.

There will also be a sprinkling of elaborately prepared résumés, some the thicknesses of encyclopedias with more detailed information than contained in a biography of Napoleon. Pictures of the wife and little ones may be included. Others use attention-getting devices on their résumés such as special paper, or exotic colors, or even different shapes. Résumés on computer floppy disks are a recent fad. While these gaudy résumés shouldn't be dismissed out of hand, be a little suspicious of someone so anxious to substitute form for substance.

Six Tips to Help Sort Through Résumés to Find Qualified Applicants

How can the manager wade through the sea of paper received to pick out the few applicants who might be good candidates for hire? Here are clues to help uncover the gold nuggets.

1. Look for résumés that are accompanied by cover letters. An applicant who writes a cover letter to go with his résumé has gone

to the trouble of making a personal response to the ad. He or she has probably carefully selected a few ads for response. (If they are mass-mailing at least they're doing a heck of a lot of work.) Read cover letters as carefully as the actual résumé. It could provide information about the applicant's personal reaction to the ad.

2. Don't discard handwritten résumés without reading them. Sometimes a person without a prepared résumé because they're not actively in the job market will find something appealing in an ad. This person might be worthwhile interviewing.

3. Be wary of overly long resumés. The maximum length should be two pages. Anything longer shows an inability to be concise or a desire to hide a lack of meaningful experience beneath a mountain of baloney. This applicant may be trying to draw attention away from qualifications and onto presentation.

4. Look for résumés that list specific accomplishments. If the accomplishments can be verified, so much the better. Resumés that list specific companies the applicant has sold to are also impressive. If they are companies or within industries that your company has targeted or sold, you have an immediate frame of reference when you interview this applicant.

5. Discard résumés that are sloppy, inaccurately written, or filled with spelling and grammatical errors. An applicant who hasn't taken the time to proofread the résumé won't take the time to do the job properly either.

6. Don't be afraid to interview applicants who are currently unemployed. Being out of work used to create suspicion. (If he's good why does he need a job?) Today, unemployment can be caused by a variety of factors that are beyond the applicant's control. If the applicant has good, verifiable qualifications, let the interviewing process decide.

How to Decipher Résumé Language

There are other tidbits of information that can be collected by deciphering the average résumé. Exhibit 5–4 is a typical résumé, along with a few conclusions (in italics) that can be reached by a careful reading.

EXHIBIT 5–4

DAN SMITH RÉSUMÉ OF QUALIFICATIONS

EXPERIENCE

Possess more than ten years experience in computer, data processing, and office equipment sales. Management experience at the district level.

CURRENT POSITION: ABC Corp. Salesperson. *He has been a district manager, but now he's back in field sales. He might not be management material.*

DUTIES: Sell word processing systems and Personal Computers to commercial accounts in Los Angeles and San Diego counties. *Note that his territory is a local one. He might object to travel.* Always above-quota performer. Tops in sales for past six months. *If he's leading the company in sales, why does he want to make a move?*

PREVIOUS POSITION: Nano-Bit, Inc. Dist. Mgr. 10/85 to 5/86. *His tenure as a district manager lasted only seven months.* Managed the western office for company selling microfiche and data retrieval equipment. Supervised four salespeople. Quota responsibility was $90,000 a month. *He doesn't say he met the quota responsibility.*

PREVIOUS POSITION: Star Graphics Salesperson. 5/81 to 12/84. *What happened between 12/84 when he left Star Graphics and 10/85 when he started at Nano-Bit? Was he out of work?* Sold graphics and film services to major corporations throughout southern California. Always quota performer.

EDUCATION: Three years Bus. Ed., Cal-State Fullerton. *Why did he leave college one year short of graduation?*

Summary: *This man appears to have good experience selling various kinds of office systems and equipment. If he's telling the truth, he consistently meets quota when in a field position. His one stab at management appears to have ended in failure. He's never traveled. Most disturbing is his wanting to leave a job where he's an apparent success and leaving college close to graduation. Is this a pattern? I'd schedule for an interview if looking for a field person, but not if seeking a possible candidate for management. He'd have to answer some tough questions about why he's seeking a move and the unexplained ten months between jobs. Also, the résumé summary claims ten years of experience and the jobs total only seven. Where are the other three years?*

How to Reduce the Applicants to a Manageable Number

Select a half dozen or so most promising resumés and call the applicants for personal interviews. The most promising can be those whose qualifications most closely match the job's requirements, or an application may be discovered with allied, but not directly related, experience. The manager may wish to consider people with different skills so the sales team will be varied and able to support one another.

How to Screen Applicants: Ten Things to Look For

Screening applicants is hard and tedious work. As a rule the manager doesn't know the people being interviewed. The best way to begin is by looking for small signals sent out by the applicant that may tell the manager more than the written history on the applicant's resumé. Some of the things to look for are:

1. Is the applicant on time for the interview? Promptness is an important quality in a sales position.
2. How's the person's handshake? A dry, firm hand is a subtle signal of self-confidence.
3. Does the person talk too fast? Is this the way the company's sales messages should be delivered?
4. Does the person joke too much, or reminisce to excess, or gesture wildly, or have any personality traits that the manager finds offensive?
5. Is the person well groomed?
6. Can the person listen with complete attention as well as talk?
7. Does the person know the industry the company services, the products it sells, and the customers it reaches?

8. Does the person appear to be well organized, consistent, able to follow a train of thought without wandering?
9. Is the person convincing and sincere?
10. Is the person responsive to new ideas and open to new techniques?

Why First Impressions Don't Mean Everything

The answers to these questions will help you form a first impression of the applicant. However, please remember that while first impressions are important, they aren't *always* correct. Don't make the wrong answer on any of these categories an automatic blackball, and do give the applicant the courtesy of the entire interview before reaching a conclusion.

How to Match the Applicant to the Opportunity

Interviewing is the process of comparing the applicants to the job opportunity. This is where the job description is invaluable. The manager is looking for a match, the person who most closely meets the description.

What Information the Manager Wants to Get Across at Initial Interviews

The first interviews should be informal, geared to reducing the candidates down to a more workable three or four people. During this first interview the manager should discuss the industry, the job opening, and what it takes to succeed. Information about the company should also be provided. While this information is being given, the manager should try to assess the candidate. The interviewer should answer questions openly, but always be more of a listener than a speaker.

What Information the Manager Wants to Obtain from Initial Interviews

Applicants should be queried about their backgrounds and experience. Managers can do screening by asking themselves two basic questions about each applicant:

1. Does this person have the right work experience and background for the job?
2. Does this person have the ability to do the job?

It's surprising how many candidates are eliminated by these two simple questions. Another surprise of interviewing is just how many candidates eliminate themselves by what they reveal about themselves.

The Worst Hiring Mistake a Sales Manager Can Make

The worst mistake a sales manager can make is to hire someone who won't put out a maximum effort to do the job. Because the sales profession necessarily allows a certain amount of freedom, there are a few people who travel from job to job, content to last a few months taking the salary or draw a company offers, stealing it really, and then wandering off in search of the next outfit sucker enough to hire them. Some of these people are presentable, glib, and with apparent excellent credentials. They sound and look good because they have made interviewing for the next job their profession. They're well dressed, the résumés are impressive, and they know all the buzz words. They look and talk like ideal candidates, but hiring one is worse than keeping a territory vacant.

Eight Clues to Help Uncover a Job Hopper

How does a manager uncover a job hopper? There are things to look for. Here are some of them.

1. The résumé provides the first clue. Does the applicant list too many jobs? Is the average tenure in a job only two or three months? Are there long gaps in the employment history?
2. During the interview, is the person vague about the responsibilities he or she held at the jobs? Is product knowledge about previous products sold inadequate?
3. Is the person unfamiliar with the business structure at the companies he or she worked for?
4. Does the person omit references from past employers?
5. Is the person full of alibis about why the last job was left? Is the loss of the previous job never the person's fault?
6. Does the person knock all former employers?
7. Does the person claim to be employed, but able to start work for your company on a moment's notice?
8. Is the person desperate to get out of his or her current employment situation?

How to Conduct Follow-up Interviews with Job Candidates

Once the job skaters and salary moochers have been eliminated, it's time to begin the second set of interviews. This second interview should be held with a reduced number of applicants, the best of the lot that have been screened from the résumés and initial interviews. If the schedule will allow, the manager should let a few days pass while some thought is given to the answers provided by the applicants. Does what they said still make sense after reflection? It may be wise to let another person on the staff conduct at least part of the follow-up interviews to get a second opinion. This will reduce the possibility that the manager has bought into a "snow job."

Three Questions Managers Should Ask Themselves About Job Candidates

During the later interviews the manager should ask himself the following vital questions about the remaining applicants:

1. Can this person do the job?
2. Will this person do the job?
3. Will this person fit in with the sales team?

Rating Job Candidates on Intangible Factors

Some managers also try to assess job candidates' intangible characteristics such as:

- Aggressiveness
- Ego
- Ambition
- Confidence
- Empathy
- Industriousness
- Positive attitude
- Creativity
- Sociability

Unfortunately, rating people on these traits is difficult because the yardsticks come in different lengths. A salesperson bursting with confidence in front of prospects may be shy when speaking with a potential employer. There are tests that claim the ability to make these measurements, but be skeptical about their accuracy.

The Most Desirable Trait a Prospective Salesperson Can Have

One trait that is desirable, and a little bit easier to identify, is a high energy level. Take the excited and excitable salesperson every time over his or her bored and blasé counterpart.

"Tiebreakers" When It's Difficult to Choose Between Job Applicants

Third interviews and fourth interviews may be necessary when the field has been reduced to two candidates who appear to have equal credentials. There are two "tiebreakers" that can be used when it's difficult to choose between candidates. These are

1. Give the job to the person who wants it the most. Chances are this person will work hardest to make a success.
2. Give the job to the person who made the best closing presentation to nail it down. All managers prefer salespeople who know how to ask for the order. Asking for the job is just another closing technique.

Getting Senior Management Approval Before Selecting Job Candidates

Field managers may wish to enlist the aid of senior managers before making the final decision. In some cases they will want to interview final candidates before giving approval for hire. One advantage to getting the boss's input is that the manager is partially off the hook in case the hiring decision goes wrong.

How to Make the Job Offer

The final interview should be scheduled to allow both parties to make a commitment. The manager commits the job offer with the terms and conditions that have been previously discussed. The candidate commits to accept the job and to work like mad to be a success. This exchange of vows completed, the background investigation completed, the applicant is presented with a written offer just so there is no misunderstanding about the terms.

Why Background Investigations Are Necessary

Sometime during the interviewing process a background check on the prospective employee must be completed before an offer is given. The thoroughness of the investigation depends on the company. A few in sensitive industries may demand polygraph tests of their new hires. Others use investigative services who may go so far as to talk to neighbors about the applicant's "moral fiber." Still others are content with a few phone calls to former employers. Remarkably, some firms make no check at all.

Checking up on people, poking into their lives, is never pleasant. The alternative, hiring people purely on face value, would have even more unpleasant consequences for sales managers. This may come as a shock to some managers, but not every person in the employment market is what he or she claims to be.

Background Investigation Courtesy

There are courtesies regarding background checks that managers should extend to job applicants. These courtesies are:

1. Never check an applicant's background unless serious about hiring that applicant if the right answers are obtained. The reason for this is that the person may be interviewing for a half dozen different jobs. His references may be happy to field one or two calls

from prospective employers, but get a bit weary after they've heard from five or six. After a time, their replies may reflect this annoyance. Repeated checking of an applicant's references may handicap the applicant's effort to get another job.

2. The manager should let the applicant know in advance that references will be contacted. There may be one that the applicant doesn't want contacted. If the reasons seem valid the manager should respect them.

3. *Never* contact the applicant's current employer. It may result in the person being fired. This seems obvious, but many employers do it regularly. If it's necessary to contact an applicant's employer to verify that phase of work history, do it after the person has accepted an offer from the company. Offers can be made contingent on verification of current employment. If the applicant's lying, he or she won't accept the terms.

4. Share with the applicant any negative information that has been uncovered during the background check. Obviously, there are limitations here. Information given in confidence shouldn't be repeated. But if the applicant has not been accurate about the number of years with a former employer or the job title held or the salary made, share this data with the applicant. Perhaps this person does not belong on the sales team, but the knowledge that the deception has been discovered will give him or her the opportunity to be more truthful on the next interview.

Three Basic Questions to Ask on a Background Check

One of the problems with asking for references is that past employers are reluctant to give former employees poor marks. One of the reasons is that we live in a litigious society, and negative comments could cause the employer to be sued. Another, more human, reason is that many managers are perfectly willing to give an old employee, no matter how poor a performer, another chance at your expense. Then how do you frame questions that will give you the information you need to make the right decisions? Here are the routine questions to ask about an applicant's previous work history:

1. What are the dates the employee worked for the previous employer?
2. What was the title the person held?
3. What responsibilities did the person have?

One Question That Shouldn't Be Asked on a Background Check

Don't ask the old employer to verify information the applicant has given. In other words, don't ask, "Did Jane Smith work for you between June of 1980 and August of 1984?" Instead, ask, "What were the dates of Jane's employment?" Match up all the answers to the information on the résumé or job application form.

How to Find Out What a Previous Employer Really Thinks About a Job Candidate

After basic information has been verified it's time to get the previous employer's *opinion* of the job candidate. Here's a set of questions that will help determine that:

1. What were the good and bad characteristics of the ex-employee? What did you like about the person? What didn't you like?
2. What kind of sales performance did the person have?
3. Did the old employee have any poor work habits? (Managers may be surprised at how many employers will tell them that so-and-so could sell, but apparently didn't want to work very hard.)

The Probing Questions to Ask About a Job Candidate

Now get to the tough questions. These are:

1. In the opinion of the former employer, where does the applicant need improvement?
2. Why did the person leave?
3. Did performance in the applicant's territory go up or down when a new person was put in?

If the old employer has any reservations about the applicant, they should come out in this questioning.

The One Essential Question That Must Be Asked About a Job Applicant

If a manager is still not sure about the former employer's opinion, ask this one critical question: "If you had a suitable position available, would you hire this person again?" The answer to that question will help nail down the most evasive and elusive of employers. If the former employer has given nothing but praise earlier for the ex-employee, but hesitates or gives a negative response to this question, the job candidate was not well regarded.

Using Other Resources to Check on Job Applicants

There are other checks that can be made in addition to verifying former employment. One of these is a retail credit check. The information on past credit history can be purchased from a local credit bureau. The theory in seeking this information is that if the person is in hock to everyone, with a couple of outstanding judgments to boot, and the leading charge card companies have appropriated that person's credit cards and put them through a food processor—chances are that the person is not very reliable.

Most companies will verify the educational history of higher-level employees by asking for a transcript of records from colleges and universities. Few companies verify high school records. Personal references are occasionally contacted, though all that's being discovered is that the applicant actually does have a few friends.

The Legal Implications of a Formal Offer

If the applicant has survived the interviews and the reference checks and is still the candidate of first choice, now is the time for the formal offer. Many employers don't like to put offers in writing, but when hiring an applicant away from another company, chances are that person is not going to leave his or her current employer until they have a bona fide offer in writing. Be very careful what goes into an offer letter. The laws have changed over the past few years. Traditionally, employers have had the right of "employment at will." That means they could fire anyone who didn't have a union behind him whenever they wanted to. But today, more than 30 states have laws that hold employers to promises they have made to their employees. That sounds right, doesn't it? We should all be held to our word. The problem is there is a gray area the size of the planet Jupiter on just what constitutes a promise.

Contract laws vary from state to state, but almost anything that is put in writing could be considered a binding contract. For example, if the job offer letter quotes an "annual" salary, that could be interpreted as offering a one-year contract, and termination after four months could be challenged. Even the job application form can be considered an employment contract unless the form includes a disclaimer.

Nine Points to Include in an Offer Letter

Assuming that every modern salesperson lights a daily candle in Clarence Darrow's memory, how is an offer letter drafted that won't land the company in front of the Supreme Court? (It's not realistic to take the position of just forgetting about putting any offers in writing. An employed, first-rate talent won't leave a good job unless the terms and conditions of an offer are spelled out.) Here's a handy little list that will protect the company on written job offers:

1. List the position's job title. This is particularly important when a new office is being staffed and the manager may have spoken to the applicant about several job opportunities.
2. Quote the salary in weekly increments. This eliminates the possibility that the offer constitutes a long-term contract.
3. If there's a probationary period, list the term and conditions of that probation.
4. Quote the commission schedule in the letter or refer to company-published commission rates.
5. Outline the expense arrangement. Be specific.
6. List all the responsibilities of the job.
7. Provide a summary of the benefit plan. Be certain to note that a full description of benefits is available via an employee handbook or other resource.
8. Include a statement that says the plan is subject to change at management's discretion. If this isn't included, the original offer becomes chiseled in granite.
9. Include a sign-off page where the new employee acknowledges the terms and conditions of the offer.

Three Sample Job Offer Letters

Exhibits 5–5 and 5–6 are examples of several job offer letters. They are meant only as suggestions. Managers should check with an attorney to discuss the legal requirements in their states. (See, we're smart enough to use a disclaimer.)

Exhibit 5–5

Mr. Jack Williams
1225 Oak Street
Mt. Olive, CA 11122

Dear Jack:

I'm pleased to offer you the position as sales representative for the office equipment division of our company. Your duties will be to sell our line of office staplers, paper shredders, and mail room supplies to office equipment dealers and major account end-users. I've enclosed a full job description that covers your responsibilities in more detail. Your territory will include Los Angeles, Orange, and Riverside counties.

The beginning salary for this position is $450 per week. There is an annual salary revue every April. In addition to your salary, you will earn a 1 percent commission on the first $1.5 million in sales. All sales exceeding $1.5 million are commissionable at 2 percent. You are also eligible for a $2,500 bonus for meeting your quota projection. Commission and bonus schedules are subject to change without notice. This year the quota for your territory is $2 million. Because you're joining us in midyear, the quota and bonus will be prorated.

Our company pays all local job-related travel expenses. Car usage is reimbursed at 32 cents a mile. Entertainment expenses must be cleared in advance.

All new employees are subject to a 90-day probationary period. After probation you are covered by our medical, dental, and life insurance programs. These benefits are fully paid by the company. After a year, you participate in our profit sharing and are eligible for our 410K plan. A booklet offering a full explanation of our benefits plan is enclosed.

Jack, I'm very excited about the prospect of your joining our company. I know you'll become a valuable asset. If you accept this offer, please give me a written reply within 10 days.

Cordially,

Mildred Sales Manager

Exhibit 5–6

Ms. Ruth Brown
911 Appian Way
Rome, GA 99988

Dear Ms. Brown:

I'm happy to offer you the position of commissioned sales rep for our company covering the states of Georgia, South Carolina, and Florida. You'll be responsible for selling our line of carpets, tiles, and floor care supplies to dealers and distributors in these states.

You will be paid on a straight-commission rate of 10 to 18 percent, depending on the product category. A commission schedule is enclosed. These schedules are subject to change without notice. Payment will be made within 30 days after the goods have been shipped and the customer invoiced. You will receive full credit for all orders coming from customers in your well-established territory.

All travel expenses incurred in covering the territory are your own responsibility. However, we do offer a $2,500-a-month expense draw against your commission. We will cover your travel expenses during the week's training period here at the home office.

You can participate in our company's health plan, which pays 50 percent of hospitalization insurance. I've enclosed a booklet that outlines the features of this plan and a form to fill out if you wish to join.

Ruth, I think you're going to enjoy working with us. I know that we're glad to have you.

Very truly yours,

Roger Perfect

Chapter Summary

In summary, finding good salespeople is a lot like mining for gold. Tons of worthless rock must usually be processed before striking pay dirt. There are legal traps worse than any cave-in. When a rich vein is tapped, however, the entire process becomes worthwhile.

Chapter Six
How to Establish Compensation Plans

The Difficulty of Developing Good Sales Compensation Plans

Nothing is trickier than developing a good compensation plan for salespeople. The sales job is different from that of a clerk or telephone lineman, and motivating the salesperson through income opportunity is different too. There are no universal standards. A good plan for one company may be a disaster for another in the same business.

The Four Basic Objectives of a Sales Compensation Plan

The first step in developing any compensation plan is knowing what the plan is to achieve. There are some fairly standard objectives. They are:

1. The plan should motivate the sales force to produce more sales and more profit.
2. The plan should be good enough to keep the best salespeople contented and attract new people.
3. The plan should be competitive with what others in the same industry are doing.
4. There should be a relatively short time frame between accomplishment and reward. Salespeople should see quick results from their achievements.

Four Secondary Objectives of a Sales Compensation Plan

Many managers will draft compensation plans with objectives that complement the basic group. These objectives are

1. The plan should be easy for the sales force to understand. They should know what they'll make on each product sold and how and when commissions will be paid. The sales force should be able to translate the monthly commission statement without a Rosetta stone nearby.

2. The plan should be easy to administer. The monthly commission run shouldn't overload the computer. Neither should the company be required to hire a half dozen more clerks just to calculate the commission statements. (If the plan is too complicated, inevitably the company will occasionally be late paying off. Also a complicated plan leads to mistakes.)

3. The plan should eliminate arguments. Who gets paid what should be cut-and-dried. Details on commission or territory splits should be well known.

4. The plan should be fair. No plan should be designed chiefly to limit the staff's income.

Six Things Salespeople Like to See in Compensation Plans

If a manager combines the primary and secondary objectives into a compensation plan, will the salespeople be satisfied? Probably, but they'll want more. What an insatiable lot they are! Here's what the average salesperson wants to see in a compensation plan:

1. They want no ceiling on income. If they earn it, they want to get it.
2. They want compensation and rewards based on factors under the salesperson's control.
3. They want frequent payments. (Hey, that's one of management's goals too!)
4. They want a plan in which the salesperson is not penalized by unrealistic quotas.
5. They want plans that don't change drastically in midstream or even year to year.
6. They want plans without holdouts or cutoffs or chargebacks, or any of the things that many companies do to whittle down a paycheck. If the company accepts, ships, and invoices the order, salespeople want their piece of the pie.

Plug these additional factors into a compensation plan and the salespeople will adore it.

Management and Staff's Common Compensation Goals

A review of management's objectives in establishing a compensation plan and the average salesperson's objectives shows that both group's goals remarkably coincide. The company wants to sell more goods at a greater profit and the salesperson wants an unrestricted and fair opportunity to make more money. Under these circumstances it should be easy to design a plan that is suitable to both parties.

How Overmanaging Gets in the Way of Establishing Equitable Compensation Plans

Overmanaging sometimes gets in the way of establishing compensation plans that get the job done for the company and are fair to the sales staff. What's overmanaging? It's the attempt to fine-tune an instrument that's playing just fine. Overmanaging a compensation plan means seeking to limit incomes by ceilings on earnings, reducing commission schedules on popular items, revising territories, withholding or taking away prime accounts, establishing impossible quotas for bonuses, and so forth. These tactics are often self-defeating because they demotivate the sales force. Make no mistake, when a plan that means reduced earnings is introduced, you're not kidding anyone with an enthusiastic presentation.

Using Incentive Compensation

Everyone agrees that the best way to achieve all the objectives listed in this chapter is to offer salespeople some sort of incentive compensation plan. That is, the more they sell, the more they make. Money may not be the top priority on everyone's list, but it's number one with most salespeople.

The Questions Regarding Compensation and Motivation

The waters get a little murkier once beyond the general consensus that incentive plans are the best way to go. Many questions arise. Should the compensation plan be all incentive? A straight-commission plan is certainly a motivator to get out there and pitch. The person gets nothing until something is sold. But a long dry spell could drive a good salesperson right out of the business. Perhaps the best way is all salary with raises to reward superperformance. Maybe that's too darn comfortable. Perhaps a salary plus commission is the answer. This gives the salesperson a bit of security when the "no's" are flying faster than snowflakes during a Montana blizzard. The added commission plan gives the salesperson the opportunity to make much more than a minimum living. But how much salary? How much commission? What about bonuses? And why not offer better commission schedules on the more profitable lines so the salespeople will concentrate on them?

The Six Most Common Sales Compensation Arrangements

There are four fairly common methods to compensate sales personnel. Let's identify and give a brief definition of each.

Straight Commission

Under this plan the sales representative gets a percentage of the dollar value of the order. This percentage can vary from item to item, with more paid for more profitable lines and less paid for popular sellers that the company has no trouble moving. Companies pay out at different times, some upon acceptance of the order, others when it is shipped, and still others when the customer pays for it. Many straight-commission reps pay their own expenses, although the company may pay extraordinary expenses such as training, trips to seminars and trade shows, and so forth.

What's good about a straight-commission plan? The company doesn't pay out a dime until results are achieved. Essentially the salesperson is underwriting the company while the missionary work is being done. Using a straight-commission plan is a good way to establish a sales force without incurring much expense. Because the commission schedule is usually higher, a successful salesperson can earn more under a straight-commission plan. Some salespeople who are confident of their abilities will work only on straight commission.

What's wrong with a straight-commission plan? The company has less control over its sales force for one thing. They're really independent agents, with the accent on independent. They aren't tied to the company by a salary structure and can be difficult to manage. Another problem is that it is difficult to get a good commissioned rep in a virgin market where much missionary work must be done. The rep who is keen enough to get the job is also keen enough to understand that some lean times may be in store before any sales are made. In a well-established territory, it's easy to get commissioned reps, but why pay a heavy commission on what are essentially reorders? Still another problem is that good reps suffering from long dry spells may drop out.

Straight Salary

Under this plan the person gets paid so much per week or month, regardless of performance. Rewards come through salary increases. This kind of plan is often used when the person is selling products with extremely long selling cycles, or products that carry huge price tags.

The advantage of a straight-salary arrangement is that sales expenses are easy to control. The salesperson gets the amount written on the paycheck and nothing more.

The disadvantage is that the salesperson is not motivated to make that special effort to achieve.

Draw Against Commission

This plan is similar to a straight-commission arrangement except the company advances the salesperson a certain amount against future commissions. If the salesperson does not achieve the amount of the draw, theoretically he or she owes the company the money.

The advantage of a draw is that it offers the salesperson a bit of security in the form of walking-around money until a good sales record can be achieved.

The disadvantage is that the salesperson can accumulate a huge company debt that future sales can't erase. If the salesperson knows the hole is too big to crawl out of, it's a powerful *demotivating* factor. Draws-against-commission plans then can work to demoralize and demotivate the sales force.

Salary Plus Commission

Under this plan the salesperson receives a salary that is not charged against future earnings, plus a commission on all sales. Generally, the commission percentage in salary-plus-commission plans is less than for straight-commission plans.

The advantage of salary-plus-commission plans is that they offer the salesperson basic security via the salary. They also motivate the salesperson to excel because of the commission portion of the plan.

The disadvantage of this kind of plan is that some salespeople may be satisfied with their salaries and not motivated to seek extra income via commissions.

Salary Plus Bonus

In a salary-plus-bonus arrangement the company pays the salesperson a fixed salary plus a bonus if a certain dollar volume of sales is achieved. The target amount is usually changed every year.

The advantage of a salary plus bonus is that sales expenses are easy to control. Bonuses are not paid unless certain sales objectives are met. The objectives can be changed in every bonus period, motivating the salespeople to stretch.

The disadvantage of this kind of plan is that it becomes tempting for management to set targets too high. When the sales force realizes that goals are probably not achievable, they frequently become demoralized.

Salary Plus Commission Plus Draw

This kind of plan is often used to entice a veteran salesperson to join a new company. Both parties realize that the salesperson's income will not be up to previous levels until he or she has a chance to get established. Perhaps the company has a limit on beginning salaries. The compromise solution is a draw against commission in addition to the salary so the salesperson won't experience a loss of income by coming to work for a new outfit. (This kind of arrangement is limited to a specific period of time.)

The advantage of this kind of plan is that it offers a company the opportunity to attract veteran talent who can have a real impact on sales.

The disadvantage is that it puts one or two people in the company on a special status. Others who are not receiving this draw may resent it. It also puts the salesperson enjoying this plan under severe pressure to perform in the near term.

Other Types of Compensation Plans

Some companies offer variations of these plans. Salaries plus commission plus bonuses are not uncommon. Temporary salaries for a few months while the salesperson is learning the product line is also a technique that many companies adopt. After a certain period, the salesperson goes on a straight-commission or draw-against-commission plan. Guarantees are also popular. Under this arrangement, the salesperson is guaranteed a certain income regardless of performance.

Sales Managers' Compensation

The sales manager's compensation is often based on a salary plus an override on the total sales produced by the salespeople who report to the manager. This override is usually a much smaller percentage than the commission schedule for individual salespeople, but because it is based on the total business produced by the district or region, the net amount can be much larger.

If the company has a bonus plan for individual salespeople, there will almost always be a bonus schedule in place for district and regional managers as well. These bonuses often depend on the district or region reaching certain sales volume figures. Other bonus plans depend on the district or region achieving certain levels of profitability. These profit-based plans are becoming more popular as companies seek to assign more responsibility to field management personnel.

The Manager with a Territory

In many instances a branch or district sales manager will also be given responsibility for personally handling one territory within his or her assigned area. The manager is normally compensated with full commission for any sales from the assigned territory plus an override from the sales of the reps he or she supervises. The problem with this arrangement is that the manager's commission rate from personal sales will be higher than the override. There is a natural temptation for the manager to "funnel" sales into the personally managed territory.

The Key to Picking a Sales Compensation Plan for Your Company

Which plan is best suited for your company? You and the fellow managers in your company must be the judge of that. There is no single best approach. You've got to design a plan that fits your company, your product line, your industry, and your sales force. *The key to any successful plan is to concentrate on producing sales and profits for the company and not on what the salespeople earn.*

The Biggest Mistake Managers Make When Developing Compensation Plans

Some managers become so concerned about salespeople making too much income in relationship to others in the company that they develop plans that stifle rather than stimulate incentive. They put caps on earnings or cut off commissions after a certain dollar volume is achieved, or they reduce commission schedules on popular but profitable lines. These income-limiting devices work against the concept of incentive-based compensation.

Compensation Plan Objectives Summary

In summary, keep the plan simple and keep it fair. Reward those best who accomplish the most, and don't worry too much if one lucky stiff has an incredible year. Do this and you'll not only keep good people, but also there will be an army of others breaking down the door.

Don't expect any compensation plan to take the place of good management. Salespeople still need direction and guidance no matter how the plan motivates them.

House Accounts: Why They're Usually a Bad Idea

What's worse than insulting a salesperson's mother? It's telling him or her that you're making the best customer in the territory a house account. A house account is one on which the company pays no commission for goods sold. They are usually large-volume customers with special needs or special pricing that leaves no room for commission payments. Contact is handled by a member of field management or directly from the home office. Salespeople hate them because they see a large opportunity that they are forbidden to go near. Some field managers may dislike them as well. Sometimes sales volume from house accounts is excluded from the district's or region's totals.

House accounts are so demoralizing to a sales force that there should be as few as possible. The best number is zero.

Five Reasons Why a House Account Is Sometimes Necessary

Sometimes the house account is a necessary evil. Here are some of the reasons to have house accounts:

1. The customer produces so much business that it demands, and deserves, service from the top-executive level of the company. This customer would feel downgraded if handled by a line salesperson.
2. Decisions need to be made regarding this customer that are beyond the scope of a line salesperson.
3. The product sold to this customer is a special one outside the regular product line. Members of the sales force are not familiar with this product.
4. There is a special relationship between the companies that resulted in this business. Perhaps they are working together on joint projects.
5. The pricing given this customer has been calculated with such a sharp pencil that there is no room left for a commission payment.

One Bad Reason to Establish a House Account

One of the reasons *not* to establish a house account is because one customer is giving the company so much business that the salesperson is making, in management's opinion, far too much money.

Also, be extremely reluctant to take away an account from a salesperson who originally established that customer. This kind of action is extremely unfair. If absolutely necessary to make changes, offer the salesperson some kind of compensation for the loss.

Why House Accounts Should Be Examined Regularly

Sometimes when house accounts have been established they remain that way, under lock and key, forever. In many cases, the reasons for originally designating the customer as a house account have long disappeared. That's why all house accounts should be reviewed periodically, perhaps every six months. Look for changes in account status or activity that mean the customer should be turned over to one of your salespeople. Most customers are best served by the close attention a local person can offer. Long-distance management doesn't work for long periods.

Field Management Responsibility for House Accounts

If there's a house account in a field manager's area of responsibility that manager will probably be required to do some work with the customer even if it is "handled" out of the home office. There is always some fetch-and-carry work necessary with large customers. Salespeople can't be expected to do these chores because there's no compensation in it. The field manager can't make any such objection. There are no constraints on his or her time. That is reason enough, from the field manager's point of view, to try to bring the account into regular status.

How to Compensate a Salesperson for a House Account

The least a manager can do for the salesperson unlucky enough to have a house account in his or her territory is to make an adjustment if quota requirements are based on the demographics of the area. Obviously, taking out a large potential customer has reduced the territory's potential. Make up for the change by reducing quota required for bonus, and so forth. Better yet, keep the salesperson involved with the account if it's possible. Perhaps the manager can convince the home office to allow a token commission for the fetch-and-carry work all accounts require. Perhaps the salesperson can be allowed to try to sell products the house account isn't currently buying. Any action that shows this kind of effort toward fairness will boost morale considerably. The staff will know that management is doing its best to be equitable.

The Reasons for Sales Contests

Sales contests are used to boost sales and/or profits over a specific period of time. Contests can be run involving the entire product line to stimulate sales during a typically slow period, or they can be used as an incentive to move more of a high-profit product. Sometimes contests are used to get the staff's attention when a new product is introduced. Contests can be run for the entire company, or they can be used to stimulate activity for a local office. They can last three months or a week. Prizes can be anything from trips to merchandise to money. They're good morale boosters because salespeople feel they have the opportunity to earn something extra. The prizes provide concrete recognition of the salesperson's performance. Contests also help stimulate intramural competition.

12 Rules to Follow When Setting Up Sales Contests

When setting up a contest, remember that the primary aim is to motivate salespeople to extend a burst of energy over a short period of time or to focus attention on specific products. With these objectives in mind, here are some rules to follow when designing a sales contest for your company:

1. Run the contest over a short period of time. A contest that runs the entire year becomes just another commission plan.

2. Keep the contest as simple as possible. If the contest has ten pages of rules, tear them up and start over again.
3. Make winning very achievable. When staff members read about the contest, make them want to rush out and get started.
4. Keep the contest a secret until it is announced. If it's not, the salespeople will stash orders that qualify as contest entries.
5. Have tiers of winners for contests lasting any longer than one week. All-or-nothing contests lead to too many disappointments. The special achievements of each staff member should be rewarded in some way.
6. Award prizes that salespeople really want. Don't run a contest where the first-place winner gets an autographed picture of the company president.
7. As the contest progresses, post the results frequently. This stimulates the intramural competition that should be a natural development of every contest.
8. Don't split hairs when it comes to awarding prizes. The morale generated by a good contest can be destroyed by quibbling over a prize. When in doubt, rule in favor of the salesperson.
9. Don't consider any prizes won as part of the salesperson's income. Of course Uncle Sam will, but the company should not. Contest prizes are something extra, a benefit of the job.
10. Make a show of the contest awards. Presentation of prizes at a special dinner or lunch helps build morale and stimulates participation in the next contest.
11. Don't run the same contest every year. The staff will get bored. So will management. The results will be boring, too.
12. Giving lasting mementos of the sales contests, such as plaques that salespeople can display on their desk or office wall.

Sales Contest Prizes

Where do the ideas for sales contest prizes come from? The easiest prize to give is money. Cash awards are always appreciated. Money is a good choice for short-term contests such as a race to see who in the office sells the most of one product category in a week.

Merchandise and Trip Prizes

Merchandise or trips are popular for long-term contests. The contestants can earn points based on performance over the period of the contest. The points can be used to "purchase" items from catalogs supplied by sales promotion outfits who specialize in incentive awards. There are many promotional companies around with catalog after catalog of attractive merchandise. Trips can also be ordered from these companies, and there are travel agencies that specialize in arranging sales promotion travel. The salespeople from these companies can help you design a contest that will attack the job you want done. Remember, these promotional companies are making a profit on the merchandise they supply, and some of your award money is going to be eaten up by their costs for administering your program.

Five Tips on How to Get the Most Value for the Sales Promotion Dollar

What's the best way to get the most for the money put into sales contests?

1. Keep the contests as short as possible.
2. Stay with cash awards whenever possible so 100 percent of the prize money is given over to contest winners rather than to merchandising companies.
3. Give the contest winners plenty of recognition along with the prizes to show that their efforts are appreciated. They'll keep the plaque long after the cash is spent.
4. Don't pile contests one on top of the other so staff members become jaded.

5. Finally, keep the contests fun. Don't exert the same pressure on salespeople to win contests as is done for them to make quota.

THREE WAYS TO KEEP SALES ROLLING IN AFTER THE CONTEST IS OVER

What can the manager do when the sales contest is over? How does the manager ensure that there won't be a letdown by staff members? How can enthusiasm be kept alive?

1. One way is to save something exciting that can be offered at the contest's end. This could be a special price promotion for the company's customers. Make the offer good enough so the salespeople are anxious to get out there with the news.

2. The end of a contest might be used as the time to announce a new product or a product upgrade. The excitement of something new gets the sales force stimulated again.

3. Salespeople who went the extra mile during the contest period developed many leads that couldn't be closed in time to qualify for any awards. Now is the time to concentrate on those leads, bring the orders home, and, in effect, extend the energy and intensity generated by the contest far beyond the closing date.

If the sales force is directed properly, the postcontest period can produce even greater sales than did the contest itself.

WHY MANAGERS MAKE THE MISTAKE OF TRYING TO DO EVERYTHING THEMSELVES

Many managers make the mistake of wanting to do it all themselves. They spend more time in the field than they do behind a desk giving direction to their salespeople. They're more at ease before customers because direct selling is what they know best. Delegating responsibility is less comfortable for them. Sometimes field managers keep the best accounts for themselves and try to handle all the area's problems on their own. The result is that they fragment themselves until there is no sense of unity or purpose within their operations. They hold onto big accounts not because they get a bigger commission percentage on these customers, although that's often a contributing reason, but because they don't trust members of their team to handle these important customers. They try to resolve the area's problems by themselves because they mistrust the information they're being given. They're continually putting out fires because there is no clear management direction for members of their team to follow.

Motivating the Manager to Manage

How can this behavior be changed? How can the manager be motivated to reduce time spent in direct selling and increase time spent managing? The answer is that the manager must be motivated to manage just as the salesperson is motivated to sell.

Those in sales for any length of time have learned that the primary motivating factor for salespeople is money. Managers must be motivated to manage by compensation plans that make it in their best interest to do so.

The Mistake Many Companies Make When Promoting to Management

Unfortunately many companies make their salespeople pay a price, an entry fee, for that first step into management. For example, they'll take a salesperson from a territory producing an income of $50,000 a year and make that person the manager of a small branch that will earn him or her only $40,000 a year. In effect, the salesperson pays $10,000 for the title on the calling card. Of course, the salesperson is told that there is a wonderful opportunity to build up that branch and that the real rewards come with the next step up the ladder. But what is the lesson that is really learned? It is that there is more money in direct sales than there is in managing. With this kind of "instruction," isn't it natural that the manager will spend more time in front of customers and less time directing his or her salespeople?

The Four Basic Rules That Will Motivate Managers to Manage

The profit motive doesn't disappear when the salesperson becomes the sales manager. Don't ignore this fact; use it to advantage. Here are some basic rules that will help you use it:

1. Never put a new manager into a situation in which he or she can expect to earn less than earned as a territory rep. Make up any differences via increased salary or beefed-up overrides.
2. Take away any incentive the new manager may have to handle an account directly. Make all commission income for the manager the result of overrides on the sales reps' sales volumes.
3. Place more emphasis, via bonuses, on the manager achieving company long-range objectives. This will force the manager to do more long-range planning.
4. Reward the manager for the profitable performance of the branch. This will force the company's field managers to start thinking the way that senior management thinks.

A Chapter Summary of Sales Compensation Plan Objectives

In summary, designing a good sales compensation plan for a sales group isn't easy. The basic objectives are to achieve more sales and profits. These objectives can best be met by a plan that rewards achievement and doesn't penalize overachievement (see Exhibit 6–1). The actual vehicles for the compensation plan (salary, commission, draw, bonus, and so forth) are secondary to the company's intent to pay their salespeople fairly for their efforts.

Exhibit 6–1
Compensation Score Sheet

Compensation Plan	*Advantages*	*Disadvantages*
Straight commission	No results—no payment. Terrific incentive. Sales costs known. No advance costs. Costs go down when sales go down.	Less control. Sales costs can be higher. Difficult to attract good personnel. Personnel often quit when faced with a dry spell. Sales failure rate higher. Difficult plan for items with long selling cycles.
Straight salary	Sales costs often lower. Good for items with very long selling cycles. Good when long product training is required. Easy to administer.	No incentive. Salespeople become too comfortable. Income not based on results. Up-front costs for company.
Draw against commission	Payment on results. Salesperson gets "walking around money." High incentive. Sales costs known.	Salespeople often owe amounts that can't be repaid. Contributes to high turnover.
Salary plus commission	Good compromise compensation plan. Salespeople not "under the gun." Still provides incentive.	Sales costs vary. Some salespeople "coast" on salary. Up-front cost for company. Incentive not high enough.
Salary plus commission plus bonus	Provides good incentive. Income can be regulated.	Uncertain sales costs. Salespeople come to regard bonus as part of regular income.

Chapter Seven
How to Control Sales Expenses

Typical Sales Management Attitudes Toward Expenses

The typical sales manager will never be mistaken for a CPA. Numbers, ledgers, and yard-long computer printouts are not his or her game. Developing operating budgets and monitoring expenses are activities that seldom rank high on most managers' "to-do" lists. They would rather spend their time thinking and working on how to bring orders home. Let the bean counters worry about the cost to get those orders. Admiral Farragut said, "Damn the torpedoes," when he ran a Confederate blockade. "Damn the expense" is the attitude of many managers when going after business.

Why Budget Preparation Is Not a Pleasant Task

So budget work is not likely to be a pleasant task for most sales managers. Keeping a lid on expenses doesn't match the fun and excitement of making sales. The problem is compounded by the belief shared by many managers and salespeople that if they could only spend a few more bucks in pursuit of new customers, they'd bring home enough orders to justify any expense.

Why Expense Controls Are Necessary

Expense controls are necessary, and in their hearts most managers know it. One of the first things a sales manager comes to understand (because the message is pounded home by the bosses at the top) is that it's not enough to bring in orders: The orders must be profitable. That means, first of all, the goods or services delivered must be sold for the right margin of profit. Second, the cost to acquire those orders must be carefully contained. Containing sales costs leads to operating budgets, and budgets inevitably lead to controls to ensure that they are not exceeded.

Six Items That Go into a Typical Sales Branch Operating Budget

In a sales branch, and even some regional setups, budgets are easy to calculate. They're simply a forecast of the amount of money that will be spent running the operation for the next fiscal period. Here are the typical expense items:

1. The salaries paid to both the inside and outside people
2. Projected commissions, bonuses, prizes, and other payments to salespeople for moving product
3. The rent and all other office expenses
4. Local advertising expenses
5. The phone bills
6. The traveling and entertainment sales expenses, if they're reimbursed, and all the other costs associated with bringing orders into the branch

That list is very simple and straightforward compared with a sales operating budget at the senior management level.

How Budgets Are Prepared and Calculated: A Typical Worksheet

Budgets are normally prepared for an entire fiscal year but calculated month-by-month to make actual spending against forecast easier to compare and control. Exhibit 7–1 is a typical budget worksheet prepared by both branch and regional sales managers.

The Importance of Accurately Forecasting Costs

Many sales managers have two typical reactions when preparing their first budgets. The first is, "All this paperwork is a pain in the neck." When they're reconciled that the job must be done, they wonder: "How can I possibly know what I'll be spending to run this operation 10 or 12 months from now?"

That's a good question. How can managers predict the future? Let's add another question. Why is the information so doggone important anyway?

Why Expense Forecasts Help Senior Management

Let's answer the second question first. Budgets, forecasts of expenses, are necessary because they help the home office determine how much money will be needed to run the operation and how much profit can be expected if sales forecasts are met. They are a system of controls that tell the home office that expenses are reasonable in relationship to sales. They also help field managers to manage. For example, if sales forecasts are not being met by a district or region, perhaps profit objectives can still be reached by trimming expenses.

Exhibit 7–1
Branch Expense Budget

Month	Rent	Salaries	Comm. & Bonus	Travel Expense	Advert.	Other Labor	Trade Shows	Office Equip.	Recruit. Expenses	Printing	Sales Promo-tions	Train.	Tele-phone	Heat & Light	Totals
Jan.	1,200	7,000	1,500	2,300	500	0	0	0	0	0	600	0	1,100	450	14,650
Feb.	1,200	7,000	1,500	2,000	500	0	0	0	0	800	0	2,400	1,100	450	16,950
March	1,200	7,000	1,500	2,300	500	0	0	0	0	0	600	0	1,000	450	14,550
April	1,200	7,000	1,500	2,300	2,000	500	3,500	0	0	0	0	0	1,000	450	19,450
May	1,200	7,000	1,500	4,000	500	0	0	500	0	0	600	0	1,500	450	17,250
June	1,200	7,000	1,500	2,300	500	0	0	0	0	0	0	0	1,500	450	14,450
July	1,200	7,700	4,500	2,300	500	0	0	0	0	1,200	600	0	1,000	450	19,450
August	1,200	7,700	1,500	2,300	2,000	500	3,500	0	0	0	0	2,400	1,000	450	22,550
Sept.	1,200	7,700	1,500	4,500	500	0	0	0	0	0	600	0	1,000	450	17,450
Oct.	1,200	7,700	1,500	2,300	500	0	0	1,000	0	0	0	0	1,000	450	15,650
Nov.	1,200	7,700	1,500	2,300	500	0	0	0	0	400	600	0	1,500	450	16,150
Dec.	1,200	7,700	4,500	2,300	2,000	500	0	0	0	0	0	0	1,000	450	19,650
Totals	14,400	88,200	24,000	31,200	10,500	1,500	7,000	1,500	0	2,400	3,600	4,800	13,700	5,400	208,200

Remember, the manager's primary objective is to produce a certain profit from his or her area of responsibility—produce it any way possible. In many companies, the manager will be just as big a hero meeting profit objectives by lowering expenses as by exceeding sales quotas. Budget management helps management in other ways. If profit forecasts exceed expectations, then the expense spigots can be opened up another turn. Putting more money into the operation could increase sales even more.

The Sales Manager's Function as a Controller and Why It's Important

Most sales managers don't like to think of themselves as controllers or bean counters, but this function is part of their responsibility. They control their staff members by determining where and how they spend their time. They also control the amount of company money to run their area of responsibility. Often field managers' promotion into the higher levels of management is dependent on how well they exercise this control. The higher the strata of management, the more important the ability to control, to calculate sales and expense projections, and to do both jobs accurately. This ability becomes more important than the actual sales skills that got the manager promoted in the first place. It is more important than any other of the traditional sales attributes.

The Branch, District, or Regional Office as a Profit Center

Many companies are setting up their field sales offices as separate profit centers. The manager in charge is responsible not only for producing a certain sales volume within the assigned area but is also responsible for producing a net profit. Their bonuses may be tied to profit That means exercising a tight control on expenses and making sure that orders are priced so they are profitable. It is remarkable how managers working under such a plan will now question expenditures and be much less likely to approve price cutting merely to obtain an order.

When the Home Office Prepares the Field Operating Budget

In some very large companies the home office does the work for the branches, districts, and regions. The budgets are handed to the field managers in a sealed envelope. All the managers do is watch the nickels and dimes to ensure the home office figures are not exceeded. The field manager's role is that of a whistle blower. If someone is spending too much money on travel expenses, the manager blows the whistle and makes them stop.

How to Prepare a Field Operating Budget

In other companies, you'll be asked to prepare a complete operating budget. This budget will include everything it costs to run your district or region. Here are most of the standard items that go into making up a typical field budget:

- Office rent
- Salaries of sales, training, and office personnel
- Commissions and bonuses on sales
- Telephone expenses
- Office supplies
- Travel expenses, if reimbursed
- Local advertising expenses
- Temporary labor
- Local trade shows
- Office equipment purchases
- Recruitment expenses
- Local printing expenses
- Incentive expenses

- Training expenses
- Incentive awards

Most of the cost figures needed to prepare this budget are obtainable from the company or from local sources. Outside vendors for needed products, such as office supplies, can provide the other cost information needed.

Include any projected increases in cost or activity when preparing a budget. For example, when adding a salesperson be sure to include not only the person's salary but also the expenses that that person will incur to run a territory. Add a percentage for inflation. If greater activity and more sales are anticipated, reflect this expectation in the budget. More activity means more phone calls, greater travel expense, more mail, more office expense, more paperwork, and more staff to handle the increased volume.

The Best Budget a Manager Can Develop

The best kind of budget, the one that will get a sales manager good marks from senior management, is the one that gets the job done for the least money. Neat and trim with no excess fat is what they like. This kind of budget takes work. It is not developed by simply copying last year's figures and throwing in something extra because this is another year.

Eight Questions to Ask When Starting to Prepare a Budget

When preparing a budget, don't take anything for granted. Carefully examine all of last year's expenses. Ask the following questions:

1. Was every expense justified?
2. Could the job have been done for less money?
3. Can a better job be done this year for the same or less money?
4. Are all the travel and entertainment expenses necessary?
5. Are any of the salespeople extravagant and spending the company's money on nonproductive activities?

6. Is the current level of sales coverage absolutely necessary? Could two territories be combined into one without affecting sales volume?
7. Are all the clerical people currently on the payroll needed? Could the company save money by using temporaries or farming out some work?
8. Could the phone bill be cut by putting in a tie line to the home office or using a different long-distance service?

If a conscious effort is made to cut down the operation's expenses, many ways will be found to do it. Just making the effort at control will make a sales manager stand out in the eyes of senior management.

Why the Sales Staff Should Prepare Their Own Budgets

The successful manager does the planning while others do the actual work. This philosophy also applies to budget preparation and expense control. Just as the manager is required to prepare a budget for his or her area of responsibility, that manager should require staff members to prepare budgets for their territories. That's a heresy at many companies who do not allow their salespeople a voice in determining expenses. But what's wrong with asking the territory reps how much money they will need to bring in the sales quotas set for them and how they'll spend it?

Give Staff Members Budget Guidelines

Staff members are usually eager to have a voice in budget creation. However, most have not been asked to forecast expenses, so the experience will be new for them. They'll probably need guidelines, limits, and assistance to do the job. The manager will be spending a lot of time with each person going over old expense records, making suggestions, eliminating extravagances. In most cases, the manager could have completed the job with less trouble. But when a person has prepared the territory expense budget, when there has been participation in the process, he or she will work harder to stay within those self-imposed limitations.

One Expense Item That's Always Under a Manager's Direct Control

Many branch, district, and regional expenses are set in concrete, beyond the manager's control, at least on a near-term basis. These kinds of expenses include office rent, which has probably been negotiated over a long-term lease; salaries; office supplies; and so forth. One item that a manager can closely control is travel expense.

How to Control Travel Expenses

The Surefire Method to Control Expenses

The absolutely surefire way to control travel-related sales expenses is not to pay them. Many companies, particularly those whose salespeople are engaged only in local travel, do not reimburse expenses. These companies feel that commission schedules are high enough so that successful salespeople can finance the cost for running a territory. Some of these companies recognize that there are inevitable differences in the costs to operate territories and may offer an increased commission rate for "country" territories.

A nonreimbursed expense system works well in some industries, such as real estate and insurance, where it is traditional. However, more and more salespeople are demanding to be compensated for legitimate sales expenses. It's difficult to recruit good people without some form of expense reimbursement.

Controlling Expenses Through Allowances

Another sure way to limit expenses is pay salespeople set amounts—an expense allowance each month for territory operating costs. There are no surprises with this system; the manager knows exactly what costs will be. There's also no control necessary because it doesn't matter if the entire amount is spent in one day. Expense allowances are popular with small businesses because they are so easy to regulate. The problem with allowances is that uniformity is not always fair. One person may be paid too much and another person not enough. The "doer" who is hustling in the territory all day, putting on car mileage, taking customers to working lunches, accumulating parking expenses, making phone calls to clients every spare minute is penalized, while the less active salesperson is rewarded with a few extra bucks at the end of the month.

Paying Expenses on a Discretionary Basis

A third system is to pay some expenses, but not others. With this kind of system, car allowances and gas might be paid for, but not parking fees, entertainment expenses, phone calls, and so forth. An alternative to this system is to pay car mileage, but nothing else. The amount paid for each business mile driven is often based on government estimates for the cost to operate a car.

The advantage of the partial expense payment system is, again, control. The company has a pretty good fix on what it will pay out. Another advantage is that the system has a bit of flexibility. If the salesperson were to do heavy driving one month, he or she would be assured of being reimbursed for that driving. The disadvantage is that not all expenses are reimbursed. Salespeople may be reluctant to incur certain legitimate expenses, perhaps order-producing expenses, because they know they won't be repaid for them. Another disadvantage is that the salesperson may inflate car mileage or gasoline expense to cover expenses spent in other areas.

Complete Expense Reimbursement

The fourth system is complete reimbursement for all legitimate sales expenses. Companies whose salespeople are required to travel frequently usually employ a complete reimbursement system. They do this because it is costly for the individual to pay for air travel, hotel rooms, meals away from home, and so forth. It's difficult to attract a high-quality salesperson to a job involving frequent travel unless expenses are reimbursed. This reimbursement is not even considered a "perk," it's assumed to be a necessity.

Obviously, salespeople are comfortable with this fourth system. They know they will be compensated for any legitimate amount they spend. Companies are not as comfortable. The complete-expense repayment system can lead to extravagances, misuse, and outright fraud. This is particularly true if the company issues air travel and other credit cards to their salespeople. The only control possible is after the fact, after the money has been spent.

Why Reimbursement Systems Must Be Controlled

The company that wishes to reimburse their sales force for all legitimately incurred travel and entertainment expenses must control the amount of money they spend, keeping expenses within the limit of operating budgets. No company wants to pay any expensive sales "entertainment lunches" that were really dinners with Aunt Hattie. That means expense accounts must be reviewed and verified.

The first step in control is to assign every member of the sales team an operating budget. Their budgets are part of the manager's overall operating budget. As previously suggested, each salesperson should be consulted to determine the exact amount of money needed to do the job. There should be some give-and-take in this process. Staff members should believe they've been given enough resources to be successful.

The Expense Report Form as a Control Tool

After the budgets are assigned, the primary control tool is the expense report form. Many different kinds of forms are available at any office stationery store. They're all designed to detail the amount of money spent on company business.

Two Sample Expense Report Forms

Two sample forms are shown on the next few pages (Exhibits 7–2 and 7–3). The kind of form best suited to a company is dependent on the kind of sales expenses that are incurred.

Exhibit 7–2
Expense Report

Name ______________________ Week Ending ______________ 19 ____

DAY	City and State	Lodging	Transportation		Automobile Expenses	Meals Itemize Business Meals Below			Local Taxi, Carfare, Tolls, Etc.	Entertainment	Miscellaneous Expenses	Daily Total
			Air, Rail, Etc.	Limousine Car Rental, Etc	Itemize Below	Breakfast	Lunch	Dinner		Itemize Below	Itemize Below	
SUN												
MON												
TUE												
WED												
THU												
FRI												
SAT												
	Totals											

Total Expenses Paid by Employee

Entertainment and Business Meals

Date	Name of Person(s) Entertained Company, Title	Time and Place	Nature and Purpose of Entertainment	Amount	% or $ Allocated to Business

Itemize Below Those Expenses Charged Directly to the Company

- ☐ Deduct from My Advance
- ☐ Mail to Home Address
- ☐ Mail to Branch Office

REMARKS:

Automobile and Miscellaneous Expenses

Date	Items	Amount

Expenses Charged Directly to the Company (Air Fare, Auto Rental, Etc.)

Date	Items	Amount

Signature

Approved

Exhibit 7–3
Weekly Expense Report

(NAME) LAST, FIRST, MIDDLE INITIAL		T.A. NUMBER		WEEK ENDING MO. / DAY / YR.
	DEPARTMENT OR OFFICE NAME	DEPT. NO.	TELEPHONE EXT.	/ /

DATE								DATE RECEIVED / /
ROUTE COVERED FROM								
ROUTE COVERED TO								DATE PAID / /
ROUTE COVERED TO								
BUSINESS AUTO MILEAGE								CHECK NO.
EXPENSE CATEGORY								TOTAL
1. AUTO MILEAGE AMOUNT								
2. PARKING AND TOLLS								
3. CAR RENTALS								
4. TAXI & LOCAL FARES								
5. AIR FARE								
6. MEALS BREAKFAST								
MEALS LUNCH								
MEALS DINNER								
7. ENTERTAINMENT KEY EXPLAIN BELOW								
8. LODGING								
9. LAUNDRY & VALET								
10. TELEPHONE								
11. OTHER KEY EXPLAIN BELOW								
12. TOTAL EXPENSE								

BUSINESS PURPOSE FOR TRAVEL	STATEMENT OF ACCT.	
	13. LESS CASH ADVANCED DATE: / /	
	14. LESS AIRLINE TICKETS IN LINE 5 PAID BY COMPANY AND USED	
	15. NET REIMBURSABLE (DUE COMPANY)	
☐ CHECK IF UNUSED AIRLINE TICKET(S) ENCLOSED	☐ DUE EMPLOYEE ☐ RETURNED TO COMPANY ☐ CASH FORWARD	

ENTERTAINMENT	OTHER EXPENSE	KEY	Explanation of Other Expense and Entertainment—Include Guest Names and Business Purpose

COMPANY	TYPE	BALANCE SHEET MAJOR ACCOUNT / REVENUE/EXPENSE / SUB TYPE / NATURAL ACCOUNT	PROFIT COST CENTER	PROJECT CODE	AMOUNT	EMPLOYEE SIGNATURE	DATE
						APPROVAL SIGNATURE	DATE
						AUDITED BY	DATE
						VENDOR NUMBER	

How to Handle the Salesperson Who Is Chronically Late Turning In Expense Reports

Many salespeople will delay sending in expense reports for weeks and even months. Then, perhaps after an angry reminder from the manager, a flood of expense reports will arrive. Most of these late reports will not include the proper receipts or other methods of verification. (Nothing more clearly demonstrates the average salesperson's aversion to paperwork. They hate to do it even when their own money is on the line.)

The manager needs the expense reports in a timely manner to properly control expenses. Expense data must be fresh to be useful. The company controller is never too pleased to see a rash of expense reports arrive at one time. The very big expense check, even though it covers many weeks, makes it appear as if the manager has allowed the sales staff to become extravagant.

One easy way to ensure the timely arrival of expense reports is to put a deadline on them. Tell staff members that expense reports more than several weeks old will not be honored. The message is, Get the information in on time or pay the bills yourself! It's a strong message that usually gets action.

The Ten Typical Items on a Travel-and-Entertainment Expense Report

The typical travel-and-entertainment expense report covers the following items:

1. Car mileage at a set rate per mile, or car allowance plus gasoline (If a company car is used, then the normal expense allowance is for gas, oil, and upkeep.)
2. Air travel
3. Ground transport in traveled cities, and so forth, limousine, bus, taxi
4. Out-of-town meal expenses

5. Parking fees
6. Customer and prospect entertainment expenses
7. Car rental in traveled cities
8. Phone expenses
9. Baggage handling, tips, and the like
10. Miscellaneous expenses

The miscellany column is the one that varies most company to company. Some companies allow their salespeople to place stationery, business card printing, local shipping, and postage on weekly expense forms. Others insist that these kinds of items be ordered centrally.

Five Specific Steps Toward Expense Control

There are some standard controls that many companies place on expense account spending. A few of these controls are:

1. All air travel arrangements must be made by a travel agent designated by the company. With the wide variety of air fares available, the right travel agent can save hundreds of dollars *per trip*. Using a travel agent assures the company that the salesperson has not booked a higher class of travel than the standards permit.

2. Only certain hotel chains may be used when overnight travel is required. If the company has negotiated corporate rates with these hotel chains, expense costs are lowered. Another method is to limit hotel costs to a certain amount, say $55 per night's stay.

3. Only certain car rental companies can be used. Again, corporate rates may have been negotiated with these rental companies. Perhaps only certain categories of cars can be rented.

4. Meal expenses are limited to certain amounts.

5. Entertainment expenses must be approved in advance. This prevents one or two members of the sales team from acting like good-time Charley.

Expense Control Through Per Diem

Another popular method of expense control is to put a limit on all travel expenses by establishing a per diem rate for both hotel and meals. This gives the salesperson the choice of spending less on lodging and more on food, or vice versa, as he or she chooses. The traveler can also decide to skimp on both and pocket a few bucks.

How to Control Expenses by Exception

When the expense reports come in for inspection, how much attention should the manager pay to them? There is no standard system. Every sales manager has his or her own method. One popular system is the "by-exception" method. This system is very simple. If the salesperson's expenses are within budgetary limits and the salesperson is performing adequately against quota, only a cursory inspection of the weekly expense accounts is made. Individual items on the report are not scrutinized just as long as the total amount spent is within acceptable limits.

By exception is a good system because the territory salesperson is never harassed or criticized for spending too much in one particular area. The salesperson's judgment is trusted and respected. The sales manager can spend less time on expense account management because he or she is interested in monitoring only the "exceptional" expense reports, the ones that exceed budgetary standards.

Some managers use the by-exception system, but pretend not to. They'll carefully inspect a few expense accounts, on the lookout for minor discrepancies. Actually, the smaller the error they can find, the better. When they spot a mistake, they kick back the entire expense report with an instruction to redo. The salesperson who has had the report rejected naturally assumes that every report submitted is viewed with a magnifying glass. He or she will be more careful in the future.

Ten Signs That Point to a Phony Expense Claim

Still, the idea of not looking at and evaluating every single entry on an expense report bothers many sales managers. They're concerned that their salespeople may be claiming expenses that weren't spent on the company's behalf. In short, they're worried about phony expense claims. There are certain signs that help identify the false expense claim. Some of these signs are:

1. The expense reports are always added incorrectly and always in the salesperson's favor. (This alone is not damning. Many sales expense reports are incorrectly totaled.)
2. Receipts are seldom attached to the expense claims. Everyone loses a receipt now and again. If the manager has one person on staff who never submits receipts, that's the person to watch.
3. The expense report claims that the same client is being taken to lunch week after week. (Who said cheaters were original?)
4. The same restaurant is used for entertainment week after week.
5. Lunch checks total more than most dinner tabs.
6. Road mileage claims end in even numbers for trip after trip.
7. Out-of-town travel itineraries end with Friday in some fairly exotic resort city.
8. The company's travel agent is bypassed because "there wasn't enough time."
9. Receipts that are submitted often don't match the dates of travel.
10. Nonprovable items, such as meter parking and local phone calls, account for more than a normal portion of expenses.

How to Verify Individual Expense Items

If a manager suspects someone of making false claims, there are ways to verify expenses. The first rule is to insist on receipts for all claimed items. No receipt, no reimbursement. The manager who wishes to go a step further will accept only credit card receipts. Handwritten receipts are fairly easy to obtain. It's a simple process to get a block of blank receipts and write in any amount the salesperson feels the company will honor. Credit card receipts are more difficult to fake. An imprinter is used to make the copy. Most credit card receipts contain the name and address of the establishment as well as the date of sale. This makes the expense much easier to verify.

Suspicious expense lunches are easy to verify as long as the manager is careful. Just call the client who supposedly was entertained and "go over" one or two of the topics that were under discussion. The client won't know what the manager is talking about if no lunch occurred. Incidentally, the manager should ask staff members for detailed reports on the discussion subjects during any expense account luncheon. It's a good way to discourage the phony entertainment expense claim. Salespeople won't want to go to the trouble, or danger, of making up an agenda. They could have just as easily gone through with the lunch.

Charting Mileage Expense Claims

One way to verify mileage expenses is to chart the actual miles from call to call and compare that figure against the amount claimed by the salesperson on his or her expense report. If they are consistent discrepancies, week after week, there is probably a cheater on the staff.

Verifying Travel Itineraries

Travel itineraries are also easy to verify. Make sure that each traveling salesperson leaves the complete travel schedule in the office, including flights, hotels where they'll be staying, and clients they're planning to see. Compare the itinerary with the sales report of customers and prospects contacted after the trip is over. Another way to keep a salesperson "honest" is to place a call to him or her at their hotel, or messages with clients to call the office just as soon as the salesperson checks in.

Checking Up on Actual Amounts Spent

Actual amounts spent on meals and entertainment are more difficult to verify. Again, the credit card sales receipt is some help, but certainly far from foolproof. Using limits assures you that only so much money can be spent, but it doesn't guarantee that these amounts were spent in advancing the company's business. There is no better guarantee than a sales staff you can trust. If your people are doing the job and spending within budgetary limits, then avoid spending too much time on individual items. If you trust your people, most of them will reward this trust with honesty and integrity.

How to Handle the Bogus Expense Claim

If a manager has discovered that one of the salespeople has turned in a phony expense claim—perhaps a claimed expense account luncheon with a client was really dinner with the spouse—what's to be done about it?

The reaction really depends on the situation and status of the salesperson. Of course gross fraud can never be tolerated. A few dollars chiseled in a free dinner is something else. If the person was someone consistently below quota, teetering on the brink of being replaced anyway, perhaps this discovery is the nudge needed to send him or her over the edge. Poor sales ability compounded by worse judgment is reason enough to get rid of anyone.

If the person who made the false claim has a good sales record and is someone the manager would like to keep, a different approach might be taken. The situation still can't be ignored. Ask the person to come in for a meeting. At this meeting the manager should carefully contain any display of righteous indignation. Avoid inflammatory words such as "thief," "dishonest," "crooked," and so forth. The purpose of the meeting is to salvage a producer, not indulge in name-calling. Begin by giving the salesperson the evidence of the false expense entry. Avoid being judgmental. In fact, help the salesperson find a way out. Ask if the person feels that the company "owes" him or her a dinner. The answer may surprise. Perhaps the person honestly feels that some small compensation is due for work done, but not rewarded. If this is the case, or if it is something similar, it's time to be magnanimous. Let the transgressor off with a warning. Be sure to let the sinner know that all expense accounts will be examined with a microscope from now on, but let it go at that. Managers who handle this situation correctly can create loyal and trustworthy employees.

What to Do About the Company's Big Spender

There's someone on every sales team who is always over budget. No matter what the system of control or the safeguards installed, this person always manages to find ways to spend too much of the company's money. To hear the salesperson tell it, the expenses were absolutely vital to the continued existence of the company. Sometimes the overspender is a flamboyant old pro who is a consistent producer. The manager wants to keep the orders coming in the door, but would like some semblance of expense containment too. What's the best way to handle this situation?

One way is to give the person a limit: "I'll pay so much of your legitimate expense and nothing more." Somehow this approach doesn't work with big spenders. A day after the limit is imposed, they're after the manager to approve a special luncheon for 32 people at the rooftop gardens. And they can make a pretty good argument for why the party should be thrown. A compromise to the big spender means cutting out the full orchestra in favor of a string quartet.

Using a Bonus Plan to Control Expenses: Sample Scales

A better solution is to give the big spender a bonus based on the expense money that isn't spent. First, work out a reasonable budget based on information about what the territory needs. Then provide a sliding-scale bonus that lets the salesperson pick up money every time he or she saves the company a few bucks.

Here's how the yearly bonus scale might work:

	Bonus
Within Budget	$1,000
Spent Only 90% of Budget	$5,000
Spent Only 80% of Budget	$10,000

Now when the big spender thinks about entertaining, part of the money spent is coming out of the salesperson's pocket. Expense totals will head for the basement.

Four Warning Signs That Indicate Expenses May Be Out of Control

Sometimes expense containment gets away from sales managers. There are four warning signs that tell them when expenses are going out of control. These warning signs are:

1. The expense reports coming in from the field keep getting bigger every week.
2. Meetings on expenses have only a temporary effect. They may be cut back for a week or so, but soon they're bigger than ever.
3. The salespeople argue that every expense is absolutely justified and cannot be eliminated.
4. The ratio between expenses and sales is reaching unacceptable proportions.

Six Steps for Getting an Out-of-Control Budget Back on Track

What can the manager do about out-of-control expenses? Fist-pounding meetings aren't the answer. That approach has been tried. Here are actions that will work:

1. Place a moratorium on all unnecessary expenses such as entertainment. Any entertainment, including picking up the check for a cup of coffee, must be approved, in advance, by the manager.

2. Provide each salesperson with information on the current ratio of expense to sales in his or her territory. Offer a choice: The quota will be raised to bring the ratio within acceptable limits or the person will cut back on expenses. *Follow through if necessary.* The people whose quotas are raised won't have very good performance records. If bonuses are based on quota, they'll fall into line soon enough.

3. Read every expense report through a magnifying glass. Verify every line item. Kick back reports that aren't properly prepared or adequately documented.

4. Make sure that all purchases for office supplies and other items go through the company.

5. Get "on" staff members about doing better advance planning so that they're reaching the most customers and prospects in the most economical way.

6. Set a good example. Managers shouldn't ask their staff members to cut back on expenses when they entertain lavishly.

Expense Control: A Key to Promotion

The entire subject of budget limits and expense containment is not appetizing to most sales managers. It's a management chore just as filling out a call report is a salesperson's chore. There's no way managers can avoid this chore, so they may as well try to handle it as well as they can. A manager's progress in the company is partially based on the ability to set goals and to reach them. A budget is an expense goal. Containing costs is the way this goal is achieved.

Chapter Summary

Compensation plans for salespeople should be designed to reward achievement. The method of compensation varies by industry, type of product sold, and the goals of company management. There is no single plan that will fit everyone. Plans that set limits on earnings frequently cause morale problems.

Operating budgets and expense containment are among sales managers' least popular administrative tasks, but they are a necessary and important part of the job. Managers who can demonstrate an ability to control expenses and operate at a profit are always considered promotion material, even more so than their colleagues who may produce greater sales volumes.

Chapter Eight

How to Make Up Next Year's Sales Forecast

What a Sales Forecast Is

Get the crystal ball out of the closet, it's time to prepare the sales forecast. What's a sales forecast? It's a prediction of the volume of sales expected over a specific period of time. Most companies require their field managers to forecast anticipated sales a full year ahead. Quarterly and monthly forecasts are also required. Longer-range forecasts are usually handled by the senior-level managers in the home office.

Why Forecasts Are Vital

Forecasts can be made in terms of dollars or units. Many times both types are useful to the company. The sales forecast is vital in decision making. Without it the company doesn't know how much product to make, what kinds of products should be made, and how many people should be employed to produce these products. This information, in turn, determines how much raw material and supplies the company needs to buy to make the products, the production schedule for the products, the inventory of finished products, the best product mix, and the amount of advertising and number of salespeople needed to sell the products. Without the sales forecast a company's products would never get to market.

The Problem of Forecasting a Full Year in Advance

But how can any manager project a full year ahead of time how much of a product will be sold? It's never easy, even for the experts. Predicting the future will always be an art as well as a science. There are so many variables. The territory is changing. The product line is changing. The customer base is changing. Personnel are changing. The managers themselves are changing. The entire hurly-burly world is changing. So how does the manager go about making a forecast that is reasonably accurate?

The Three Classical Methods of Forecasting

There are three classical methods of forecasting. They are the *qualitative method,* the *time-series analysis and control,* and the *casual model.* Forget them now that you know what they're called. They're all too complicated for our purposes. We're going to use simplified versions of some of the techniques of these methods, but we'll do it in a way that the statisticians who do classical forecasting would not recognize. Don't worry about this. The important thing is not the method of forecasting, it's *what* is forecasted. The payoff in forecasting is based on being right.

The Easiest Way to Forecast

The easiest and most foolproof system for the field sales manager to follow is to forecast what the company has forecast. If the boys in the home office are projecting a 20 percent increase in sales for the entire company, that's what is forecast for the manager's area of responsibility. The manager's forecast will never be challenged if it simply goes along with senior management's idea of what is to come. Predict what they predict and the manager can't go wrong. Sounds too cynical? In many companies managers have no choice but to follow the home office's lead. The one latitude they have is to parcel out the number they're given to the members of their sales teams. They're asked to make a forecast, but the numbers have already been chiseled in stone and reverently handed down from the mountaintop.

This system even works, to a degree, with the senior sales managers who originate the sales forecasts. Their "bogey" is often handed down by the head of the company or a division chief.

How to Use Historical Data as a Basis for a Sales Forecast

Historical data is a good starting point from which to make an accurate forecast. Here's where to start:

Defer those things that are difficult to determine. Go back to the iffy stuff later. First, get a solid foundation of bedrock for the forecast, one that is based on facts. Where are these facts obtained? Look at the past. What does history reveal? How much did the district or region or company produce in sales last year? The year before that? And the year before that? Get the idea? When faced with making next year's forecast, run to the files and pull out last year's numbers. In fact, get out the past five years' sales figures if they are available. What's to be done with these numbers? They're to be used to make *historical sales observations.* Using historical data is a classical forecasting technique. The system is surprisingly simple.

Write down the sales figures the district has accomplished, month by month, for each of the past five years. Use the following chart to help keep the numbers in perspective (Exhibit 8–1). The result is a good historical picture of the district's sales activity.

Exhibit 8–1
Sales by Month, Past Five Years*

	1982	1983	1984	1985	1986	Percentage of Yearly Sales**
	PRODUCTS/ SUPPLIES	*PRODUCTS/ SUPPLIES*	*PRODUCTS/ SUPPLIES*	*PRODUCTS/ SUPPLIES*	*PRODUCTS/ SUPPLIES*	
JANUARY						
FEBRUARY						
MARCH						
APRIL						
MAY						
JUNE						
JULY						
AUGUST						
SEPTEMBER						
OCTOBER						
NOVEMBER						
DECEMBER						
TOTALS						

*Sales by model have not been included because the models may have changed over five years.

**The percentage of yearly sales column helps the forecaster predict seasonal variations because it shows the contribution each month makes to the total yearly sales figure.

The Benefits of a Historical Chart

This kind of chart helps in several ways. First, it provides a clear idea of the growth, or lack of growth, that the manager's specific area of responsibility has been experiencing over the years. This footprint of the past can help track the future. If sales have been growing at a steady rate of 10 percent a year, it might be safe to project a similar growth rate for the coming year. If the growth has been geometric, increasing by 5, 10, 20, 40, and 80 percent over a five-year span, projecting an increase of even 80 percent again this year might be too conservative. (But remember that geometric growth rates inevitably decline. Make sure this isn't the year the rocket starts leveling off.)

The second thing the five-year chart does is to help spot and forecast seasonal variations in business. Do the figures indicate that company sales always undergo a slump during certain periods of the year? The five-year historical chart offers dramatic proof. The manager can look like a genius if the charts help predict an increase over the entire year, but a slight downturn during the summer quarter.

Using Variable Data to Fine-tune a Sales Forecast: A List of Six Common Variables

Charting past years' activity is the fact foundation of a sales forecast, but it's only the start. Companies don't need managers capable only of making straight-line predictions based solely on historical data. Anyone with a ruler and pencil can make this kind of forecast. Now is the time when the manager must calculate the variables. Here are some of the most common variables that affect a sales forecast:

1. What are the market conditions in the area? Is the place growing or going to seed? Are companies expanding or moving out?
2. What's the competitive factor? Has the competition announced a hot new product that's going to steal away customers? Are

their pricing policies killing you? Are they particularly active in this area?

3. Is the product line getting moldy around the edges? Have prices remained competitive?
4. What's the condition of the sales team? Is it an experienced crew or a group of raw recruits?
5. What's the general mood? Are businesses optimistic? Does the sales team have good morale?
6. What shape is the industry in? Is it still growing by leaps and bounds? Is it stagnating?

What Data Not to Include in a Sales Forecast

Some forecasters like to include an assumption of economic conditions, but, again, that gets too complicated. The person making the forecast gets all tangled up making assumptions based on assumptions. It becomes a scientific version of tea leaf reading. Stick with an evaluation of market conditions.

The Role of Art in Forecasting

No manager can ever know the complete answers to all of the questions related to market conditions, but it's possible to get a handle on most of them. The art in forecasting is determining how much of a role these factors will play in next year's sale. The manager's judgment comes into play here. A hot new product might mean a 4 percent increase in sales. A territory that may be vacant for a few months might translate to a few points decrease. Be sure to evaluate all factors. A price increase might mean fewer sales, but a higher dollar volume for each order. Use the worksheet in Exhibit 8–2 to help massage the numbers.

EXHIBIT 8–2
SALES FORECAST WORKSHEET

	Last year's sales figures	________
(Plus)	Percentage allowance for price increase	________
(Plus)	Allowance for new products	________
(Plus)	Allowance for anticipated new business	________
(Plus)	Allowance for one additional sales person	________
(Plus)	Allowance for major account signed midyear	________
(Plus)	Allowance for state contract signed at year's end	________
(Plus or Minus)	Known buying plans for major customers	________
(Minus)	Allowance for territory anticipated vacant for two months	________
(Minus)	Allowance for competitor's new models	________
(Minus)	Allowance for economist's prediction of business downturn	________
(Minus)	Allowance for losing major customer	________
	This year's projection Total	________

HOW TO USE SALES STAFF MEMBERS TO HELP PREPARE ACCURATE FORECASTS

The manager doesn't lock the door to the office and stay barricaded until the forecast is finished. He or she uses the resources of the entire sales team to help. Both the territory people and the field manager who report to the person making the forecast are responsible for delivering the numbers that that manager has promised to the home office. It makes sense to seek their participation and contribution when developing those numbers. Use them to provide additional input on market conditions, circumstances in individual territories, and confirmation of business conditions.

Why the Field Sales Force Is the Best Source for Accurate Forecasts

Some professional forecasters, mostly the home office variety, have doubts about the average salesperson's ability to make accurate forecasts. But then the elite, the anointed, always have reservations about the uninitiated who haven't gone through the appropriate rituals. Field managers and the territory salespeople can be the most reliable sources for filling in the variables and confirming the projections made by using a historical forecast. They have the "feel" of the marketplace.

The field sales forecast can be the most accurate projection of all if staff members are given proper guidelines. This is particularly true of near-term forecasts. Field salespeople are in a better position than anyone else in the company to judge the immediate outlook for sales in their territories. If the home office tells a manager what to expect for the next 30 days and the sales force says something else, trust the sales force.

Using National Accounts as a Forecasting Barometer

Large national accounts are another important information source for making accurate forecasts. The buying plans of major customers are valuable indicators of economic and market conditions. They also suggest the success or failure of specific product lines. When the major accounts say they're going to stop buying a particular product, often the rest of the marketplace follows suit.

Instructing the Field Sales Force in How to Make a Forecast: A Forecasting Chart

When asking for forecasts from the sales staff, begin by giving them precise instructions. Provide them with material to work with, such as the accompanying chart (Exhibit 8–3). This chart asks the salesperson to project, customer by customer, what products will be sold and the total estimated dollar value of orders from these accounts. Note that the chart has space for identified and unidentified new customers. No salesperson ever knows, in advance, where all the new business will come from.

Why Field Forecasting Charts Measure More Than Business Potential

This chart will give the manager much valuable information about the field sales force's perception of what's going on in the field. First, it tells the manager each salesperson's estimate of next year's total sales. It also provides an important insight into the salesperson's attitude. The products that they think will be sold is another important category. If every salesperson reduces sales and quantity estimates for one particular product, perhaps it is the first rustling of a problem on the wing. Consider the possibility that something may be wrong with that product. Lower estimates of sales to important customers should also be an alarm warning of possible problems that the manager may wish to discuss with the salespeople handling those customers.

Avoiding Blue-Sky Forecasts

It's important to emphasize to staff members that blue-sky projections aren't wanted. Every manager likes to see optimism, but not unbridled enthusiasm that can be a disaster for the forecaster. Demand that the sales force make conservative forecasts.

Avoiding Pessimistic Forecasts

Obviously, forecasts can't be too conservative. Some salespeople will project zero sales if they're allowed. How does the manager

Exhibit 8–3
Yearly Projection of Products Sold by Customer

EXISTING CUSTOMER	PRODUCTS SOLD	MONTH OF ORDER	$ VOLUME	NEW CUSTOMERS	PRODUCTS SOLD	MONTH OF ORDER	$ VOLUME

SALESPERSON____________ TOTAL $ VOLUME EXISTING CUSTOMERS____________

TOTAL $ VOLUME NEW CUSTOMERS____________

TERRITORY #____________ GRAND TOTAL____________

avoid the overly cautious projection? Never link the salesperson's quota, bonus, or commission schedule to the forecast that is required of that person. Every salesperson will deliberately forecast conservatively in order to obtain an easily reachable sales target from the company.

Comparing Forecast Data

Always save all the forecasts the sales force makes. A historical record of their forecasting tendencies can be accumulated. When the material from the sales managers and territory reps comes in, compare their numbers with the historical forecast. Here's how this kind of comparison will look (see Exhibit 8–4). Compare both sets of numbers with the goals the company has set. If all three sets of numbers agree, or even come close, the forecast is completed. It can be sent up the line to senior management with the knowledge that it's the best estimate possible and that this opinion is shared by others.

Exhibit 8-4
Sales Forecast Comparison Worksheet

HISTORICAL FORECAST (ADJUSTED)________________

SALESPERSON'S FORECAST________________

COMPANY PROJECTION________________

What to Do When Forecasts Don't Agree

The estimates made by several levels within the company will seldom agree. Most territory salespeople will make very conservative projections, some predicting less sales than last year's numbers even in an up market. A few will be wildly optimistic, listing iffy prospects as sure things. The ability to sort through these judgment variations is largely based on the manager's knowledge of the personalities of the sales force. (After a few years the manager will have the historical record of past forecasts to help identify the forecasting tendencies of staff members.)

Adjusting Forecasts

The manager should adjust the territory forecasts based on past knowledge of the sales force. How do the figures match up to the historical forecast after adjustments? If the numbers come close, don't rush the forecast off to the home office just yet. Contact the salespeople whose numbers have been adjusted. Let them know of the reevaluation. Ask them if they feel the adjusted numbers are within the range of possibility. The manager shouldn't use rank to force "yes" answers. Truth is being sought, not a commitment to try hard. If the salespeople agree with the analysis, the forecast is completed. If they don't, there is more work ahead.

The Give-and-Take of Forecast Meetings

Meetings between managers and territory salespeople to discuss forecasts are often similar to other buyer/seller situations. The "seller" is the sales manager who is trying to push the idea that the new forecast will be a piece of cake. The "buyer" is the salesperson who has all these obstinate objections for why the job can't be done.

In these circumstances the sales manager shouldn't sell so hard that he or she doesn't listen to the salesperson's objections. It's important to hear and understand the reasons why the salesperson thinks the job is impossible. It's also important to make adjustments if the salesperson's arguments can't be answered. If an account representing 20 percent of the territory's business has moved away or been lost, there's no point in "convincing" the salesperson that he or she can make it up by signing many small new customers if the average new-business orders represent only a 10 percent per year increase.

Using Networking to Make Sales Forecasts: The Delphi Method

Still another technique in gathering information to make accurate forecasts is to network with other sales managers. What do they think about market conditions? Are they projecting big increases in business? Their optimism, or lack of it, can help the manager frame a forecast.

Incidentally, this system of inquiry is called *the Delphi method* and is a time-honored forecasting technique. The name goes back to ancient Greece, where people seeking answers to difficult questions would consult the oracles at Delphi. So you see, forecasting has always been tough.

The manager using this system doesn't want to poll the company's competitors, because they may not be straightforward. The best system is to establish a network of colleagues and friends in allied, but noncompetitive industries, who trade information with one another.

The Most Critical Factor in Forecasting

After referencing all the factors the final forecast will be developed. It started with a historical base, adjusted for all the variables that could affect sales, adjusted for the buying plans of major accounts, and adjusted for the input from peers. It should roughly agree with the adjusted forecasts from the sales force and the numbers you know the home office wants to achieve. If it's done right it's a forecast that can be stacked up to anything produced by the statistical whizbangs on their supercomputers. Send it in to the home office.

There's one final item the manager must take care of. This is absolutely the most critical factor in forecasting. *The manager must make the forecast come true.* The manager who can do that year after year will be called a forecasting genius.

Ten Actions to Take During a Sales Drought

Often structural changes in an industry, or other factors, can be the cause of a severe sales drought. The competition may have introduced a new product that has taken the industry by storm and caught your company off guard. Perhaps the entire industry is downsizing, closing plants by the score and laying off employees by the tens of thousands. Maybe the branch or region has undergone unusual sales personnel turnover. Whatever the reason, sales in your area of responsibility have experienced a long dry spell. Quota is not only unreachable, it is unthinkable. Here are ten corrective steps to take during sales droughts.

1. Find out the root causes. Action can't be taken to correct a situation until there is clear understanding of what caused it.
2. Don't give up calling on prospects and customers even though they're in no mood or position to buy. You'll be Johnny-on-the-spot when conditions change.
3. Think through what you're doing. Is it appropriate to this new situation? Maybe the old solutions won't work anymore. When conditions change, you have to change along with them.
4. Keep up your spirits. Focus on any positive developments. Avoid doom-and-gloom sessions. They are self-defeating.
5. Fight harder for the remaining business. Let the marketplace know that your company is going to be among the survivors.
6. Help your customers face these difficult times. Do they need longer payment terms? Less expensive solutions to their problems? Anything you do to see them through will be appreciated and remembered.
7. Avoid panic. This is no time to gut the sales force, reduce prices below the profit level, or make wholesale changes that haven't been carefully considered.

8. Improve efficiency. Things are slow, so there is time to work on internal procedures, quality control, and staff training.
9. Investigate selling to other industries and through additional channels. Don't, however, abandon the customer base your company has served.
10. Restructure quota assignments based on the new reality. Working toward goals that everyone in the organization knows are unreachable is terrible for morale. Assigning new quotas based on reality will boost everyone's spirits.

What to Do When a Forecast Is off the Mark

At some time during every manager's career, no matter how much time is spent forecasting or how hard the manager works to meet it, the results will be nowhere near what has been projected. If the entire company is off by a similar margin, the manager has no real problem. There may be some moans and groans from senior management, but the manager is in no real trouble (except, of course, the entire company may be in trouble if no one's meeting projections).

The serious problem for sales managers is when their operations are sputtering while everyone else is hitting on all cylinders. A manager faced with this situation six months into the fiscal year should ask senior management for permission to make a midyear correction.

Why Midyear Corrections Are Sometimes Necessary

A midyear correction is an adjustment to the sales projection made halfway into the fiscal period. They're used when goals set at the beginning of the year are hopelessly out of reach. They're useful to the company because the correction allows top management to make a realistic appraisal of the numbers that will actually be reached. They can adjust budgets, production schedules, profit objectives, and so forth. Corrections are also important to the sales staff. Morale sinks very low when salespeople realize that their quotas cannot be met. If bonuses are out of sight, some members of the team will stop trying hard. No matter what the reason, they will blame the company for setting the numbers too high. A midyear correction wipes the old slate clean and establishes a new starting point. Sometimes reduced bonus money is promised to those meeting the new objectives. It gives salespeople realistic goals to shoot for when previously set goals are demonstrably unattainable.

How to Sell Senior Management That a Midyear Correction Is Necessary

The manager's hardest sales job is convincing senior management that a correction is necessary. It can be done by specifying the circumstances. (Circumstances that couldn't be predicted when the forecast was made, such as several big accounts moving out of the area.) The arguments must be very powerful, very logical, and, above all, irrefutable. There may be much grumbling, but senior management is vitally interested in what the actual results will be in every area. There's no point in insisting on relying on a forecast that has proven to be unreachable.

How to Make a Midyear Forecast

If and when senior management agrees to a correction, have a new forecast already prepared. Consult members of the sales staff to assist with this new forecast. Get new numbers based on their estimates for the next six months. This is a fairly near-term forecast, and the input from the sales team should be more accurate than any other data source. Massage the numbers based on knowledge of how the individual salespeople forecast. Be sure to consider the conditions that caused the first half figures to be off. Turn in the revised figures to the home office.

An Important Tip About Midyear Corrections

Revisions are always easier for top brass to swallow if the manager projects that some of the losses for the first six months will be made up in the next period. That's not a suggestion that the manager present an overly optimistic revision so it will go down easier. Be as accurate as possible. The bullet was bitten when the manager admitted the forecast was out of reach. Meeting the revised figures can be vital to a sales management career. Senior management's perception of performance is just as important as actual performance. Performing at quota is the key to a "good" perception. If the forecast can't be met, try to revise it to one that can be met.

What Managers Can Do When They Have No Input into Their Sales Targets

In many cases field sales managers have no voice in sales forecasts and projections or in establishing district or regional quotas. The numbers are dictated to them by the home office, and the only say they have is in slicing up the total district quota and parceling it out to individual members of the sales team. Oh, there may be a big national meeting during which the big boss asks for everyone's verbal assurances that next year's numbers can be met. Woe be it to anyone who voices a negative opinion at one of these inspirational tent meetings.

Often field sales managers in these situations just take the burden that they've been handed and try to do the best job they can. There's nothing wrong with this attitude, and it may be the best way to "get along" in a company. However, it doesn't hurt managers to make their own, private, forecasts. For one thing, it gives them some practice in the art so they'll be able to handle the chore when they're the ones handing out the targets. For another, it gives them insight into how top management thinks. If the historical record of the district or region is compared against the assigned quota for the past few years, the manager can obtain an idea of the growth pattern senior management hopes to achieve.

How to Raise an Objection to an Unreasonable Sales Forecast

The manager who has privately prepared a sales forecast has gathered ammunition that can be used to raise an objection if the company's assigned figures are too high. Management may not like to hear that a mistake has been made, but it's better to make this claim before the year starts than to wait and try to excuse a subpar performance, after the fact, on the basis of an unrealistic quota.

The first thing for managers to do when their forecasts don't agree with quota assignments is to check and double-check their own numbers. Those responsible for quota assignments have had a lot of practice making forecasts. They're more likely to be right. If the numbers still don't mesh, get the sales team's forecasts. What kind of job do they think can be done? (Get information from the sales staff, but never enlist them in a disagreement with the home office.)

Managers who have made these checks and reviews and still feel the job can't be done should contact their direct superiors. This is not an action to be taken lightly. Don't even consider approaching the next level of management if there are only minor variations between the quota assignment and the homegrown forecast. There's a standard wisdom in business that says, Don't go to the boss with problems, only solutions.

If quota can't be made, the manager should know exactly what is possible. That is, have the alternate forecast prepared with full justification for how and why those numbers will be reached. This justification could include a historical perspective of sales in the district, plus the sales force's own estimates of next year's production in their territories.

What to Do When Objections over Quota Assignments Are Ignored

Sometimes reason doesn't work, particularly if the manager works for a company that doesn't seek input from the field when setting objectives. The senior managers who made the forecasts may not be in a position to retreat from their predictions before the year has even started. However, it does put the manager on record of making a statement about this year's quota assignment. The manager won't be popular when the protest is made, but also won't be subject to quite as much pressure when projections aren't met. A midyear correction may be easier to obtain.

How to Negotiate Goals with Senior Management

In some companies, next year's targets can be negotiated. The home office asks for a forecast from their field managers, massages the numbers, and sends back next year's quota assignments. Invariably, the numbers coming back call for more sales than the forecasts supplied by the field managers.

Often, these quotas from the home office are not carved in stone, but they are written in indelible ink. They can be changed, but only if the manager can muster convincing, factual arguments. The manager's own forecasts, plus the sales team's forecasts, provide the foundation for these arguments.

Don't quibble over small variations. The key to rising in most organizations is to establish the reputation as a "can-do" person. The manager who keeps telling superiors that the job can't be done is not going to establish that kind of rep. Managers must demonstrate willingness to stretch. However, the manager who is positive that quota assignment is not reachable should speak out. If the arguments and figures are convincing enough, it's possible to obtain a quota reduction.

What to Do When the Sales Staff Says Next Year's Goals Can't Be Met

This is a reverse of the circumstance discussed in the past few previous paragraphs. What's to be done when the sales staff tells the manager that the forecast is unreasonable? Perhaps the manager thinks the numbers are a stretch, but reachable. Perhaps the manager had the numbers handed down from a higher authority. What to do when a member of the sales team comes to the manager and says that next year's numbers are impossible to meet? Don't throw the person out of the office. The manager wants the option to make the same plea to senior management

Listen to the person's arguments. What's unreasonable about the quota assignment? Why can't it be met? It's likely that the person won't have an organized presentation. There may be references to big customers lost, or a changing territory, or fierce competition, but few specifics.

Answering Objections to Quota Assignments

When answering an objection about an individual quota, give the team member some insight into the quota assignment given to the entire area. The territory quota being complained about is only a tiny portion of the total. Let the person know that he or she wasn't being singled out. Next, ask the salesperson to develop a forecast for the territory. If the company number isn't reachable, what is? Ask for a full listing of business expected by existing accounts plus the orders anticipated by new accounts. At the very least this action causes the salesperson to analyze the territory and plan the year. The salesperson may take several days, or even a week, to prepare this information. Meanwhile, research the territory. When the salesperson comes back with the requested information, the manager is ready with an account-by-account rebuttal. If, for example, the salesperson's forecast shows an increase in new business of 8 percent, the manager may be able to demonstrate that this territory has consistently produced a 12 percent increase in new business.

What to Do When a Salesperson Can Prove That a Quota Assignment Is Too High

During the discussion on quota be prepared for the possibility that the salesperson is correct in the assessment that the quota assignment is too high. If the manager can't show the person where the business is going to come from, then that manager should be willing to discuss an adjustment. The manager will want the same sort of pliability from superiors. The adjustment isn't necessarily a reduced quota. Perhaps the manager can offer the salesperson a slice of a vacant territory or credit for what had been a house account. Demonstrating flexibility is a great morale builder. The staff will recognize the manager's willingness to listen to arguments.

The Last Word on Forecasts and Quota Assignments

Forecasting isn't one of the black arts, it's part science, part educated guesswork, part experience, part being a good listener, and all hard work. Nobody's forecast is right all the time. This can be unfortunate, because quota assignments are based on forecasts. In the end, plug in all the available facts, listen to everyone's opinion, take a best guess at a number, and then work like crazy to make that guess come true.

Chapter Nine

How to Set Up Branch, District, and Regional Offices

The Argument Against Office Space for Sales Representatives

Many managers feel that a plush sales office is a handicap, a magnet that draws salespeople out of the field. Why make it comfortable for the sales reps? They're supposed to be out in their territories standing in front of customers. So who needs office space? Isn't an office likely to lure salespeople away from their primary responsibility? These managers have a good case. Why does a selling organization need office space in areas remote to the home office? Why can't all field salespeople work out of their homes?

Seven Reasons Why Branch Office Space Becomes Necessary

There are many reasons why office space becomes necessary. Here are some of them:

1. When the manager wishes to keep closer control of the people on the staff. The manager saddled with a younger, less experienced staff may feel that daily supervision and coaching is necessary.
2. When there's an administrative operation that is handled at the branch level, such as order processing.
3. When the company's servicing operation is run out of the same location.
4. When some product or spare parts inventory is locally maintained and shipped.
5. When the manager would like to establish a local telemarketing setup.
6. When there's a need for office support services such as proposal and quotation writing, stenographic services, copy machines, phone answering, and so forth.
7. When the company has grown to the point where a prestige location is needed for corporate identity.

These reasons, and others, call for the establishment of branch offices. The problem that growing companies face is exactly when to establish branches, and where they should be located. It's a problem their field sales managers are often called upon to solve.

Shared Facilities: A Popular New Approach to the Sales Office Space Problem

An intermediate step between working out of the home and renting office space is now available. Many companies use shared office facilities for their sales reps. This kind of arrangement has been growing in popularity for the past few years. The way shared facilities work is that a company or individual contracts for a large amount of office space in a central location or handy suburb. The company then slices up this space into very small offices. There's a desk and a chair, and a file cabinet, and a lamp, and not enough room to do a pirouette. This kind of space is perfect for salespeople who don't spend much time in the office, but need a retreat where they can go lick their wounds.

What Shared Facilities Offer

These facilities usually offer standard office support such as secretarial service, copying, phone answering, mailing, and so forth. The rates are generally high considering the amount of space, but a good buy nevertheless because it's still less expensive than renting a complete office and contracting for the additional services. It's a good compromise between no office at all and expensive, leased facilities. The telephone answering is usually a tad more personal as well. Because there's a contact between the telephone receptionist and the salesperson, the receptionist can divulge a bit more information than "I don't know when he'll be back."

When Shared Facilities Are the Best Solution to the Sales Office Space Problem

Shared facilities are the best solution when a central location and some support services are needed for the one or two salespeople in that locality.

The Ten Signs That Tell the Manager Exactly When a Branch Office Is Necessary

It's time to consider the establishment of a branch when one or a combination of the following conditions occur:

1. When there're more than several salespeople who will be working out of the same geographic area.
2. When a branch or district manager will be working out of the same location.

3. When the company needs a local physical location to store inventory, spare parts, or provide service.
4. When the company wants to maintain a strong physical presence in the community.
5. When there's a need for permanent secretarial and office help.
6. When outside support people, such as marketing-support reps, will be working locally.
7. When sales personnel need close supervision and constant motivation.
8. When the company needs a place to conduct customer demonstrations and/or training.
9. When there's a need for a local facility to recruit and train new help.
10. When the company requires a local communication point, a command post, a rallying center.

If one or more of these conditions prevail, then consider establishing a branch.

Ten Questions That Help the Manager Establish a Branch Office Location

Deciding to establish a branch office creates as many questions as it answers. Some of the things the manager must think about include:

1. Exactly where will the branch be located? In what town and where in that town?
2. How many people will be staffing that office?
3. Who will be in charge of that facility? (Don't try to establish a branch office without a lead person in charge. This is the road to chaos.)
4. What are all the functions of the office? Is it just a place where salespeople shuffle papers? Will it be a display and demo facil-

ity? Inventory location? Service center? Training area? Shipping point? Administrative facility?

5. How many square feet are needed to fulfill all the required functions? Has the space estimate allowed for planned growth?
6. How much is the budget for the space? Don't begin looking for an office until the company provides guidelines on how much can be spent.
7. Is a prestige address needed to impress clients, or is someplace off the beaten path adequate?
8. Is the space accessible to the workforce and is reasonable transportation available? Are the sales staff likely to be tardy because the office is hard to reach?
9. Is good parking available? Most salespeople use cars. If they can't park close by, or if they need to spend big bucks for garage fees, the manager is going to have one unhappy sales force.
10. Is it central to the business area? The office may as well be close to where the customers and prospects are.

Getting Help to Acquire Field Office Space

That's a fairly big laundry list and the manager should get help to check off all the items. Most large companies have a real estate department to assist. Managers working for smaller companies are on their own. Big company or small, the field manager will probably be asked to help scout out locations. Don't go alone. The first thing to obtain in the search for good office space is a knowledgeable commercial real estate agent.

Using a Commercial Real Estate Agent

A commercial real estate agent can do the legwork while the manager is out in the field promoting the company. Level with the agent.

Tell him or her your budget for office space and how much space is needed. If the goals aren't realistic, a good agent will say so. Perhaps the search needs to be confined to another part of town, or perhaps the branch will have to do with less space.

How to Calculate the Costs for Office Space

When inspecting space with the agent, costs will be quoted to you by the square foot. To calculate the monthly rental fee, multiply the cost per square foot by the number of square feet. For example, if the space available is 1,000 square feet at 70 cents per foot, the monthly rental charge would be $700. A thousand square feet at $5 per square foot would be $5,000 per month rental. Simple, isn't it?

Additional Office Costs

The company is expected to pony up for all leasehold improvements. That means if office partitions are wanted or if power must be brought to certain rooms or if paneling is desired on the walls, the company pays for it.

Lessor Concessions

That's the way it's supposed to work, but landlords, and real estate agents, are just as anxious to close deals as the rest of us. They'll frequently make concessions to get good tenants. One of the concessions most often offered is for the landlord to pay for all or a portion of leasehold improvements. The lessee may also be able to get a discount from the quoted rate for space. This discount would probably come in the form of a few months' free rent because the lessor wouldn't want existing tenants to know that rates had been lowered.

How to Negotiate a Good Office Lease

The ability to negotiate a deal is directly related to the amount of excess office space in town and the amount of space a tenant wishes to lease. Are half the offices in town empty? Count on getting concessions if the company would be a prestige tenant. Is the company looking for more space than contained in the Yankee Stadium? Real estate agents will be panting at your door offering deals. However, if the company is looking for two small, private offices with a tiny receptionist's area, then there's not much negotiating leverage. One nice concession that can often be negotiated in a new building where the company will be the prime tenant is to call the building by the company name.

The Legalities of the Commercial Office Lease Form

When space is found that's right for the company and the best deal possible has been negotiated, it's time to sign the lease. These leases are really not all that different from rental apartment lease forms. According to most of these forms, the tenant is required to pay no matter what, and the lessor is off the hook, no matter what. That's because the lessor's lawyer drew up the lease form. A company's own attorney can take a look at the lease form. In most cases, he or she will suggest a few minor changes and charge a healthy fee. (If business is slow, the lawyer may insist that this lease is the most outrageous document ever seen and offer to slug it out on the company's behalf all the way to the World Court.)

In-house legal departments handle the lease negotiations for many large companies. Small companies seeking to rent relatively little space are stuck with the lessor's standard form. The one thing to remember is to be sure that any concessions wrung out of the lessor are listed in the lease form. See Exhibit 9–1 for an example of a standard lease form.

Exhibit 9–1
Lease
(General Form)

1. PARTIES:

This Lease is made and entered into this ________________ of ________________________________, 19_____ by and between ______________________________________ (hereinafter referred to as "Landlord") and ____ (hereinafter referred to as "Tenant").

2. PREMISES:

Landlord hereby leases to Tenant and Tenant hereby leases from Landlord, on the terms and conditions hereinafter set forth, that certain real property and the building and other improvements located thereon situated in the City of ________________________________, State of ________________________________, commonly known as

____
(here insert address)

and described as ____
(here insert legal description)

____
______________________________________ (said real property is hereinafter called the "Premises").

3. TERM:

The term of this Lease shall be for ______________________ commencing on ________________________________ and ending on ____

4. RENT:

Tenant shall pay to Landlord as rent for the Premises, the sum of

____

($________________) dollars per month, in advance on the first day of each month during the term hereof. Rent shall be payable without notice or demand and without any deduction, offset, or abatement in lawful money of the United States to the Landlord at the address stated herein for notices or to such other persons or such other places as the Landlord may designate to Tenant in writing.

5. TAXES:

(a) Real Property Taxes.

Landlord shall pay all real property taxes and general assessments levied and assessed against the Premises during the term of this Lease.

EXHIBIT 9–1 (CONTINUED)

(b) Personal Property Taxes.

Tenant shall pay prior to the delinquency all taxes assessed against and levied upon the trade fixtures, furnishings, equipment, and other personal property of Tenant contained in the Premises.

6. UTILITIES:

Tenant shall make all arrangements and pay for all water, gas, heat, light, power, telephone, and other utility services supplied to the Premises together with any taxes thereon and for all connection charges.

7. ALTERATIONS AND ADDITIONS:

Tenant shall not, without the Landlord's prior written consent, make any alterations, improvements, or additions in or about the Premises.

8. HOLD HARMLESS:

Tenant shall indemnify and hold Landlord harmless from and against any and all claims arising from Tenant's use or occupancy of the Premises or from the conduct of its business or from any activity, work, or things which may be permitted or suffered by Tenant in or about the Premises, including all damages, costs, attorney's fees, expenses, and liabilities incurred in the defense of any claim or action or proceeding arising therefrom. Except for Landlord's willful or grossly negligent conduct, Tenant hereby assumes all risk of damage to property or injury to person in or about the Premises.

9. ASSIGNMENT AND SUBLETTING:

Tenant shall not voluntarily or by operation of law assign, transfer, sublet, mortgage, or otherwise transfer or encumber all or any part of Tenant's interest in this Lease or in the Premises without Landlord's prior written consent, which consent shall not be unreasonably withheld.

10. DEFAULT:

It is agreed between the parties hereto that if any rent shall be due hereunder and unpaid, or if Tenant shall default and breach any other covenant or provision of the Lease, then the Landlord, after giving the proper notice required law, may reenter the Premises and remove any property and any and all persons therefrom in the manner allowed by law. The Landlord may, at his option, either maintain this Lease in full force and effect and recover the rent and other charges as they become due or, in the alternative, terminate this Lease. In addition, the Landlord may recover all rentals and any other damages and pursue any other rights and remedies which the Landlord may have against the Tenant by reason of such default as provided by law.

EXHIBIT 9–1 (CONTINUED)

11. SURRENDER:

On the last day of the term of this Lease, Tenant shall surrender the Premises to Landlord in good condition, broom clean, ordinary wear and tear and damage by fire and the elements expected.

12. HOLDING OVER:

If Tenant, with the Landlord's consent, remains in possession of the Premises after expiration of termination of the term of this Lease, such possession by Tenant shall be deemed to be a tenancy from month to month at a rental in the amount of the last monthly rental plus all other charges payable hereunder, and upon all the provisions of this Lease applicable to such a month-to-month tenancy.

13. BINDING ON SUCCESSORS AND ASSIGNS:

Each provision of this Lease performable by Tenant shall be deemed both a covenant and a condition. The terms, conditions, and covenants of this Lease shall be binding upon and shall inure to the benefit of each of the parties hereto, their heirs, personal representatives, successors, and assigns.

14. NOTICES:

Whenever under this Lease a provision is made for any demand, notice, or declaration of any kind, it shall be in writing and served either personally or sent by registered or certified United States mail, postage prepaid, addressed at the addresses as set forth below:

TO LANDLORD AT: ______________________

____

____

TO TENANT AT: ______________________

____

____

Such notice shall be deemed to be received within forty-eight (48) hours from the time of mailing, if mailed as provided for in this paragraph.

15. WAIVERS:

No waiver by Landlord of any provision hereof shall be deemed a waiver of any other provision hereof or of any subsequent breach by Tenant of the same or any other provisions.

16. TIME:

Time is of the essence of this Lease.

____

____

____

Exhibit 9–1 (continued)

____

____

____

The parties hereto have executed this Lease on the date first above written.

LANDLORD:

By:____________________

By:____________________

TENANT:

By:____________________

By:____________________

The Mechanics of Running a Field Sales Office

Most companies put their field sales managers in charge of branch office operations, although some companies will appoint office managers for this task. No matter how a company handles it, the senior sales executive in the branch is heavily involved in the day-to-day operation. Many managers who would rather be working to increase the sale of company products are surprised at how much time this operational managing takes.

Seven Things That Must Be Done Before a New Sales Office Is Opened

There are many things that must be done before an office is open. These things include:

1. Installing a phone system. In a sales environment a phone is needed on every salesperson's desk, a switchboard up front, the ability to make conference calls, enough lines so customers won't get busy signals, the ability to route calls to others, the ability to "hold" calls, the ability to hook in computers and facsimile machines, and so forth. Does the company want to "network" between office machines? Will there be telemarketing in the office? Perhaps the company wants to be on-line to customers' offices so the customers can input orders directly into the system. In the old days, getting all these services was simple, Ma Bell was called. Now

there are many different suppliers of phone systems. Private companies can sell everything from the switchboard to the telephones to leased lines. Competition means that all these products are available from a variety of sources. Competition also means that some companies in this new industry have good performance records and others do not. Shop communication equipment and services carefully.

2. Designing the physical layout of the office. Who's going to sit where and why? Who gets private offices? Where are the secretaries and receptionist going to sit? Where are the file cabinets going to be, and how many of them are needed? Where's the location of the demo room? The conference room? Do the salespeople need privacy? (J. P. Morgan, the financier, believed that all desks should be open so that people could see that business was conducted in plain sight without secrecy. But Morgan never had to contend with a dozen salespeople on the phone all at one time.) If management doesn't want people to have privacy, at least there should be some acoustical divisions. Will partitions between desks be a sufficient sound muffler?

Considerations for department separations are also important. Where's the Service Department going to be? How about the location of Parts Inventory? Where will the office supplies be housed? If these decisions are made in advance, the move to an office will go much smoother. One way to plan is with an office layout form (Exhibit 9–2). Sketch out on this form exactly where everything is to go.

3. Buying the necessary office equipment. How many computers will the office use? The copy machine has become a necessity for every office. The size machine needed depends on how it is used. Will the copy machine be used to help prepare customer proposals and presentations, or will it just be used to record copies of letters and memos? Is a fax machine necessary? Is the branch going to be on-line to the company's home office?

Exhibit 9–2

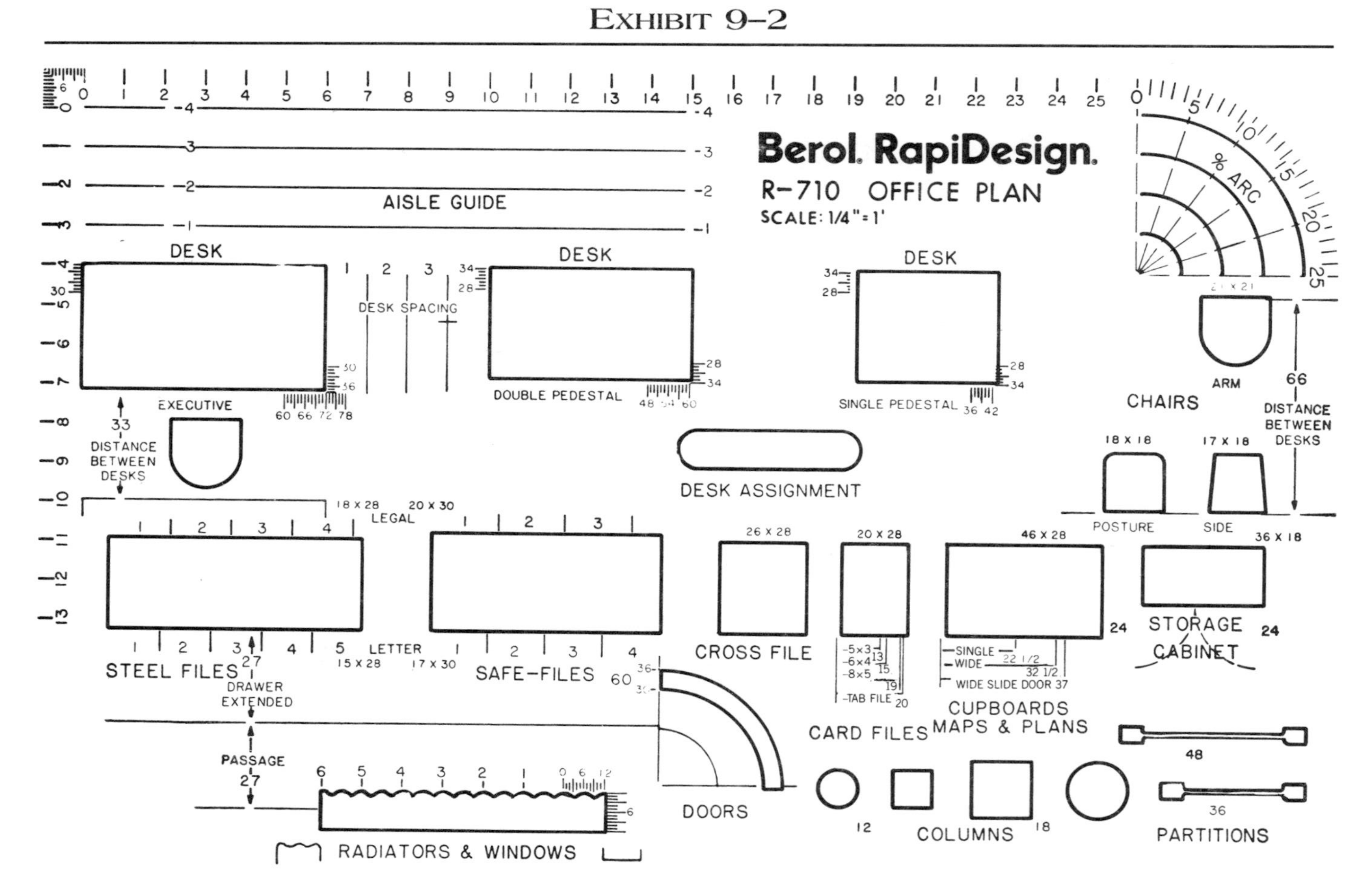
Berol. RapiDesign.
R-710 OFFICE PLAN
SCALE: 1/4" = 1'
AISLE GUIDE
% ARC
DESK
DESK SPACING
DESK
DOUBLE PEDESTAL
DESK
SINGLE PEDESTAL
EXECUTIVE
DISTANCE BETWEEN DESKS
CHAIRS
ARM
DISTANCE BETWEEN DESKS
POSTURE
SIDE
DESK ASSIGNMENT
LEGAL
LETTER
STEEL FILES
DRAWER EXTENDED
SAFE-FILES
CROSS FILE
TAB FILE
SINGLE
WIDE
WIDE SLIDE DOOR 37
STORAGE CABINET
CUPBOARDS
MAPS & PLANS
CARD FILES
PASSAGE
DOORS
COLUMNS
PARTITIONS
RADIATORS & WINDOWS

4. Consider the personalities in the office. Whose ego will be bruised if not assigned a private office? Which two salespeople should not be placed close to one another? What secretary needs to have a slightly better desk and location because of her senior status?

5. Select the office decor. Is this to be a prestige location visited by customers and prospects? If so, better fixtures, more attractive appointments, more expensive furniture will be needed. An interior decorator could be used on this project. If the location is strictly a headquarters for the sales staff, more Spartan fixtures will suffice. The place shouldn't be too comfortable if salespeople are supposed to be outside most of the time.

6. Take care of the power requirements. What kind of power will the office need? How many outlets? Where should those outlets be? (Plenty will be needed in the demo room.) Will the office include sophisticated electronic equipment that requires an uninterruptible power source? Are surge protectors necessary?

7. Make allowance for the mailroom facilities. Even if products are not being shipped from this location, a small area must be set aside for mailing letters and small packages. Minimum requirements include a postal meter and scale, some wrapping capability, a zip-code directory, and so forth. If products are being sent from this office, then much more equipment for wrapping and shipping will be necessary. In this instance the manager must also be concerned with the location's dock and storage facilities.

The Physical Move into a New Sales Office

Expect the physical move to be a trial. There'll be a week or so when business can't be conducted as usual. No matter how well the move is planned, files will go astray, the phone system won't work right, the power situation won't be much better, the space allotted for a specific function just won't be adequate, there'll be a quarrel over a corner office with a window. It's a good idea to keep all field salespeople in the field as much as possible during this shakedown period. They'll only add to the confusion if they're around.

Smoothing Out the Details

Once the office is in place, the manager is responsible for seeing that it runs smoothly. That means seeing that the mail gets out on time, ensuring that the clerical staff is happy and productive, intervening with the landlord because the company hasn't been allotted enough parking space, authorizing local purchases of office supplies, verifying the office phone bill, and so forth. Of course, all these duties will be in addition to the field sales manager's primary responsibility of meeting quota.

Chapter Summary

The opening of a new branch is a test of managerial skill and organizational ability. Plan carefully. Senior management will be watching to see how well this task is performed.

Chapter Ten

COMMUNICATIONS TECHNOLOGY AND THE SALES MANAGER

THE CHANGING DYNAMICS OF THE FIELD SALES FORCE

First a correction: The world isn't going through a computer revolution; what is happening before our eyes is a communications revolution. Sure, computers are a vital ingredient, but they are the medium through which the communications revolution is taking place. The big story is the myriad number of new ways in which information and ideas are being transferred.

Revolutions turn everything upside down, and in a revolution everyone is affected, including sales managers and salespeople. Exactly how is the subject of this chapter.

Advanced communications technology is changing the dynamics of the field sales force in a fundamental way. It is changing the very structure of business. Sales managers can't remain aloof from these developments because they affect how the manager of the future will function. "We are in the middle of the most transforming technological event since the capture of fire," says John Barlow, founder of the Electronic Frontier Foundation.

Sales managers must be able to understand and be able to use these revolutionary technologies if they wish to keep pace with their peers *and if their companies wish to keep pace with their competitors.*

Why are these developments so important? Communication is the stock in trade of every salesperson. They have always been conduits. The salesperson's job is to reach prospects and inform them of the company's products and services. They tell the company just what the prospect needs from the organization so that the prospect can be converted to a customer. They perform countless service functions: checking order status, correcting problems, suggesting product applications. Anything that can improve communication is vital for slaespeople to learn and understand.

Electronic Communications 101

Some of the basic advances in communications technology in the past several years that have caused these profound changes include:

1. "On-line" information. Via a laptop computer, a field salesperson sitting in a customer's office can dial up the home office computer and learn the inventory status of any product. ("We've only got two gross left, Joe. If you want them, better give me your order today.") That same laptop can enter the order, price it, track it, and give the preferred method of shipment. All administrative functions, sales figures, marketing information, daily reports, schedules of salespeople and managers can be available on-line.

2. Facsimile transmission. This technology is often scorned by on-line purists because it is so basic, but the simplicity of fax is what makes it so popular. Put the documents in the feeder, dial the phone number, and press the "send" button. Heaven for computer phobics! Salespeople working a territory can send in orders from their hotel rooms at the end of the day via a portable fax. Many hotels have fax machines available, and more than a few offer special rooms with fax machines in them. Okay, it's not on-line, but it beats the mails or even next-day delivery services. It also beats phoning in orders because all the information is transmitted in writing. Nothing gets

lost in translation. Fax transmission can also be used by managers to update field salespeople on price changes, special offers, contest announcements, upcoming sales meetings, and other company business.

3. Beepers and pagers. Ever miss an important order because you couldn't be reached during the time when the prospect had to make a decision? ("You should have returned my call, Janet. I gave an order for one thousand pieces to Consolidated just this morning.") Salespeople in the field don't have the time or the opportunity to call their offices every half hour for messages. Beepers and pagers alert them to opportunities and emergencies. They eliminate the out-of-reach salesperson. The downside is that a beeper going off during the course of an important meeting can be an annoyance.

4. Cellular phones. In 1986 there were five hundred thousand cellular phones in operation. Today, there are about 28 million. Any salesperson or manager working a large metropolitan area and stuck in glacier-speed traffic during those golden selling hours knows why. Cellular car phones allow some of that "dead" time to be put to good use for making appointments, talking to certain customers, and contacting the home office. The monthly service fees are high, (which is why the phones themselves are inexpensive) but these service costs are gradually coming down.

5. Phone mail. Phone mail is a bad idea whose time has come. It is a communication retreat rather than an advance toward the future. The systems are, essentially, small electronic mailboxes that allow callers to leave messages without the intervention of a human operator. Phone mail has been enthusiastically embraced by companies seeking to reduce the number of live bodies on the payroll (phone operators and secretaries) while maintaining the same level of service.

The body count may have been reduced, but so has the level of service. Anyone who has suffered through a drone of recorded messages and asked to select from a menu of seemingly inappropriate options gets the *real* message quite clearly. It is that the company using phone mail considers its time more valuable than the caller's time. For salespeople trying to reach decision makers, phone mail has become a formidable barrier, worse than the most imperious "gatekeeper" secretary.

6. E-mail. Want to communicate an important message to a colleague who isn't available? Leave a message in his or her electronic mailbox. The message shows up on the recipient's computer screen. He or she can respond in kind. This procedure is now largely intramural, but more and more companies are beginning to connect to one another via E-mail. Some companies have hooked some of their important customers to their internal E-mail systems, allowing administrative personnel within those companies to directly connect with one another.

7. Teleconferencing. Have a meeting with important clients clear across the country? Is it important to see their faces during the negotiations? Delay that phone call to airline reservations. Travel expenses are getting more outrageous every year, and long-distance travel itself merely to see one or two clients is inefficient. (There's only so much work that can be done in an airplane seat that's three inches shorter across than the width of the passenger's butt.)

The answer for many companies is an alternative called teleconferencing, meetings between the two parties, each settled comfortably in their home cities, during which the images of both sides are displayed on oversized television screens while the conversations are conducted. While not quite the same as being there in the flesh, teleconferencing is a major improvement over telephone conference calls because the parties can see one another's reactions.

Many large companies have set up teleconferencing centers in their offices, and centers are available at some hotels. Quick-print franchises, which are trying to position themselves as home office support centers, are also setting them up. Teleconferencing, obviously, can also be used for intracompany business, such as sales meetings. This saves the travel expense of bringing the troops into the office. ("Picture phones" are also being developed that allow two individuals to see one another during their telephone conversation. Sending images over a phone line, however, strains its data-handling capacity. In most systems, the images are jerky.)

8. On-line between customer and supplier. Many companies are now linked via computer to their key suppliers. These customers can enter orders on-line, verify inventory, track the order, obtain shipping data, and enter other computer realms where they are allowed access. This permits a much closer association between customer and supplier.

Why On-line Communications Between Customer and Supplier Means Less Control for the Account Salesperson

Those who believe that the advances in communications technology are merely tools that assist salespeople in doing a better job are mistaken. They will change forever the relationship between the sales rep, the customer, and the supplier. Here's how:

On-line communication allows for closer relationships between customers and their key suppliers. The buyer who needs a product can enter the order directly with a key supplier without a salesperson's intervention. The customer engineer can directly contact a supplier product manager via intercompany E-mail to verify product features or ask about a new application. It is still the salesperson's responsibility to introduce new products, inform the customer about new applications, and generally ensure the customer's satisfaction, but the need for the "service-type" call is diminished. The salesperson's role as intermediary is less vital.

These developments mean that individual salespeople will have less personal control over their accounts, particularly when these accounts are large and "connected." The sales rep will be unable to control the flow of information to the customer. Contacts between customer and supplier will be made at varied levels. This translates to fewer salespeople with a "following" of customers who can be carted like a portable treasure from one company to another. If the salesperson leaves an organization, the well-serviced account is likely to stay behind.

The End of the Weekly Sales Meeting?

Here's a fundamental change that seems slight but has a profound impact on the relationship between the sales manager and the sales team. It is no longer necessary for a sales team to gather together in a central location for daily, weekly, or even monthly meetings.

Sounds like heresy, doesn't it? The sales meeting has been a standard sales management tool ever since an Egyptian cemetery plot salesman convinced a pharaoh that the Valley of the Kings would make a terrific spot for a tomb. With advanced communications technology, however, bringing the squad together to receive the word is just another ancient rite that has lost much of its validity.

Without the meetings, how's the manager going to find out what's going on in the field? How is the manager going to determine, first hand, who's busting their hump and who's eating popcorn at matinee double features? (Some managers convene short meetings every morning just to be sure the troops are awake, dressed, and ready to hit the streets.) How are the troops going to get the latest dirt?

Communications technology takes care of these concerns. Two-way communication between manager and salesperson can be established via voice mail, E-mail, fax machines, laptop computers, electronic notepads, pagers, cellular phones, and other devices. The manager can monitor the salesperson's progress, or lack of it, through computer tracking programs that reveal what's going on in a territory far more accurately than any five-minute dialogue during a meeting. (More about these programs in another chapter.) Sales and marketing information is available on-line. When group interaction is desirable, teleconferencing is an acceptable, and less expensive, substitute to bringing everyone to a central location.

Face-to-face contact will always be part of sales management. Technology is no substitute for the relationships that develop from personal contact, but the weekly or daily "shape-up" meeting just isn't necessary anymore.

Should Salespeople Come into the Office?

In the last chapter we reviewed the circumstances under which a branch office is necessary. More and more managers are asking themselves if it's necessary for outside salespeople to ever come into the office. For many companies, the answer is an emphatic no. There is a national trend toward telecommuting, and nowhere within an organization does it make more sense than for field salespeople. Providing space, even a small desk and telephone, for salespeople who should be spending most of their time in the field is expensive. Many companies ask their field salespeople to maintain in-home offices, thereby cutting down on the space needed at the branch, regional, or central office.

Three Advantages of Outside Salespeople Working Out of Their Homes

1. More sales calls. Instead of coming into a sales office, salespeople can be out in their territories ready to work at the start of each business day. With new communications technologies, there's no longer a reason for them to come into an office, except to "shape-up," that is, prove that they are awake, dressed, and ready to work. If that is necessary, the manager doesn't trust his or her team.

2. Less office space needed. Why maintain desk space for people who use it only on a part-time basis? Also, less warehouse space is required. Sales materials can be inventoried in the in-home offices of the sales crew. In fact, some branch offices could be eliminated entirely.

3. Fewer gripe sessions. One of the standard "features" of sales meetings is the inevitable gripe session, during which salespeople complain about the company's pricing, deliveries, quality, the impossible quota, the hostile marketplace, and just about everything

else under the sun. These sessions can be demoralizing because they focus on how tough the job is. Without so many sales meetings, there will be fewer opportunities for salespeople to get together to reinforce negatives.

Three Disadvantages of Outside Salespeople Working Out of Their Homes

There are disadvantages to salespeople working directly out of their homes. Manager must be aware of these disadvantages and take them into account when setting up a sales force that will be working out of their homes.

1. Less control. For managers who are control freaks, not coming face-to-face with salespeople on a frequent basis can be a problem. These managers don't get to grill each salesperson regarding what is on today's schedule. (This kind of information is available from various computer programs.) They don't get the assurance that the salesperson is out of bed, dressed, and ready to work.

2. Loss of camaraderie. This is a serious disadvantage that the sales manager must address. It's hard to develop team spirit when team members never get to see one another. Team goals mean nothing. Friendly rivalries and competitions are difficult to establish.

3. Alienation. The salesperson who is out in the field for long periods and doesn't get to meet home office personnel and peers begins to feel disassociated and alone. A feeling develops among field salespeople that they aren't a part of the organization, that they don't really know what's going on in the company. The sales manager can address this problem by scheduling quarterly training meetings, making frequent updates, sending personalized notes, conversing with the sales staff over the phone, encouraging peers to talk to one another about common problems, scheduling sales calls with field personnel, teleconferencing, and using complete candor and openness during conversations.

Nine Things to Consider When Furnishing an In-Home Office

The decision has been made to shoo all the field salespeople out of the branch, regional, or home office. They are now Flying Dutchmen, banned forever from home port! What is the essential equipment and furniture they will require to set up offices in that spare bedroom? No single list will fit every situation, but there are standard options:

1. A desk. It needn't be J. P. Morgan's old rolltop or Swedish oiled teak. Any large, flat writing surface, such as an old table, will do.

2. A file cabinet. If the salesperson is going to keep files, store literature, and maintain records on customers and prospects, then a place is needed to put this stuff where it can easily be retrieved. Incidentally, for home office decoration on the utilitarian but cheap side, two, two-drawer file cabinets can be used as a base for a flat writing surface, creating an inexpensive but useful desk.

3. A fax machine with built-in telephone. Now that the home office has banished all field salespeople, management will need an inexpensive communication tool to keep the field sales force informed. The easy and inexpensive way is via facsimile transmission, the low-tech response to high tech. The salesperson will find the fax machine handy for sending out written quotes and follow-up letters. Multipurpose fax machines can also serve as low-speed copiers, so the occasional document can be copied and filed. The appeal is in their simplicity. Time required to learn how to operate a fax machine is all of 15 seconds.

4. An answering machine or answering service. The salesperson will, hopefully, be spending most of his or her time in the field. If the company office won't be taking and relating messages, an answering machine or answering service is the best alternative solution. Depending upon the urgency of returning incoming calls, a beeper or pager service may be preferred. (Some fax machines come with built-in answering machines. The advantage is an all-in-one office device that doesn't take up much room.)

5. Dedicated word processors. Word processors with visual displays are a good compromise for computer phobics who are required to dash off an occasional letter, proposal, or quotation to prospects and customer. They are more advanced than typewriters and easier to use than computers. They are also relatively inexpensive.

6. Desktop computers. The requirements for a desktop computer in a salesperson's in-home office depend upon the situation. For independent reps running their own businesses, a desktop is certainly handy because it can be used for many kinds of small-business applications—from accounts receivable and payable, expense control, inventory control, and so forth. For the company salesperson working out of an in-home office, the requirement for a desktop is not quite so obvious. Most sales reps don't do any serious number-crunching, the applications that computers handle best. Proposals and quotations can be handled easier and with less cost by dedicated word processors.

7. Laptop computers. Laptops make more sense, especially for the field sales rep who is on the road. The big question for any sales manager when deciding if a laptop is applicable for the salespeople in the company is, *does the company have the software to support the applications the manager wants automated?* Another chapter addresses the issue of sales force automation (SFA) in detail.

8. Electronic notepads and palmtops. Some regard electronic notepads as nothing more than exotic, digitized day planners. They are an electronic alternative to the traditional lined notepad, to-do lists, appointment book, Rolodex file, and alarm clock. Some have fax capability. If you prefer that a customer address be displayed on an LCD screen rather than looking through an address book for it, these notepads are for you. Others consider them gadgets. Palmtop computers are still a product in search of a market.

9. Office services. A number of businesses have grown in the past several years specifically to service the expanding SOHO (small office, home office) market. Salespeople working out of their homes should make connections with one of these centers. They offer services such as copying, mail drops, packaging and mailing, fax trans-

mission, printing proposals and presentations, and so forth. Some rent computers, word processors, and typewriters on an hourly rental basis.

The "Soft" Costs of Too Much Equipment

Be sure to evaluate the "soft" costs of supplying each in-home salesperson with a desktop computer, laptop, or other electronic device. A soft cost is the time required to keep the doggone things running, time that keeps salespeople in their home offices rather than in the field. Managers certainly don't want their salespeople sitting at home "surfing the Net" during golden selling hours instead of out there in front of prospects and customers. Still, more and more companies require their reps to have a computer.

The Overriding Consideration When Selecting Equipment for Reps Who Will Be Working Out of Their Homes

When selecting equipment and software for field reps who will be working out of their homes, keep one thing uppermost in mind: The intent of all the hardware and related support systems is to free up more of their time for selling, *not to turn them into office clerks.*

Establishing a Database

"Database" is a popular sales and marketing buzzword. Demystified, it simply means information, records, or lists of some kind stored in retrievable form so they can be used and/or manipulated over and over. For example, the list of homes a real estate agent has for sale could be considered a database.

The reason they've become popular is that, through the ubiquitous computer, the information in a database can be massaged and used many different ways. Want a list of customers that never order unless the company offers a special? A computerized database can give it to you in a jiffy. The database can be helpful in identifying high-potential prospects, targeting the right markets, and developing effective sales and marketing strategies.

What Goes into a Database

For sales managers, the most popular kinds of databases are just what you might imagine: lists or profiles of prospects and customers. To be useful to a sales manager, an effective customer database should contain the following minimal information:

1. Name, address, and phone number of customer
2. Account number company has assigned to that customer
3. Industry designation
4. Size of company
5. Record of purchases*
6. Credit established and credit history*
7. Salesperson assigned to customer*
8. Record of visits salesperson has made to customer*
9. Names of important contacts within customer's organization*

Does that appear to be similar to the basic requirement for any customer record, including the old-fashioned three-by-five-inch card in a rotary file? Of course, it is! It has just been glorified by giving that record a fancier name. Of course, other basic information may be required as well, depending upon the desires of company managers maintaining the database.

---

*This kind of information is not static, which means that the database must be constantly updated.

Seven Places to Obtain a Database If You Don't Have One

If everyone on your block but you has a prospect or customer database, there are any number of sources for obtaining (buying) one. List acquisition can run anywhere from $1.00 to $3.00 per name. Many lists are now available on floppy disks or CD-ROMs. Traditional sources include:

1. Direct-mail firms. The largest and most comprehensive databases are offered by direct-mail service bureaus, which also handle mailings for their customers. These firms can provide lists in every category from school administrators to presidents of furniture companies. They charge per thousand names. Lists can be purchased on mailing labels for one-time use or on floppy disks and CD-ROMs for multiple use.

2. Magazines. Has your company developed a new, revolutionary automatic pistol that shoots four hundred rounds before reloading? The readers of a magazine such as *Guns and Ammo* would be logical prospects to buy it. Obtaining a database list from a special-interest magazine is an excellent way to target a specific market. (The "rifle" approach.)

3. Newspapers. Subscribers to newspapers are prospects for a variety of products. Newspapers sell their subscriber lists but often print others than can be purchased for the cost of the publication.

4. Associations. Trade associations often sell the database lists of their members. Got the perfect product for office supply stores? Contact NOPA (National Office Products Association) and talk to them about buying their list of members.

5. Government agencies. Some government agencies sell lists to private industry. For example, it is possible to buy lists of new-car registrants from some state automobile-licensing bureaus.

6. Computer firms. Some computer firms have gone into the business of digitizing lists and putting them on CD-ROMs. It is possible to buy databases categorized by zip codes, electronic Yellow Page directories, and various other distinctions.

7. The Internet. The worldwide communications network is a great database source. More about the Internet later.

Six Ways to Create Your Own Database

Don't have a database and don't want to pay for one? Create one from scratch. The information you need to build your own completely "customized" list is currently available in the organization now. Here's where it has been lurking:

1. From the address books and files of the company's salespeople. The company reps know the customers and prospects within their territories. Make up a form with the information you need in your database and ask the salespeople to fill it out for every customer. No, *insist* that they fill it out. Follow up, because a few reps won't complete the task without being pestered.

2. From company billing and credit records. Within these records is a pertinent database in raw form, including buying patterns.

3. From libraries and directories. Libraries maintain all kinds of industrial directories listing every kind of corporation and government agency. The information is there for anyone willing to take the time to extract it. Better yet, buy the appropriate directories, many of which are now on floppy disks or CD-ROM, and save the transcription job.

4. From newspapers and magazines. The business sections of local newspapers frequently carry lists of the largest and fastest-growing local firms. Magazines such as *Fortune* have annual issues listing prominent firms in various categories. Of course, the magazines also offer their subscribers' names for sale.

5. From local trade associations. Every association meeting you attend will usually cheerfully supply a list of all the attendees.

6. From Yellow Page ads. Does your company make a special composite replacement shoe heel that will last forever? The local

Yellow Pages directory will list every shoemaker—your logical prospects—in town.

Four Suggestions When Selling by Fax Machine

Many of the messages popping up on fax machines these days are advertisements to sell something. To many recipients, this kind of solicitation is an annoyance and business intrusion. To others, it is an effective and inexpensive way to market. Making offers via fax is certainly less costly than telephone solicitation. When marketing via fax:

1. Know the recipient. Is the offer likely to be of interest?
2. Make a strong offer. To gain interest, make the deal exciting.
3. Test the offer. Send sample batches to selected prospects before mass faxing.
4. Send the offer when phone rates are least expensive. This is usually at night after regular business hours. Many fax machines can be set automatically to "broadcast" messages to many recipients long after everyone has left the office.

The Internet

This will be an overview of the Internet, but don't be concerned, it will not be a technical description. No computer hardware will be described or recommended. There will be no paragraphs that begin or end with mysterious codes such as: "http/www.snowjob/."

First, a definition: The Internet, originally established in 1969 as a military communications system, is an international communications network that connects individuals, companies, government agencies, and educational institutions together via personal computer. Simply put, persons or companies with computers on the "Net" can exchange information with one another.

No one yet fully understands exactly how this phenomenon will shape the future, but it is already reshaping the present. Children in a school in Muncie, Indiana, can exchange lessons with students in London, England. Employees in two different companies can trade data on-line. Companies can offer products for sale through electronic "catalogs."

Estimates of how many individuals are tied to the Net range from 15 million up to 40 million. The list is growing daily, and the growth rate is accelerating. (In 1994, American consumers spent more dollars on computers than on television sets.)

Enthusiasts are convinced that the Net's huge body of potential consumers offers an unprecedented sales and marketing opportunity. Theoretically a company could offer something for sale that would be seen by up to 40 million "surfers." More than 370 Internet "shopping malls" have been established. Last year, about two-and-one-half-million North Americans bought something via the Internet.

Others feel that the numbers and the scenario are much too rosy. They claim that the Net is still a refuge for computer mavens. It is true that accessing the Net can be a tedious process. Rather than "surfing," wading through hip-deep water might be a more appropriate description for those who are not fully initiated. Not everyone has the patience for the delays, disconnects, errors, and so forth. Even computer guru Bill Gates admits that the "Internet is not quite ready for prime time."*

There is also a tremendous dropout rate. Many computer users are happy to accept free trial offers by on-line services such as Prodigy, CompuServe, and others, but immediately cancel when the trial period is over and they are required to pay.

Another reality is that the total number of Net users is segmented into special-interest groups. Just logging on isn't going to give any company access to every user. At best, marketing on the Internet is fundamental niche marketing.

---

*One computer consultant advising those who wish to set up a location in an electronic shopping mall suggested that the vendor make it "intellectually challenging." Any vehicle with that requirement isn't tuned to mass markets.

Access to the Internet

The first step in getting access to the Internet is selecting a service provider. This is a crowded field with a wide number of local and national providers, such as America Online, Prodigy, and CompuServe. Most of these providers charge a small setup fee and a monthly fee. Others charge hourly usage rates as well. A caveat: Creep before you crawl, and crawl before you walk. Learn what you are doing. Support can be expensive, and some Internet access providers expect a certain amount of competency (computer literacy) from their users.

Soliciting on the Internet

Advertisements for every kind of product from weight-reduction pills to tractors are appearing in electronic mailboxes. The reason is that it is easy and inexpensive to target millions of on-line users with the touch of a key. Companies such as Email America sell retailers E-mail addresses. (At publication, 5 million addresses cost $99.00) To send an advertising message to 100,000 of those users costs less than $5.00. What an advantage over direct-mail costs!

Of course, many E-mail users find these advertising messages an intrusion. There is as yet no data on how effective they are.

Electronic Bulletin Boards

There are about 60,000 electronic bulletin boards on the Internet. Text-based (words only), they provide information to a small group of subscribers. Most bulletin boards serve a particular city or locality and are accessed by a single phone number. They make money by selling ad space on their "boards." Membership is inexpensive, usually less than $100 a year. Up to now, the content of many boards has been sleazy, but they do provide an opportunity for niche marketing.

The World Wide Web

A commercial network called the World Wide Web has been formed. It is an information storage system linking resources internationally and consists of a collection of graphic sites (words and pictures) scattered around the Internet network. In this arena, selling isn't considered bad manners. The Web is the multimedia region of Internet. It has been called "the embryonic royal road through cyberspace" and is becoming the Net's commercial or business network. With an estimated two million regular users by the end of 1994, the Web has become popular, primarily because it is so much easier to use and offers both color and graphics. Another advantage is that is doesn't cost much to develop a presence. Space can be rented for as little as $50.00 a month.

Don't assume, however, that usage changes will be your only cost. Designing the electronic "page" to stimulate prospect interest may require expert help. As a rule of thumb, the less handholding you require, the lower the price is likely to be.

All sorts of businesses are "setting up shop" on the Web by establishing what is in essence an electronic Yellow Pages ad. These ads can contain much more information than would be practical in a conventional hard-print ad. For example, the description of a product might be followed by a colorful picture, a complete set of specifications, suggested applications, prices, and even an order form. The right ad is important. Getting the prospect's attention is still the key to success in any form of marketing.

The Difference Between the Web and Bulletin Boards

Bulletin boards allow for more interaction because the user has, in essence, entered a remote computer. The Web may eventually have more sites than stars in the Milky Way, but it is slower because graphics can be downloaded into the searcher's computer.

Electronic Catalogs

Now that the World Wide Web is a reality, why not distribute an entire product line electronically? Computer browsers could scan through the pages, get complete information on the products, check out the prices to make sure they are competitive, and place their orders on-line. According to a recent study by Arthur D. Little, 75 percent of computer users would purchase products from electronic catalogs if prices were similar, or less, than printed catalogs. They would also *reduce their purchases from conventional sources.* That last tidbit of information is causing many suppliers to investigate electronic commerce.

For the supplier, the process sure beats mailing out two million catalogs that may be obsolete by the time they arrive. If need be, pricing can be updated every day to reflect current costs or to meet competitive situations.

How to Start Marketing on the Internet: Eight Things to Know

If the idea of electronic marketing appears appetizing, here are a few basic baby steps:

1. Explore the options. Subscribe to at least one basic service to get your feet wet. Just browse for a while to learn the ropes. Some Internet junkies resent "newbies" (new users).
2. Set goals. Develop a modest plan and work out a budget.
3. Know where you are. In many Internet forums, hard selling is considered bad form. Save that kind of effort for the World Wide Web.
4. Have limited expectations. Not every product is suited to this form of marketing. Don't be taken in by quoted statistics on the number of Net users. They aren't all prospects, and they can't all be reached.

5. Don't switch your principal occupation from sales manager to Web programmer. It will take forever and the results will likely be shabby. Get expert assistance.
6. Realize that there are no secrets on the Net. Anything good you do will quickly be copied.
7. Understand that nobody is in charge. This is a new game, and the rules are being written as it is played.
8. Be wary. For example, make sure you'll be paid for what you sell. The Internet allows a certain degree of anonymity. Highwaymen abound on the Information Superhighway.

The Information Superhighway

The Information Superhighway theoretically takes the Internet one step further by connecting computer networks to one another *and,* ultimately, to TV sets and telephones. The information revolution is rapping hard at the door of every American home. Some believe that the greatest potential revenues will come from interactive television rather than computers. TV sets are easier to use and everyone has one.

Home Shopping Networks

Home shopping networks offer products for sale to consumers through TV cable programs. This medium was once considered a revolutionary way to move products. Stories circulated about incredible volumes sold through this channel. Sales and marketing managers lined up, hat in hand, to get their company's products into the stream. What actually happened might provide a lesson for those who predict such a rosy future for the Internet.

This turned out to be an expensive way to move product, and the kinds of products that could be directly sold via a TV hard pitch were limited. The shopping networks are still active, but they are no longer considered the marketing manager's savior. Tune in to any shopping network: The products offered are inevitably high-margin items for which comparison pricing is difficult, such as jewelry and collectibles. Factory closeouts, which the sellers buy at distress pricing, are also popular.

For sales and marketing managers, consider this channel a possible dumping ground for obsolete merchandise, but not a vehicle for steadily building sales.

Selling on the Internet is sometimes considered bad form, sort of like being introduced to a stranger at a cocktail party and immediately pitching him on the benefits of a life insurance policy. More and more Internet users, however, find the impulse to try to sell something to the person on the other end irresistible.

CHAPTER SUMMARY

The "cyberspace" revolution is almost upon us. It will change forever every aspect of business, including sales and sales management. It will change forever the relationship between the company, the customer, and the salesperson servicing the account. In fact, these areas will be among the most heavily impacted.

The revolution is coming all right, but not at the express speed some enthusiasts predict. Also, the results won't be exactly what the experts predict, because revolutions always deliver unexpected consequences. Still, you might as well get on board while the bus is still creeping along, because we are going "there" whether you like the route or not.

Chapter Eleven
How to Develop a Sales-Training Program

The Value of Sales Training

Sales training is like motherhood and the flag. It's hard to find anyone who has a word to say against it. The reason is plain. For salespeople to perform successfully, they must be familiar with all aspects of their jobs. We hear much about "natural" salespeople, but they're more myth than reality. Few are born with the ability to sell. Closing-technique genes are not interwoven into DNA patterns. Product knowledge is not an instinctual memory such as the kind that sends the swallows back to Capistrano each spring. Sales skills must be learned, and heaven help the company that allows its sales force to learn them haphazardly.

The Manager's Responsibility Toward Sales Training

For managers, training staff members is an integral part of their jobs. Their future success depends on how well they handle this responsibility. The better a staff is trained, the better they will sell. The more they sell, the better the manager looks. So a good part of every managerial assignment is being a teacher. Managers may even have to teach things that they never knew themselves.

The Ten Reasons Why Continuous Sales Training Is Necessary

The concept of continuous sales training is not revolutionary. Just about every sales-oriented organization believes that an ongoing sales-training program is necessary. Here are some of the reasons why they think so:

1. The costs for making direct sales calls seem higher with each new study on the subject. Higher costs make it imperative that these calls not be wasted. How can the manager ensure that staff members are squeezing the most out of every call? Give them the benefit of a sales-training program.

2. Competition gets keener every year. Companies are scratching and fighting for every inch of business. The ones who will get it are those whose salespeople are better trained, know their product lines better than they do their spouses, and know how to serve the customer.

3. Failure is an expensive luxury. When a salesperson fails, a new one must be trained to take the position. Recruitment is time-consuming, a good territory goes untended for a long period, customers are ignored, business is lost.

4. A poorly trained salesperson reflects on the entire company. Nothing is more tedious for a manager than mopping up after someone who didn't know how to do the job. The customers and prospects in the territory no longer have much respect for the organization. Once customers begin asking one another, "Have you noticed the quality of their people?" the company's reputation is finished.

5. A training program is the best way to instill company attitudes and company priorities into the sales crew. In other words, a

training program is the best place to indoctrinate salespeople regarding the kind of behavior expected from them.

6. Personal weaknesses, poor work habits, and other problem areas are often revealed during a training class. The manager is in a better position to determine who needs more help after the class is over.

7. A good training program is an important motivator. The well-trained salesperson is confident when facing any sales situation.

8. Today's products are more complex and technical. Customers buy from salespeople who show them how their products solve problems. There can be no "finding a need and filling it" without adequate product training.

9. Customers expect professionalism from their vendors. A well-trained, responsive sales force is a sign of this professionalism.

10. Without training, salespeople grow stale and restless or burn out. The best way to ensure a fresh, lively sales force is through a continually updated training program.

It's obvious from this list that sales training is absolutely necessary. Every sales manager needs to have a training program to develop a professional staff that will get the job done. Where does the manager go from here?

Why Managers Should Begin Training Programs with Themselves

The first person to train is the one who needs it the most and who will derive the most benefit from it. That person is you! You can't teach others unless you know yourself. Even better than knowing, you must *understand.* The difference is between knowing what's right and knowing why it's right. (That's why companies almost always pick salespeople to become sales managers. Former salespeople understand field sales problems because they've encountered those problems themselves.)

So your first training chore as a manager is to become knowledgeable. You have a head start because you know a lot from experience. They didn't pick you to be a manager because you're a dummy. But there may be fuzzy areas, neglected skills in your background. Perhaps you were a great prospector who never learned to close too well, but made up for it by the sheer volume of prospects you were able to generate. That system worked for you as a salesperson because you were responsible only for your own production. As a manager you can't afford to neglect any of the selling skills. You must learn how to close effectively so that you can pass on this knowledge to every member of your crew.

FORMALIZED TRAINING PROGRAMS

Managers working for large companies are fortunate. Most major companies usually have some sort of formalized sales-training program in place. They may send the manager to specialized sales schools, supervisors' schools, time management schools, and so forth. They use staff training specialists and independent sales consultants to reinforce training programs. Large companies normally hold regularly scheduled product-training sessions and may provide full-time field trainers.

WHAT TO EXPECT FROM A FORMALIZED TRAINING PROGRAM

Managers with companies who have formalized training programs should take full advantage of these training opportunities. Learn the product line better than anyone else in the company. Learn the theory behind various sales techniques. Most important, observe how the teaching is done. Teaching skills are vital for the manager's next task, which is to communicate what has been learned to the people on the sales staff.

What Managers Teach During Sales Training Courses and Where They Teach It

The Classroom

Sales training almost always takes place in one of two locations. The first place is in a classroom. This is the formal side of sales training. These classrooms are set up to be similar to the classrooms found in high schools and colleges. They're populated with chalkboards, slides, flip charts, films, instructors, tests, and, unfortunately, occasionally bored students. A bored student is not the best absorber of information, so the first rule in teaching a sales-training class is to make the sessions lively and interesting.

How to Present Sales-Training Material

The manager makes a training course lively by being absorbed by the material being presented. That's right, *absorbed*. This training is vital to the incomes and success of the people in the class and the manager's own success as well. The material is made interesting by varying the presentation, doing some verbal instruction, some discussion, some audiovisual instruction, some hands-on training, some case studies, some team competition, some role-playing, some quizzing, some written testing—in short, a bit of everything.

The Least Successful Teaching Techniques

Of all the techniques listed above, the one that's least likely to succeed is straight, uninterrupted, verbal instruction. Students don't respond well to lecturing because it involves only two of their five senses: hearing and seeing. The straight-out lecturer also contends with the natural skepticism of salespeople toward the blowhard. The more the instructor talks without interruption, the less the students think the instructor knows. Using flip charts, films, slides, and other audiovisual aids is only marginally better. The instructor is still only involving two of the students' senses.

How to Get Students Involved in the Course Material

The instructor who wants to get students interested gets them involved with the presentation. The easiest and least intimidating way is through group discussion. Invite questions, ask for comments, suggest problems without dictating solutions. The instructor should make sure the interplay is not just between teacher and class, but between class members as well. The instructor serves as the discussion leader, guiding conversation so it goes where it's supposed to go. The instructor shouldn't ridicule wrong answers; the class will usually know when something isn't right. At the end of the discussion, summarize the conclusions, or let the class summarize for themselves. Material learned this way is likely to stay with the trainees much longer than a straight lecture, no matter the qualifications of the lecturer.

Using Case Studies as a Teaching Tool

Using case studies to educate is the method favored by the Harvard Business School. This system of study is really more applicable to marketing rather than sales training, but it can be useful because case studies identify specific problems. Because the situation actually happened, the student can match his or her answer against the real-life solution.

Using Competitive Spirit to Make Classroom Work Challenging

Dividing the students into teams and then posing a problem to solve can make a training session fun. The salesperson's natural competitiveness makes everyone want to "win." One way to keep the class occupied during the evening is to give each team a problem just before the class breaks for the day and ask for solutions first thing in the morning.

Role-playing as an Overrated Teaching Tool

Role-playing seems a natural sales-training technique. The idea is to simulate situations that are likely to occur in the field. It's easy and seems useful to have someone in the class behave as the "guardian" secretary, then ask one of the trainees to try to get past her to see the decision maker. However, the situation is artificial. The person playing the role is not a real secretary and not likely to give realistic responses. The person chosen to challenge the secretary is likely to feel pressure by performing in front of his or her peers.

Six Topics That Should Be Included in a Basic Sales-Training Class

The best place to begin training a new salesperson is in the classroom. Unless the company has staff trainers, the manager is the person who should give the class because field training is a primary sales management responsibility. Here's the "basic" course:

1. Selling skills. (What else?) Teach the nitty-gritty of how to prospect, how to make a survey, how to make a presentation, how to handle objections, how to write a proposal, how to close, and how to keep the customer near and dear.

2. The product lineup. The salesperson must know what he's carrying in his bag, what it does and why that's useful, how it's priced, how many other competitors are selling something similar, why his stuff is better, and so forth.

3. Territory management. The trainee must be taught the best way to run a territory, how to plan calls, how to manage time, and so forth.

4. Company history. Tell the trainee something about the company, its place in the industry, how it got there, and where it's headed. Who's who in the organization is always a good thing to know.

5. Nitty-gritty details. How does the salesperson process an order? What's the commission schedule and when is it paid? What kind of literature is available? What's the policy on expenses? Where does a new fish go to get a problem solved? What kind of reports are required? Giving the sales trainee this kind of information during the training session will save the manager a lot of follow-up later.

6. The motivational message. The instructor has a captive audience, so why not use a bit of time to inspire? New hires find the going tough enough when they go into the field. Give them something that will help carry them over the rough spots. Develop a positive attitude within the sales crew.

The Length of Classroom Training

Classroom training should be short. It's difficult to keep attention at a high level for more than two or three days.

Scheduling Multiple Training Sessions

Obviously, in many circumstances, more than one training session will be needed. One solution is to schedule multiple training sessions several weeks or months apart. This strategy keeps the attention level high during each session. It also gives the trainee the opportunity to quickly try out what's just been learned in field situations. Another benefit is that the students aren't kept away from their territories for too long a time.

Why Classroom Training Is Never Enough

Formal training is never enough. No salesperson's education is finished upon completion of classroom sessions, no matter how intensive. When the books have been laid aside, the next step is field training, where the "graduates" can apply their classroom knowledge to real-life situations. In fact, classroom and field training are two sides of the same coin. They should be coordinated to ensure maximum development and growth of the sales force.

Field Training: Five Reasons Why Managers Shouldn't Put Raw Recruits with Old Pros

For some companies, field training means sending the new salesperson out to work a few days or a week with an experienced representative. The trainee watches and theoretically absorbs every trick and shuffle while the old pro does his number. Some companies call this training, but it is likely to do more harm than good. Here's why:

1. The "Old Pro" is probably not a good teacher. He or she has not been taught how to train. There's no way to measure the actual useful knowledge the trainee will obtain during this field "experience."
2. The Old Pro is likely to have some poor work habits you don't want the young trainee to absorb. The veteran may also have some cynicism you won't want thrust on an eager young mind.
3. Observation is a good learning technique, but the trainee is getting none of the theory about why the Old Pro is doing the things that need to be done to get the order.
4. If the Old Pro has a bad few days, the trainee may get discouraged.
5. The Old Pro is not being paid to train. He or she may resent the request. Sales coverage in the experienced person's territory may suffer during the time the two are together.

So putting a trainee with an experienced salesperson for a few days is not training, and it could be a disaster.

Who Has the Primary Responsibility for Field Training?

How then should field training be implemented? Remember what was said earlier? The manager is the primary training resource in a sales operation. The manager works with new people to educate them and develop their skills.

Three Things Not to Do as a Field Trainer

Before addressing what should be done as a field trainer, let's take the time to discuss what *not* to do.

First, field training is *not* allowing a new salesperson to tag along after the manager to watch him work. The trainee may learn a few things from observation, but not enough to function in the field alone. He or she will learn by doing. The manager assists the learning process by forcing the person to plan, both before and after the call, and by correcting mistakes in a positive way.

Second, field training is *not* something that is restricted to staff members who are having problems, or are inexperienced. The improvements made in the sales technique of an experienced salesperson may prove to be much more valuable to the company than the problem corrected with a marginal person.

Third, the salesperson that the manager spends the day with will observe the manager's work habits as well as sales technique. If the manager starts the day late or spends the morning in the coffee shop or drinks at lunch, the person being trained may think that's the path to success. The manager working in the field with a member of the sales staff should set a good example by working hard.

The Proper Way to Conduct Field Training

The first training step the manager should take is to set up the time when he or she will work with the trainee. It's a bad idea to show up in the salesperson's territory unannounced or spring an early-morning surprise in the day the manager wishes to spend with the salesperson. Give the trainee good advance notice. Part of the manager's evaluation is to determine how well the salesperson can plan a productive day. The advance schedule also gives the manager an opportunity to check out the salesperson's recent call reports and review the territory being visited.

The Field Trainer as a Coach

The field trainer is really a coach. In coaching, the best technique is to guide the trainee into doing the job on his or her own.

Joint Calls

One of the most popular training methods is for the manager to take a trainee along on joint sales calls. These calls break down into three types:

1. Those calls in which the sales manager takes the lead role and the trainee acts as an observer.
2. Those calls in which the trainee takes the lead role and the manager acts as an observer.
3. Those calls in which the manager and trainee both interact with the prospect or customer.

When the manager takes the lead in a call, it becomes a learning experience for the observant trainee. (The lessons can be "force-fed" by a question-and-answer period after the call is completed.)

When the trainee takes the lead, the manager is in a position to assess the salesperson's performance and determine which skill areas need improvement.

When the two share responsibility, the manager has, in effect, designated the trainee an equal for the tenure of the call. It's important for the manager to maintain this equality throughout and not "take over."

It's often a good idea to switch roles during a field training session, with the manager taking the lead on one call, the trainee leading on the next.

Why "Rescuing" Is a Bad Idea

One action that defeats the training process is for the manager to interrupt and take over a sales situation because the trainee is floundering. No manager wants to let a potential sales opportunity slip away, but remember, the main purpose of field training is to make the salesperson self-sufficient. That won't occur if the manager pulls the trainee out of every hole. Make the occasional interruption to get a call back on track, but once the manager takes over a sales situation, it's difficult for the trainee to regain the initiative. His or her stature with the prospect has been diminished. The prospect is likely to address comments and questions to the "boss."

Using Questions as a Training Tool: Ten Prompting Questions That Help a Sales Trainee Plan a Sales Call

One of the best methods of coaching is through questioning. The questions should all be designed to make the trainee think about the call and the sales process. Here are some typical questions to ask a new representative before a sales call:

1. What are your objectives on this call? In your mind, what will make this call successful?
2. Have you researched this prospect? How big is this company? Who's in charge of the buying decisions for our product line?
3. Do you have an idea of the products you specifically want to recommend here?
4. Who is this prospect buying from now?
5. What's your fallback plan if the prospect won't see us? Is there anyone else in the organization whom it might be valuable for us to see?
6. What objections are likely to come up?
7. What kind of questions are you going to ask?
8. What, if any, material do you plan to leave?
9. Do we currently have customers with businesses similar to the prospect's? What are they buying from us?
10. How do you plan to close?

All of these questions force the trainee to plan calls, at least all those calls made with you more thoroughly. They are designed to ripen the trainee into an experienced salesperson who will think about every call before it's made.

How to Handle a Sales Call with a Sales Trainee: Three Things to Remember

1. During the actual call, try to let the trainee run the show. The manager should consider his position to be similar to that of a field admiral on board a naval vessel. The admiral may be the senior officer, but the ship's captain is in charge of that particular voyage.

2. While the manager doesn't want to sacrifice any potential orders or customers, the prime objective is to train the salesperson to be self-sufficient.

3. Remain in the background, out of the way. The manager should ask to be introduced by name only, or as a "colleague." If the prospect knows the manager is along, he'll likely begin ignoring the salesperson, addressing comments and questions to the manager. The prospect may also try to change the agenda, effectively freezing the salesperson out of the subject.

A Manager's 14-Point Checklist to Help Critique a Trainee's Sales Call

The manager's focus during the call is observing how the trainee is handling the situation. There is a fairly standard checklist that fits most sales situations:

1. Was the trainee prepared?
2. Did the trainee have any knowledge of the prospect's operation?
3. Did the trainee seem comfortable during the introduction and presentation?
4. Did the trainee engage the attention and interest of the prospect?

5. Did the trainee make a good, effective presentation?
6. Did the trainee listen more than he talked?
7. Did the trainee explain the benefits?
8. Did the trainee gain the respect of the buyer?
9. Did the trainee answer the objections?
10. Did the trainee recognize any buying signals?
11. Did the trainee focus on the right products?
12. Did the trainee try to close at the right moment?
13. Did the trainee leave the correct material with the prospect?
14. Did the trainee promise the prospect a further course of action?

See the training checkoff list (Exhibit 11–1).

After the Call Is Over

Obviously, the manager is not sitting in the prospect's office with a clipboard, like some sort of business-oriented Woody Hayes, checking off the answers to these questions. Instead, the manager should be making mental notes that will be shared with the trainee after the call is completed. Now is the time for the aftercall critiquing session. These sessions are touchy. No matter how diplomatically the observations are made, they are still going to come out as *criticism* of the trainee's performance.

Eight Prompting Questions That Help a Trainee Plot Call Strategy

Before making these observations, ask the trainee more probing-type questions, forcing him or her to plan a strategy that will capture this prospect. Some strategy-planning questions should include:

1. Evaluate the call. How do you think it went?

EXHIBIT 11–1
FIELD TRAINING CHECKOFF LIST

ACCOUNT_______________________________________ DATE_________
NEW PROSPECT?____
TIME_____________ LENGTH OF CALL____________________________
PERSON SEEN____

Advance preparation	Good____	Fair____	Poor____
Knowledge of customer	Good____	Fair____	Poor____
Introduction technique	Good____	Fair____	Poor____
Gained prospect's interest	Good____	Fair____	Poor____
Presentation skills	Good____	Fair____	Poor____
Explained benefits	Good____	Fair____	Poor____
Rapport with prospect	Good____	Fair____	Poor____
Answered objections	Good____	Fair____	Poor____
Product focus	Good____	Fair____	Poor____
Recognize buying signal?	Good____	Fair____	Poor____
Closing skills	Good____	Fair____	Poor____
Left correct material	Good____	Fair____	Poor____
Future action plan	Good____	Fair____	Poor____

Comments: ____
____
____
____
____
____

2. Was the person seen as the decision maker? Was he or she open? Do you feel that other departments might be involved?
3. What's your next step with this prospect? Are you going to do a survey? Give him a demo? Write a proposal? Try to close?
4. Our competitor appears to be very solid with this account. Did you see any weak points that you might exploit?

5. Evaluate the company. Did it seem lively or slow-moving? Did their office equipment and procedures seem up-to-date? What about the attitudes of their personnel?
6. Will more time with this prospect be a worthwhile investment?
7. What kind of company support do you think you'll need to make an order happen?
8. What is the single most important factor in obtaining an order from this prospect?

All of these questions cause the trainee to think about the call that's just been completed and contemplate what steps should come next. If the manager causes the salesperson to do this analysis on every call, then the coaching job has been successful.

How to Handle the Critiquing Session: Using the Observation/Question Technique

Now the call is ready to be critiqued. This is the Monday morning quarterbacking session that should take place immediately after the trainee has been encouraged to plan the next step with the prospect. It's done after the planning session because critiquing can be an ego deflator. The discussion is about how the trainee conducted the call and ways it could have been improved. These comments, while critical, are meant to help the trainee improve his or her actual call techniques. Examples of these kinds of observation/question techniques are as follows:

1. The purchasing agent reacted negatively when you tried to close. Do you think you should have waited until you answered all the objections that were raised?
2. You didn't have the one brochure the buyer wanted to see most. Do you check your presentation binder before each call?
3. You missed an important product benefit in your presentation. Do you fully understand how that benefit helps this particular prospect?

4. You ignored the buyer's assistant. Are you sure that person won't be involved in the buying decision?
5. You quoted a two-week delivery schedule on a product that has a month's lead time. Are you familiar with all our lead times?

Of course these comments are all criticisms. The manager has made observations regarding what went wrong in the call, and the question follow-up is used to soften the impact of the remarks on the trainee. The manager can soften it further by showing that the mistake is not serious or by admitting to experiencing similar problems.

Why It's Important Not to Be Overly Critical

It's important not to offer too many criticisms at one time. First, it is extremely demoralizing for a new salesperson to hear that everything that's been done could have been done better. Second, the salesperson will absorb only so much material from a single coaching session. When critiquing a call, try to focus on only the most important areas the salesperson needs to work on.

Five Ways to Suggest Actions Needed for a Trainee's Improvement

At the end of a field training session the manager may notice certain weaknesses in the trainee's sales skills. It's best to end on a positive note, so addressing these issues the right way is important. Begin by emphasizing all the good things that were accomplished during the period. Be generous with praise. (If it is genuine.) Try statements such as:

"I noticed improvement in your analysis skills today. At the last call we made, you zeroed right in on the prospect's problem."

"Your demonstration on the Model 5000 Hermisphere is first-rate. I may call on you to give it during our next classroom training session."

These positive remarks are a prelude to presenting the list of things the trainee must work on. When going over this list, give the reasons why these skill areas are important. For example:

"The first prospect we saw today was in no position to buy anything. You need to work on qualifying prospects. No salesperson ever has enough time. That's why it's important to spend every minute with those prospects who have a need for the product, the authority to buy it, and the funds to pay for it."

Follow this up with an offer of assistance. "I've prepared a list of qualifying questions. Work these questions in on every preliminary call. You'll be surprised at how much more effective you will become. When I check back with you next week, you'll probably have several success stories for me."

The tactic then for discussing skill weakness areas with trainees is to

1. Begin by praising the trainee's accomplishments.
2. Engage in a frank discussion of the problem areas.
3. List the reasons why improvement in those areas is important.
4. Make suggestions on how improvement can be made and offer assistance.
5. Follow up on progress.

Four Suggestions on Reinforcing Good Habits

Correcting problems is important. Just as vital to a good training program is noticing and praising the good things the trainee does right. Whether they are learned or instinctive, good selling habits are the basic building blocks needed to construct the complete, self-sufficient salesperson.

All of us tend to repeat what we have performed successfully in the past. Praise from the manager equates with success in the trainee's eyes. Here are some ways to parcel out praise:

1. "Your knowledge of that product application is very thorough. The explanation you gave made the benefits clear to the prospect. She certainly seemed interested. Looks like you've established a solid prospect. Let me know what happens with this one."

2. "I couldn't help noticing that you stopped the demonstration and went directly for a close the minute you recognized a buying

signal. That was exactly the right thing to do. I'm pleased that you were so alert."

3. "This was a pretty good day! We got a lot done because your call schedule was so well organized. I'm impressed by your work habits."

4. "We must have spoken with eight people at Chaos, Inc., before we learned the name of the decision maker, but you kept right on digging. Keep up that kind of persistence. It will pay off."

The Six Stages in Selling and Buying Cycles

The average amount of time between first uncovering the prospect and obtaining the order is called the selling cycle. Some products are sold on the first call or not at all (the "one-call close"). For others, the average incubation period before an order is obtained may be anywhere from a week to several years.

It's important for new salespeople to understand the selling cycle for your company's product line. If they don't learn this important information, they may become discouraged or, at the very least, make inaccurate forecasts. Selling cycles can be identified in the following way:

1. Prospects have a problem for which your company's product offers a solution, but they don't know they have the problem.
2. The salesperson finds the prospect and uncovers the problem.
3. The salesperson offers the solution. This step can be broken down into
   a. Verbal presentations
   b. Demonstrations and testimonials
   c. Verbal agreement that the solution has value
   d. Written proposals
4. The prospect checks budgetary considerations.
5. The prospect investigates *alternative solutions*. (This may seem unfair, but it is real life. Most prospects will check out other vendors to see if a better or lower-cost solution exists.)
6. The prospect makes a decision.

Incidentally, salespeople who continually complain about the company's noncompetitive pricing are probably arriving late during the buying cycle. Some enterprising competitor has been there first and uncovered the prospect's need. Their solution fits what they do best. Your people can only offer a lower-cost alternative.

Ways to Relieve Pressure During a Field Training Session

There are several things to remember during any field training session. The first is that the person being trained is under strain. He or she is well aware that a judgment is taking place. The manager should do everything possible to ease this pressure. During the day the manager should take the lead roll in a call or two. The trainee should be allowed to observe the manager in action. Some of the techniques that have been talked about can be demonstrated and the trainee can be given a few minutes reprieve from inspection beneath the microscope. Another good procedure is to be generous with praise. When the trainee does something right, say so. Part of the job is building confidence.

How to End a Day's Field Training Session

At the end of the day, review the activity. Summarize the day's accomplishments. Go over the things that must be done to follow up with each prospect. List the things the trainee must work on. Emphasize all the positive events of the day. Finally, *let the salesperson know that this is just one of a series of regularly scheduled field training sessions.* A single day in the field with a trainee, no matter how fruitful, will not be worthwhile unless it is followed up. For training to be effective it must be a continuous process, going on as long as the manager has responsibility for the area.

Training Programs for Veteran Salespeople

One of the most difficult jobs for a manager is training or retraining a veteran salesperson. How can a manager reeducate the "Old Pro" who has seen it all and "forgotten more than the manager will ever know?" Many veteran salespeople do not take kindly to instruction. They view it as an insult, a questioning of their abilities and experience. Yet, they may need training as much as the rookie on the job for the very first day. How does the manager get the veteran to accept this badly needed training?

Rules When Retraining Old Pros

The first rule is don't tinker just to tinker. If a manager is lucky enough to have a superperformer on the staff who is consistently out-achieving everyone else, don't force-feed this person an unwanted training program just because the company manual states that everyone will go through the exercise. Don't be in a hurry to make this person discard unorthodox methods because they don't correspond to popular theories on how sales should be made. Accept the idea that there are a few salespeople who have found a secret sales formula that works for them and them alone. It can't be transferred, and adding or deleting an ingredient sometimes ruins the formula altogether. Just enjoy the orders and let the superstar alone until there's hard evidence that the formula isn't working anymore.

How to Retrain the Old Pro Who Has Gone Stale

Superstars aside, there are still many veteran salespeople who need additional training. Their work habits may have become sloppy, or their knowledge of the product line isn't up-to-date. In many cases, Old Pros need their emotional batteries recharged. How does the manager accomplish these training objectives without damaging the egos of the veterans?

Three Easy Training Pills for the Old Pro to Swallow

Classroom training is the easiest pill for the veteran to swallow. If classes are regularly scheduled, the veteran isn't offended when asked to attend, because everyone has to go. New-product training sessions are also an easy "sell." After all, even the veteran can't be expected to know much about a brand-new item in the product line.

Pride won't be bent or bruised. New company policies are still another way to "educate" the Old Pro. In all of these instances, always try to include some sales techniques classes as part of the curriculum, in effect slipping in the material under the veteran's nose.

Field Training the Veteran Salesperson

Field training sessions are the most difficult for the Old Pro to swallow. After all, doesn't he or she already know every trick in the game? Additional training is not going to teach him or her anything new! If the veteran has been a steady performer for the company, it's up to the manager to protect that person's ego. The aim is to build skill, not destroy confidence.

Setting Training Objectives for Veterans: Sample Dialogues That Won't Bruise Egos

One way to suggest a training session to a touchy veteran is with a set of clearly stated objectives. For example:

"Charley, you've always been between 90 and 100 percent of quota. That's good, but I know you can do better. With your talent and dedication, you should be over 100 percent every year. I feel with a little help you can put together some pretty impressive numbers. Let's spend a little time together."

Another way is to bring out a problem that concerns the manager. For example:

"Jane, your close ratio has gone down steadily for the past few months. Perhaps you're not spending enough time qualifying your prospects. Maybe it's something else, but we have to find out. Let's work together two days next week. Maybe I can see something that you're missing."

Still another way is through outrageous flattery. Here's how this works:

"Ed, you've got the best-organized territory in the district. Do you mind if I tag along one day next week and take notes? Some of the other people here might benefit from your example." (Shame on you if you don't mean it.)

Using a Sales Trainee to Retrain an Old Pro

A variation of this last method can be used to revive a tired veteran. Assign a rookie to the veteran after first telling the Old Pro that it's important for the new person to learn the ropes from the very best. Ask the Pro to set up a training schedule for the rookie. Of course, this could create a problem with the rookie not being properly trained. The manager must prevent his by supervising the training operation. Ask to review the training schedule that the veteran develops. Through observations and questions make the veteran revise the training schedule until it is complete. The veteran is forced to review the basic selling techniques that made him or her successful for so many years. By using the veteran in a controlled way, the manager is really training two people at once.

Going Back to Basics: The Ultimate Training Tool for Veterans and Rookies Alike

When a veteran salesperson can't get untracked, there's no better cure than a thorough review of basic sales techniques. The principles of salesmanship that work for the rookie can be used to revive the veteran. The manager should treat the veteran like the rawest recruit. How many calls are being made daily? How good is product knowledge? Are presentations professional? Are the demos first-rate? Are closing techniques up-to-date? Hammering home the basic skills may make it possible for a manager to salvage a veteran who has gone sour.

The Status of Sales Training in Many Small Companies

Small companies often hire only experienced sales representatives because they feel that they can't afford to spend any money on training. They also often want immediate production from their salespeople, an instant "bang for their buck." The result is that the typical sales force in the small company that doesn't believe in training is highly erratic, each salesperson using different techniques and methods. Even written proposals and quotations may be different as the salespeople decide for themselves the best way to pursue a prospect. Good salespeople going through a bad time are almost never salvaged, poor sales techniques are not corrected, and performance moves up and out like the tides.

How a Small Company Can Set Up and Run an Effective Sales-Training Program

Seminars

There are many things a small company can do to get their people trained. If the company is too small to support a formalized in-house training program, it can arrange for its people to attend seminars. Those given by organizations such as the American Management Association, are run by professionals with many years of sales and marketing experience. Most are well run and pack a lot of information and practical how-to technique in short sessions.

They cover such a variety of sales-oriented subjects, most companies can find a seminar that answers its particular need. The seminars can be expensive, with price tags ranging anywhere from $500 to $2,500 dollars, but they're a bargain when compared with the time and effort of putting together your own program. Some of these seminars are given during the weekends so no valuable field sales time is lost.

The Sales Evangelists

One word of caution: Make a thorough investigation of the course material before you select a seminar. There are a great number of sales evangelists out there bringing their inspirational, almost religious, messages of happiness through better selling to whomever will pay for them. They fire people up, make them burn with enthusiasm. However the "fix" may wear off quickly.

How to Check Out a Seminar

If management's objective is to obtain training on basic or advanced selling skills, or learn management techniques, use a group such as the American Management Association. No matter who is used, learn what the contents of the course are. Read the course material. Check with other companies who have attended. Get their evaluation of the value of the seminar. Send one person before you consider sending a group.

Subscribing to Sales Journals and Bulletins

Small companies can also subscribe to sales journals and bulletins such as the kind put out by the Dartnell Corporation. These monthly bulletins usually run about four pages. They offer practical tips and suggestions on selling and constantly remind the salesperson to always take the professional approach.

Using Local Educational Facilities as a Training Tool

Local universities and colleges are additional training resources that can be tapped by the small company. Most offer nighttime courses in sales and marketing. Paying the tuition for salespeople who wish to take these courses is an inexpensive way to develop seasoned personnel.

The local library will have shelves filled with books on selling and sales training. The sales manager of a small company might play the part of an instructor and assign the same reading material to every person on the team. Use Saturdays to discuss the material, and the company has just implemented an inexpensive training session.

The Sales Manager as an Educator

Finally, the sales manager of a company is the best resource for ongoing field training. When working with the sales staff he, or she can make every call a training call, using questions, observations, and more questions to develop a professional staff. When speaking to a staff member on the phone about sales problems, the manager can guide the person to the right solution rather than just dictate an answer. Admittedly, this takes more time, but the person may not call again with the same problem.

The Two "Nevers" in Sales Training

There are two "nevers" to remember about sales training. The first is that salespeople can never be overtrained. The second is that sales training never ends.

Chapter Twelve

How to Motivate Sales Personnel

What Motivation Is All About

"Motivate" is a word that's on every sales manager's lips almost every day. Some managers speak of nothing else. They use it like a secret and mysterious password that they hope will magically change the ordinary salesperson into Captain Quota Buster. What does "motivate" mean and why is it such a popular subject with sales managers? Peter Drucker said, "We know nothing about motivation. All we can do is write books about it." There are many theories on the subject, from the simplistic "everyone is motivated by lust and greed," to Maslow's overly complex motivation pyramid (Exhibit 12–1).

Noah Webster scribbled in his dictionary that to motivate means doing or saying something that causes a person to act. In other words, when someone is motivated, a still body goes into motion.

EXHIBIT 12–1
MASLOW'S PYRAMID

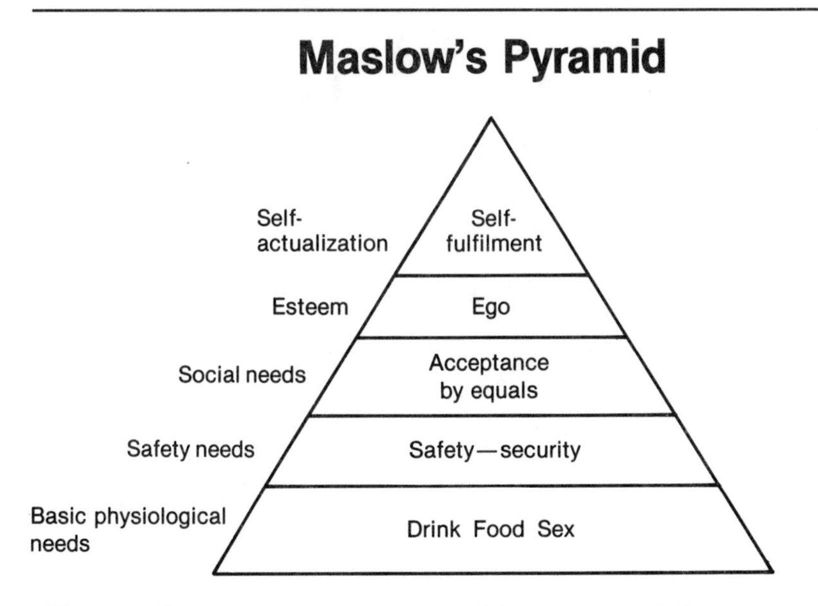

Some Questions on the Need for Motivation

How does the manager get members of the sales team excited? How are they energized into action? How are they *motivated?* More important, why do they need to be motivated? Isn't the compensation plan with income partially or entirely based on performance supposed to take care of that problem? What's going to propel them if it isn't money?

Compensation and Fear as Motivators

Yes, the compensation plan is a motivator. If the company's compensation is similar to that of most companies, the harder the crew works, the more they get paid. Then why should direction be so difficult? Why can't the manager just tell the gang what to do and wake up to find it done? Every salesperson has heard the old joke about the manager who ran a sales contest where the winner got to keep his job. Why shouldn't every manager make that a creed? Perform or get out. Does the promise of money combined with the threat of dismissal sound like a good motivational program? Managers should shake their heads no, because things don't work that way.

Why Motivating People Is a Difficult Problem

Motivating salespeople is one of the most vexing and complicated problems a manager faces. It's bothersome because many managers feel that the compensation plan, which usually rewards according to accomplishment, should be motivation enough. If the salesperson isn't going to hustle to make more bucks, it seems that little else will make him or her try harder.

But money's only part of the answer. (It's a very big part of the answer, and don't let anyone tell you differently.) Compensation is the basis for our economic society. (It's important to everyone, and most managers wouldn't want a salesperson who isn't interested in making more cash.)

Using Motivational Techniques Based on Human Nature

Other motivational techniques must be used to get people moving the way managers want them to move. All of these techniques are based on human nature.

One Assumption to Make When Developing Motivation Programs

When thinking about ways to motivate the sales crew, start with an assumption. That assumption is that the sales staff are out there working. Perhaps they're not working the right way, but that's up to the manager to correct. If there are a few people on the payroll the manager suspects of spending every afternoon taking in double-feature matinees at the local theater, they should be let go. They aren't part of this discussion. Motivational theory doesn't work on anyone who won't even try. The manager must start with people who are seriously interested in doing the job. Your problem is not literally to get people moving, it's to get them moving in the right direction, at a faster pace and with both eyes on a clearly defined goal.

The Manager's Job as Motivator

The manager's job as a motivator is to take people who are sincere, channel their efforts, get them to work harder, work smarter, and produce more consistently. The goal is to help the company make more profit and to make the operation's performance look better. The manager's motives are selfish, so acknowledge that. Don't try to sell the program on the basis of its being entirely for the benefit of the sales staff, although motivation has a beneficial effect on the person being motivated. It usually means a higher income for that person, a better chance at promotion, and a good feeling of self-accomplishment. Managers should not feel that they are manipulating others when they motivate them to perform at their best.

18 Things, Other Than Money, That Motivate People to Perform Better

What, exactly, besides compensation motivates people to perform at their best? Here are some of the common "dynamite sticks" that managers put under their salespeople.

1. Peer pressure. The best people on any sales staff are true competitors. Their incomes are important indicators of their success. Just as important is how their incomes relate to the incomes of other members of the sales team. They feel that relative income is a truer gauge of how they measure up. The best salespeople want to compete in every way possible. Are more sales calls per week a target?

Put up a chart on the office wall listing the number of calls made by each person on the team. Do other things to emphasize intramural competition. *Always* display monthly sales performance records in a prominent place. Not one person on the staff will want to be on the bottom of that list. Run local contests. The prizes don't have to be large. Do everything possible to stimulate the natural (but friendly) rivalry that exists among good sales performers.

2. Recognition. One of the most important motivational factors for a salesperson is acknowledgment for a job well done. It's not enough to call the person into the office and offer him or her a handshake. (Remember about peer pressure.) Let the good performer know that his or her efforts are appreciated. Show this appreciation in front of everyone. Mention a good sales effort in the company newspaper if the company has one. Allow a top achiever to address a company meeting. The salesperson needs to be recognized for superior accomplishment.

3. Credit. Salespeople must know that they are getting proper home office credit for all the good things that happen in their territories. Some new sales managers are so anxious about how top management regards their own performances, they sometimes emphasize their own roles in landing big accounts and orders and downplay the salesperson's participation. This is a big mistake. Nothing demotivates a sales crew faster than the feeling that the boss is stealing their thunder.

4. Awards. Even an inexpensive plaque given to a salesperson at a presentation ceremony in front of the sales staff will motivate the sales crew. If the plaque doesn't hang on the office wall, that's because the salesperson has taken it home to hang in the study. Give pins that identify superperformers. They'll be worn with pride.

5. Contests. The best contests are those that involve the spouse, such as a trip for two. That makes the salesperson a winner in the spouse's eyes.

6. Trust. Salespeople will work harder for managers they trust. Is the manager's word good? When a promise is made is it kept? Does the manager trust good performers enough to leave them

alone and let them handle their jobs in their own way? Let staff members know they're trusted and they'll work harder.

7. Potential for unlimited earnings. Why is this category listed here rather than under compensation? It is because "caps" or ceilings on earnings are extraordinary demotivators. The salespeople on staff must feel they will receive every penny they earn in commissions. Nothing deflates the wind from a salesperson's balloon faster than the knowledge that the company will allow him or her to make so much and nothing more. Management is telling them that it pays to try to achieve only so much. If income must be regulated, do it via quota assignments and bonus setups. If the commission plan is tied to gross profit, so what if one salesperson made more than the manager, or even the company president? Perhaps that salesperson made the greater contribution to the company that year.

8. Opportunity for advancement. Everyone likes to feel that there is a chance for a better job, a chance for a bright future. That's why promotion from within whenever possible is so important. Let the staff see that superior performers are rewarded for their efforts. (That's why mature companies who offer little chance for advancement must pay more to keep good personnel. The best of the crop will get restless and leave unless they can't match their current compensation elsewhere.)

9. Stability. Does the company reel from crisis to crisis? Does top management come and go through a swinging door that never stops? Do prices and policies change with every new moon? If so, there will be trouble keeping good people and more trouble motivating the people that are kept. Incidentally, that "forget about what we did before, we're off to a fresh start now" story can be sold only so many times.

10. Good products. A reliable product line that offers customers a fair value is one of the best motivators of all. A hot product line is more exhilarating than sex. On the other hand, salespeople enjoy challenges—but they don't like being told by customers that the product line is junk, or overpriced, or never delivered on time. They

want to spend their time selling, not putting out endless strings of brushfires.

11. Decent and fair treatment. Are the salespeople bullied? Are they put on notice if they fail to make quota for one month? Are they humiliated in front of others? Does management play favorites, passing out plum assignments to special pets? Does management feel that the best way to get top performance is through intimidation? This is a lousy motivational technique—the salespeople are being motivated right out the door and into other jobs.

12. Affection. Surprise! People work better and work harder if they believe they're liked. Try building the sales crew's self-esteem by holding them in esteem.

13. Realistic goals. Are the quotas reachable, or just percentages based on management mindset increases? Do staff members have any input into their quota assignments? Is management willing to make adjustments if it's proven that quotas have been set too high? If the goals aren't achievable, why should the salespeople break their backs to try to reach them?

14. Input. Give the sales crew a voice in what goals to seek and how those goals can be achieved.

15. Decision-making responsibility. One powerful motivator is showing trust in people by giving them some leeway to negotiate with prospects. If they must come to management to knock a dime off the price to land a big contract, they'll know that their abilities and judgments aren't respected. Give them guidelines, sure, but let them have some say in cutting deals.

16. Training. The best way to show the crew that there are better things planned for them is to offer regularly scheduled training classes to improve sales skills, product knowledge, time management, and so forth.

17. Variety. Doing the same thing year after year gets stale, particularly if the only change in the order of battle is a quota that keeps going through the ceiling. Try to give the veteran people new assignments every so often just to prevent burnout.

18. Achievement. The synthesis of all the motivating factors is achievement. It brings satisfaction, the knowledge that a job has been done and done well. To give staff members the opportunity for achievement, first give them a set of attainable goals.

The Manager's Attitude as Motivator

These factors are in no particular order of importance because there is no order of importance. What motivates one person will leave another cold. No matter what technique or series of techniques used, there is no better motivator that staff members can have than the knowledge that management always has their best interests at heart. If they believe that management always wants the best for them then the motivational job is easy.

Sales Contests: A Quick-Fix for Slow Sales

One of the "quick-fix" ways to motivate the sales crew into action is through a sales contest. From the sales crew's view, a contest provides them with a chance to earn something extra. The something extra could be anything from cash to a trip to Fiji. From the manager's view, the contest helps focus the crew's attention on a particular product or gives impetus to a specific time period.

Contest Time Periods

Contests should be held over relatively short time periods. Long-running contests tend to lose the sense of urgency that you want to create. A contest that runs the entire business year is not a contest at all, it is just part of the overall compensation plan.

Contest Objectives

The first thing needed for a contest is an objective. What does management want the contest to accomplish? Is the goal to try to focus the sales crew's attention on a brand-new product just introduced into the line? Is it an effort to cram more sales activity into what has typically been a slow time of year. Perhaps management wants the sales crew to concentrate on a few very profitable items that the company sells. A sales contest might be the answer for any one of these problems.

Simple Sales Contests

One of the easiest contests to devise and administer is the short-term sales contest for the local office. Let's say management wants to dramatically demonstrate how more demos lead to more sales. A contest is announced that gives $200 cash to the person on the crew who does the most demos over the next five days. The rules of the contest stipulate that sales don't matter, demos do.

Each day a record is posted of the verified demos done by every member of the sales team. At next Monday morning's regularly scheduled sales meeting, there is a short ceremony, the winner is handed the $200, and every member of the sales staff who did better than the normal number of demos is congratulated because more sales will surely result. If there is a large crew, first, second, and third prizes would be advisable, because by midweek one or two persons might move so far ahead of the pack that those near the bottom might be discouraged and stop trying.

The Most Common Type of Sales Contest

The most frequently used contests are those that focus on total sales volume or percentage of sales over quota. Obviously, those contests that use percentages of quota are more equitable because sales territories are not equal in volume, potential, or maturity. The winners of these contests can be those who achieve the best sales records. Frequently, preset goals are given as bogeys, with all those exceeding certain dollar figures or percentages of quota, winners. Longer contests of this type can run for a month, a quarter, or even six months. Again, anything longer loses the interest of the contestants, except those at the very top. Even a six-month contest is a bit of a stretch. However, some managers prefer longer-term contests because the prizes can be more sumptuous. These prizes can range from trips to television sets to good, old cash.

Merchandise Prizes

Some companies award contest points that can be redeemed for merchandise from companies who specialize in sales promotion merchandising. The advantage of using a point system is that it allows prize awards on many different levels. People not near the top of the standings will keep trying their hardest to win smaller prizes. The promotion company takes care of the problem of providing the actual award. The disadvantage is that the merchandising company must make their profit too. Many of the contest dollars budgeted for awards do not go to the company's salespeople, but rather to third-party contest administrators.

Publicizing the Contest Results

Frequent posting of contest standings is extremely important to recognize those who are achieving their goals and spur on to greater efforts those who are not. If the sales crew is well scattered throughout the region, then a contest bulletin with the weekly standings should be sent to each member. Long-term contests do have a positive effect on those salespeople who are just short of goals near the end of the contest. They try like mad to make it over the top.

Contests Focused on Profit

A third type of contest focuses not on total sales or quota performance, but rather on total profit. This kind of contest is useful if the salespeople have leeway in product pricing and if different products carry different margins. After all, it's not how many orders the salesperson brings into the house, but how profitable these orders are. A profit-oriented contest is a good way of teaching this valuable lesson. This contest is a bit more difficult to administer because the profit calculations must be made and posted for every salesperson. Obviously, this kind of contest is not suitable for a company who doesn't wish to let their salespeople know what the profit margins are.

Team Sales Contests

A fourth type of sales contest simply puts one group against another in a challenge to see who can produce the most sales over a specific period. This kind of contest often produces the most competitive spirit because it's *mano e mano* with no holds barred. Even though the stakes may be small, often people will try harder to win in this kind of contest. The downside is that they're also hoping that their contemporaries fail. Perhaps management doesn't want to foster this kind of attitude.

How to Get the Most Dollar Value Out of a Contest

The way to get the most "bang" for the buck in any kind of sales contest is to make it as fair as possible, with every member of the sales team having an equal chance to win so that slow starters aren't discouraged. It's important that enthusiasm not wane halfway through the contest. That's why levels of prizes are useful. Publicity is important at the beginning and during a contest. The purpose is to foster intramural competition. Advance notice or rumors of a pending contest is a disaster. Salespeople will hoard orders that meet the contest requirements and enter them after the start date. Contests should be fun. It's important not to needle or pressure those not doing well. Staff members will dread the next contest. Finally, repetition leads to boredom. Contests have their greatest impact when they're not used too often.

How to Keep Sales Coming in After the Contest Is Over

One of the problems with contests is that they lead to a post contest depression. Everyone has been busting their butts through the entire contest period. The winners have collected their prizes and the losers are grumbling about some people's luck. The sales staff has worked at high energy levels and are exhausted. How does management keep spirits and sales activity high? One way is through close monitoring of activity through the contest period. If the sales crew has been making an extended effort during the contest period there will inevitably be a number of prospects they weren't able to close in the required time period. These uncommitted, but still live, prospects make a wonderful springboard for the selling period that immediately follows the contest.

Go over these prospects with each of the salespeople. Learn the reasons why they weren't closed. Maybe the timing wasn't right. Perhaps there is a concession or a promotional consideration that can be made that will help turn these prospects into customers.

Get more personally involved in the sales effort right after a contest. Offer to call on uncommitted prospects with salespeople. Make sure they aren't ignored just because the contest is over. What management is doing is ensuring that the extra efforts extended by the sales staff during the contest period have not been wasted. If all leads are followed up and all prospects worked as hard as possible, the postcontest period can yield more business than the actual contest itself.

A sales promotion hard on the heels of a contest is another way to keep the staff's spirits high. Now is the time to offer a baker's dozen on product orders or free supplies with certain dollar-value shipments.

How to Use the Promise of Promotion as a Motivational Tool

The promise of promotion has always been a good motivator for sales personnel. Most salespeople fancy themselves as potential managers. They'll work harder if they believe there is a career path leading upstairs in the company. That's why growing companies who are rapidly opening new offices and promoting people to field and staff management usually have an easier time keeping sales personnel than do more mature outfits where upward mobility depends on somebody already in management dying or retiring.

Assessing Promotion Possibilities

One of the first things managers should do is to assess the management possibilities for the people who report to them. The easiest way to do this is to examine their own career paths. What was the way they got promoted? Is that same avenue open to others? How long did they have to wait, and what had to be accomplished? Was the rise fairly typical, or did a manager get promoted because of extraordinary circumstances? Next, examine the company's structure and policy. How many people are being promoted every year? What's the typical profile of a new manager?

The manager wants to examine these things in order to counsel staff members who are ambitious to be managers. Let them know how to go about getting promoted. Let them know the traits that management is looking for. If the manager is part of the recommendation process, let the people know the traits that are personally important. Be candid about the possibilities. If there isn't much movement in the company, say so. People aren't idiots, they'll make the observation anyway.

When a Good Salesperson Isn't Management Material

If the manager is approached by someone who isn't management material, there should be some frankness regarding the traits that he or she lacks. Also, aspiring managers should know about the downside of promotion. If the manager of a small branch won't make as much as a top-producing salesperson, let the eager ones know that fact. It will save disillusionment later.

Holding Back a Promotion

Never hold anyone back from promotion just because that person would be difficult to replace. In fact, one of the ways for the manager to move up the corporate ladder is to acquire a reputation as a developer of managers.

What to Do When There Are Two Good Management Candidates

The manager with two good candidates for promotion is lucky. Support them equally. Stay on the sidelines, except to tell them both what's required. Let them fight it out in the trenches. The intramural competition could produce some excellent sales results for the entire operation.

What to Do When There Are Few Opportunities for Promotion

If there are no management positions likely in the near future, perhaps semimanagement jobs could be established, such as senior staff members who would supervise the trainees and less experienced salespeople. These seniors could be compensated by means of an override on the sales made by the juniors who report to them. This would give senior people a bit of experience for the time when branch or higher managerial positions become available and would give the manager the luxury of having closer field supervision for less experienced personnel. The availability of these senior positions would be a motivator for the entire sales staff.

Why It's Wrong to Give False Hopes About Promotion Opportunities

The lure of management is a strong motivator. Some companies trade on this desire, making all their salespeople "management trainees," or dangling promotion opportunity like a carrot in front of a donkey. Don't practice this deceit, but use this motivator in a more ethical way. Level with staff members about the opportunities for management in the company and what they need to accomplish to get there. It's the best way to avoid disillusionment and bitterness. It's also the best way to get staff members moving in the right direction.

How Managers Can Motivate Themselves

Many a manager has started like a flare, shining bright and hot for a time, then burned out early. They go so far and no farther. How can managers prevent this fate when they're so busy working with their people, keeping their energy levels high, making sure they're improving themselves and moving in the right direction? How do managers motivate themselves? How do they keep their direction headed straight toward the promised land? How do they prevent themselves from running hot and cold? How do they maintain a consistency of performance that moves them that next step up the ladder? Yes, most managers have a boss who's supposed to be handling that chore, but likely he or she is many miles away.

The truth is that every manager is supposed to be self-motivated to some degree. It's another responsibility like getting the sales forecast in on time. Here's how to do it.

The First Step in Self-motivation

The first step is simple. Managers should begin by doing just what they've told their salespeople to do. They should establish their own goals. Just what *is* the promised land as far as they're concerned? Is it that next step up, perhaps from branch to regional manager? Is it an income goal? Money is never a bad objective. Perhaps they've set some sales goals for the area that exceed company quotas. Maybe they want to aim for making their area a higher-profit center.

Selecting Different Kinds of Goals

Many managers tend to select only long-term goals. Frequently they want to aim for touchdowns. Some intermediate benchmarks should also be established so progress is easier to measure. Those who don't set these intermediate goals are likely to become discouraged because that goal line is so far away.

Motivation Through Personnel Improvement

Managers should learn to be excited by the progress of the people who report to them. Watching ideas take root and people grow can be a great motivator. Managers should learn to take pride in the development and maturity of staff members.

Motivation Through Competition

Managers should be motivated by competitive factors, both external and internal. Of course, they want to do better than the competition. After all, they're still salespeople at heart. They should also be anxious to match the performance of their operations with those of other managers in the company. The desire to measure up well against others can be a strong motivator.

Motivation Through Wielding Influence

Managers can be motivated by the influence they exercise with top management. Senior managers seek the counsel of those they respect. Those who are asked for advice are beginning to have a voice in shaping the company. Trust placed in a manager can be flattering and motivating. It suggests the opportunity to rise still higher.

A Summary on Self-motivation

Managers should use all the tools to motivate themselves that they use to motivate their own people. There are no secrets, only common denominators that work in both directions.

Chapter Thirteen
How to Run a Sales Meeting

The Essential Ingredient in Every Sales Meeting

Managers who have reached the conclusion that they have something very important to convey have passed the first litmus test for a successful sales meeting: *They have a purpose.* If the statement appears obvious, think back to all the meetings attended that didn't have a reason for being, except to hear a manager rant and rave for hours about everyone's poor performance. The first requisite for a good sales meeting is to have an excellent reason for calling one.

The Seven Common Reasons for Calling a Sales Meeting

Some of the more common reasons for holding a sales meeting are:

1. To inform. What's going on in the company these days? What's happening in the field? The sales meeting is a wonderful place

for information exchange. New-product announcements can be exciting when done with flair at the sales meeting.

2. To plan. How is the company going to get more business, more new accounts? How are we going to get more sales from existing accounts? How are we going to promote those wonderful new products that are coming down the pike?
3. To inspire. Many sales meetings are like evangelical happenings, bringing the gospel to the faithful.
4. To educate. To tell the sales crew about the new products, or have a session in sales techniques, or have some hands-on training, are all popular reasons for sales meetings.
5. To reward. Some sales meetings are restricted to top achievers. They are holidays disguised as meetings for tax reasons.
6. To evaluate. Some top managers see members of the sales crew only once or twice a year. The sales meeting is a good place to talk to person behind the numbers.
7. To build camaraderie. Often the national sales meeting is the only time of the year that the entire sales crew is together in one place.

Know the True Cost of a Sales Meeting

Meetings are expensive and time-consuming. Space often must be rented. Travel arrangements must be made. The troops must be fed and cared for. However, these are not the only costs the company incurs. Sales meetings take the sales staff out of the field. Golden selling hours are wasted. Learn to calculate the *expense* of the travel arrangements *plus* the cost of the lost selling time.

How to Determine the Kind of Meeting You Want to Hold

Managers must decide exactly what kind of a meeting they wish to hold. Is the attendance going to be bigger than a joint session of

Congress, with the manager dramatically posed behind a podium, giving the straight scoop to the silent troops? Will this be a small-group discussion with the accent on everyone's active participation? Will it be an awards ceremony to honor superior performers, or has this meeting been called to introduce a new product line?

Why the Kind of Meeting Determines Its Structure

Why are the details of a meeting so important? Because the kind of meeting that is planned determines the style of the session, the advance arrangements necessary, who will attend, the location, the tone of the meeting, the room size, the physical layout of the meeting room, and even the seating arrangement.

The Small Office Meeting

Many managers hold very small meetings in the office. This is the least expensive meeting to call because it doesn't cost the company money for space rental. The informal office meeting is part of the normal work routine. Often it is haphazard, called to discuss a particular problem. Sometimes it is a regularly scheduled planning session. This meeting is usually free-form, with no agenda, drifting on the tides of chance from one topic to the next. Short-term objectives are set, information exchanged, and problems resolved. A meeting such as this is necessary and takes the least time from the selling day.

The Negative Implications of an Office Meeting

However some managers feel that meetings in the office don't pack enough impact, and staff members could be distracted by the ebb and flow of normal business. Everyone has seen an office meeting disrupted by "emergency" phone calls. During breaks every salesperson seems to rush off to check for phone messages, or even tries to reach a few important customers on the phone. Just about every office meeting seems to get restarted late because all the salespeople can't be rounded up.

The Advantages of Moving Meetings Out of the Office

To avoid distractions and accent the importance of the message to be delivered, some managers prefer to hold even ordinary meetings in local hotels. Almost all good hotels can provide meeting rooms and appropriate paraphernalia, such as slide and overhead projectors, chalkboards, easels, and so forth. These hotels can also provide lunch and serve refreshments during the breaks. The advantage of holding the meeting outside the office is that the salespeople are all together and can't run back to their desks at every break. Schedules are easier to maintain. Many managers feel that these advantages are worth the small cost of a meeting room.

Calling the Larger Meeting

Larger meetings, or those deemed particularly *important,* are often held in hotels or resorts. Because of their relaxed atmosphere, resorts are often chosen when award ceremonies are the principal reason for the meeting. Being at the resort for a few days is part of the award. Spouses are often allowed to accompany their mates, and the tone at these meetings is relaxed and informal. Sometimes product launches are also made at resorts because management is trying to create the impression that good times are coming.

Six Advantages to Planning a Meeting Far in Advance

Scheduling larger meetings as far in advance as possible has several benefits. They are:

1. The more time available, the better the meeting will be prepared.
2. Space and logistical problems can be resolved far ahead of time.
3. Airline fares for those who travel to the meeting are usually less expensive if reservations are made far enough in advance.
4. The desirability of involvement by other company departments can be determined.
5. Advance notice gives the sales reps time to button up their territories so fewer sales are lost. They also have time to consider any problems they wish to discuss with managers in private meetings.
6. It's easier to arrange for guest speakers.

Site Selection for Sales Meetings

If salespeople are being brought in from other parts of the country, to minimize travel time and expense the manager may wish to select a central location for the meeting. If a large number of salespeople are concentrated in one area, that's another good reason to hold a meeting nearby.

Travel Arrangements

After site selection, the first thing managers must consider is how all the attendees will get there. If the company has an in-house travel department, let them tackle the problem. Some companies allow the reps to make their own travel arrangements. This could cost a few extra bucks in travel expense, as many reps will not choose the least expensive way.

There are so many different fares and rate schedules available today that a good travel agent can be invaluable in sorting through the various options and selecting the least expensive fares. They usually know the lowest rates and the reliable carriers.

Arrange for everyone to arrive at the hotel the night before the meeting starts. This guarantees full attendance with no late, out-of-breath, arrivals.

Hotel Accommodations

If the meeting's large or important enough to be held in a hotel, it's a good idea to put up attendees at the same location. That way they shouldn't have any problem getting to the sessions on time. If a large enough block of people will be staying at the hotel, the management may throw in the meeting rooms at no extra charge.

To be certain everyone knows where to be, and when to be there, ask the hotel to post the meeting schedules, including the rooms, on a bulletin board. Several hotel chains have gone electronic, and meeting schedules are posted on in-house television channels.

A Short List of Meeting Requirements

Here's a short list of meeting requirements:

1. A site
2. A hotel that can provide meeting rooms, hotel accommodations, and cater the food requirements
3. A travel consultant to make the hotel reservations as well as handle the travel arrangements

Inspecting the Site of the Meeting

It's a good idea to make an inspection visit to several potential meeting sites before making a final choice. Negotiate rates and other considerations with the hotel convention manager. Like any other, the hotel business is competitive. They're usually anxious for your business, and discounts can be arranged.

Meeting-Room Size

The size of the meeting room depends on the number of people who will attend the meeting. Use the hotel's catering or convention service for guidance on meeting-room size. They'll know from experience how large a room is needed to accommodate the planned crowd.

Scheduling

Now, what kind of a meeting is planned? For what will be primarily an awards ceremony, keep the schedule light. The people are being brought in to pat them on the back, not make them sweat. A training or a planning session might have a heavy schedule with work planned for both day and evenings.

How to Arrange the Seating

Who does the talking determines the seating arrangement. The best seating setup for a group discussion is a round table. A "U" or open "V" shape is best for larger group discussions. With every one of these shapes each member of the discussion group can see the faces of the participants. (It's nice to see who you're shouting at if the meeting becomes heated.) For other types of meetings, different seating arrangements are more desirable. A schoolroom-type seating system might work best for a training session (Exhibit 13–1). If the audience is large and the primary aim of the meeting is to pass along information in one direction, from manager to staff (that's called a "cascade" meeting, from the top down), a row-type seating arrangement is preferable, with the speaker on a stage or dais so the audience can look up while they're listening to the inspiring message.

Exhibit 13–1

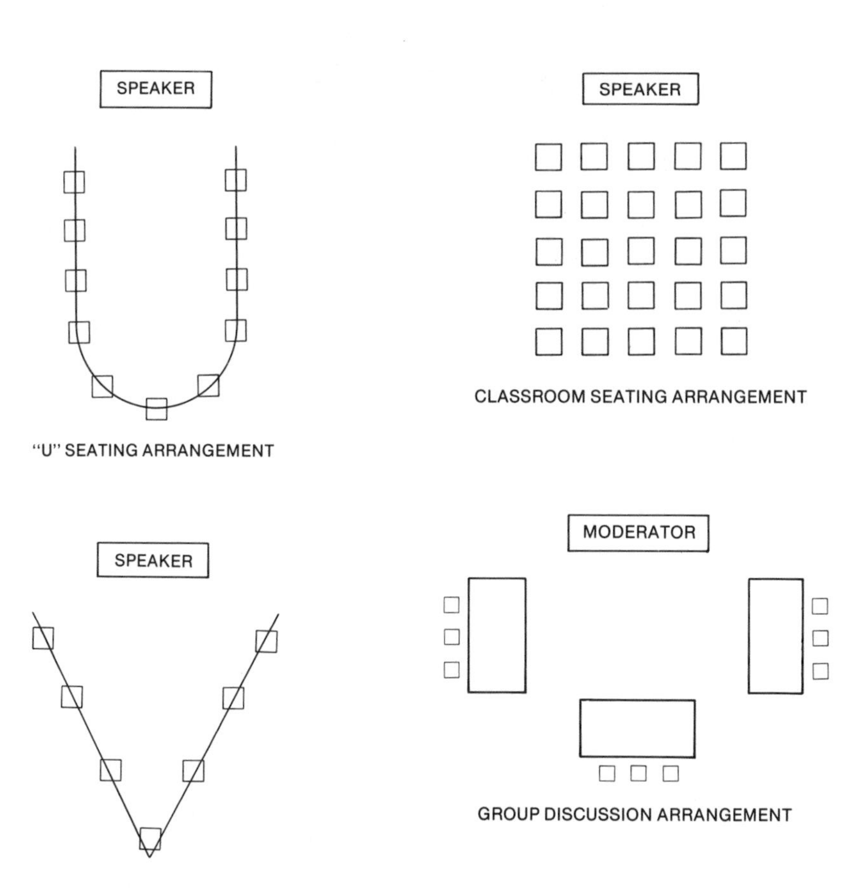

Sound Systems and Other Meeting Props

If the room is large, a sound system is an absolute requirement. Any good hotel has this kind of equipment. Incidentally, all the gadgets the hotel is expected to provide should be specified well in advance. Don't wait until check-in time to tell the hotel that a slide projector is required or that a room is needed with ten electrical outlets near every table. They may not be able to provide these items on short notice.

Four Questions to Ask Yourself When Developing a Meeting's Agenda

An agenda is a list of the topics management wishes to discuss. It can be as long as the manager likes, and any topics can be included. After all, it's the manager's meeting. However, there are several questions managers should ask themselves when selecting agenda topics. These questions are:

1. Is the topic fresh? Nothing deadens the mind of the listener faster than stale material. If the subject's been chewed to death at past meetings, let it rest in peace at this one.
2. Is the topic relevant to everyone in the room? If there are subjects to discuss that pertain only to a few individuals in the group, then do it in private meetings or break up the meeting into smaller groups.
3. Is the topic important? Don't use a big meeting to discuss trivial subjects. This doesn't deaden minds, it freezes them at absolute zero.
4. Is the planned presentation lively? If the company is embarking on a new program, it's vital to stimulate the enthusiasm of the sales crew. Don't forget basic selling skills just because the sales staff may be veterans.

A Typical Meeting Agenda

On the following page is a typical agenda for a sales meeting (Exhibit 13–2). Once the agenda has been made, print enough copies for everyone attending the meeting. If requested, the hotel will distribute these copies when the attendees register, or place them in the room where the meeting will be held. The advantage of having the hotel distribute the agenda in advance is that the attendees get to study it after they register. The disadvantage is that it's safe to bet big bucks that several people won't bring their copies to the meeting room.

Exhibit 13–2
Sample Sales Meeting Agenda

7:30–8:00 a.m.	Coffee and rolls
8:00–8:15	Welcome, Bill Brown, Regional Sales Manager
8:15–9:00	Review last quarter's performance, R. Webster, Branch Manager
9:00–10:00	This quarter's objectives, Bill Brown, Regional Sales Manager
10:00–10:15	Coffee break
10:15–11:00	Competitive activity review, Mary Lacey, Salesperson
11:00–12:00	New product introduction, Jack Dunston, Senior Salesperson
12:00–1:00	Lunch
1:00–1:30	Credit policy changes, William Blake, Credit Manager
1:30–2:00	Order processing review, Lana Kinsey, Head of Order Processing
2:00–3:00	Leasing, Sandra Lindly, Leasing Rep.
3:00–3:15	Afternoon break
3:15–6:00	Hands-on training, new "Alpha" product All participate, conducted by Al Simmons, Director of Training
6:00–7:00	Dinner
7:00–9:00	New compensation plan, Bill Brown, Regional Sales Manager

Five Reasons Why It's Important to Use Different Speakers at a Meeting

The sample agenda lists several different speakers and indicates that most of the afternoon session is broken up into group discussions with a wrap-up session after dinner.

Using different speakers is desirable for several different reasons:

1. It's easier on the manager's voice if others are taking a turn at the microphone from time to time.
2. This can be called the Clint Eastwood lesson: In his movies he doesn't say much, but when he speaks those around him had better listen if they wish to stay healthy. Managers who are on stage less, saying less, make what they say seem *distilled,* more important and precious because of scarcity.
3. The manager won't have to research or prepare a speech on every topic on the agenda. Others will help carry the load.
4. The other departments in the company get a chance to address the sales crew. Letting other departments speak also gives the sales crew a chance to question them.
5. Members of the sales crew get a chance to speak in front of a large audience. This is excellent practice for the budding managers on the team.

Breaking Up a Sales Meeting into Specialized Sessions

The afternoon of the sample agenda is broken up into discussion groups because it's tedious for salespeople to sit and listen to speakers all day long. Small panels can tackle various subjects and present the results to the larger group at the evening session. Training sessions also help to break up the day. If new equipment is to be presented, the afternoon session is a good time to give people hands-on training. They'll be relieved at the chance to be active.

Sales Meetings Evening Sessions

Managers can expect gripes about any evening sessions. Don't schedule them if this is a reward-type meeting. But if this is an important meeting with vital topics on the agenda, don't worry about the gripes. Managers can't be afraid to let their people know that this is serious stuff. One of the best ways to demonstrate just how serious it is, is to program a day crammed full of work. Use the meeting's schedule as an example of the company's determination, its dedication to excellence and success. After all, the meeting is taking away valuable time from fieldwork. If working through the evening will cut out an extra meeting day, that will be one more day that the staff will be where they should be, out in front of customers. Meetings are important, but don't expect orders to flow through the doors while you're holding them.

Scheduling the Meeting's Breaks

Schedule refreshment breaks during the morning and afternoon, a lunch break, and dinner. Make these breaks long enough to allow the attendees time enough to do some telephoning. (A bank of phones in the lobby is one thing to look for when selecting a hotel site.) This is particularly important when conducting meetings that last several days. The salespeople will have enough time to collect phone messages, make a few calls, and perhaps do a little business. However, restart the sessions on time. Don't allow stragglers to come wandering in late.

Private Meetings

Allow enough time during the evening dinner break to conduct short private meetings. These meetings can be valuable when held with members of the sales team who work in distant areas or with company representatives from other departments who aren't often seen. They are also valuable when discussing topics relevant to only one or two people on the staff. Private breakfast and luncheon meetings can also be used for evaluation purposes for new members of the sales team or someone struggling.

Food and Beverage Service

The food and beverage service must be coordinated with the catering staff of the hotel. Timing is extremely important. The refreshments must be there, ready to be consumed, when the meeting breaks. If the stuff is late, the meeting will never get started again on schedule. If possible, the best place for the refreshments is outside the actual meeting room. Food service set up inside a meeting room can be a noisy distraction. Lunch and dinner are usually catered by the hotel in separate dining rooms. This allows working material in the meeting rooms to be left undisturbed during the break periods. Request the hotel to provide coffee, tea, juice, and rolls a half hour before the beginning of the morning session. Late-risers who missed breakfast can get something in their stomachs.

It's not enough just to make these arrangements with the catering staff of the hotel; they should be verified at check-in. At this time confirm that the equipment requested for the meeting rooms is there.

Using the Hotel's Catering and Convention Services

Get acquainted with an individual on the hotel's catering staff who can be contacted if things go wrong. (It's a safe bet that something will go wrong.) If the food's not there on schedule there will be someone to call. A member of the convention staff can assist if something is wrong with the meeting room or the equipment. Also keep standby devices available in case something goes awry with the hotel's equipment. For example, an easel with a large blank pad can help salvage a presentation if the slide projector breaks down.

Some Details That Can Make for a Successful Meeting

Remember to pay attention to the small details. They can make the difference between a successful meeting and one that's a flop. For example, if the planned meeting is large or involves several different departments of the company, have name tags available to help identify everyone. Asking the attendees to stand and introduce themselves at the beginning of a meeting takes only a few minutes and puts names to faces. Blank pads of paper should be available for those attendees who wish to take notes. An official minutes-taker who sends out a summary of the details of the meeting to all attendees isn't a bad idea either. At lunch and dinner arrange the seating so people sit at different tables at each meal, meeting as many fellow employees as possible.

Smoking has become an important issue, with smokers and nonsmokers dug in to opposing trenches. There won't be any ceasefire in the near future. At least divide the room into smoking and nonsmoking areas. Better yet, allow smoking only in the hall outside the meeting room during the breaks.

How to Address a Meeting

After the details are handled, the agenda is set and the audience is assembled looking upward at the speaker with rapt, intent faces waiting for the *word*. What happens next? That's obvious. The talking starts.

Many people experience butterflies during their first presentations before a large audience. How will the audience receive their message? Franklin Delano Roosevelt had some good advice that pertains to all speakers: "Be sincere, be brief, and be seated." Let's add two more "be's." Be prepared and be yourself.

Everyone dreads laying an egg at the podium. There's good reason for the fear. In some companies career advancement depends on an executive's ability to speak well before groups. The people who report to a manager and that manager's peers are watching the performance too. Under these conditions, speeches can be agony.

13 Tips on Speaking Before an Audience

One of the best ways to avoid jitters before a speech given to a judgmental audience of coworkers and superiors is to be prepared.

1. Know what is to be said and practice it until the remarks are down cold.
2. Research the material.
3. Pepper the talk with anecdotes and examples.
4. Pause and take a breath before beginning. It's not necessary to start rattling off the message the minute the podium is reached.
5. Don't read the speech, there's nothing worse—deliver it.
6. It's almost impossible to talk too loudly, so let them have the full impact of the message.
7. Try to look at various faces in the audience. Make eye contact.
8. Don't forget to sit down when finished.
9. Conviction is a powerful ally. If you're convinced that your message is important, that sincerity will shine through.
10. Don't try to force an unnatural style that doesn't reflect your personality. The audience will recognize that you're strained. For example, almost everyone feels that humor is a good audience relaxer—but if jokes aren't part of your normal style, then don't try to tell them because you've taken temporary custody of the podium.
11. Use language the audience will understand. You're there to communicate, not to demonstrate the size of your vocabulary.
12. Be brief and to the point. Nothing deflects the attention of an audience as much as a speech that runs on and on—long on sound and wind, woefully short on substance. If you deliver such a speech when you do have something important to convey, the audience won't be listening anymore.

13. If you practice the first 12 tips and still have a bad case of nerves each time you step before a podium, get some experience. Join Toastmasters, or some other public-speaking club, and practice making speeches before managers with similar fears.

Why Meetings Don't Run on Schedule

Why can't sales meetings ever run on schedule? There are two principal reasons. The first is that the speakers do not measure the time needed for their remarks and frequently run over their allotted schedules. The second is that salespeople adore the sounds of their voices and will take as much time during discussion and question-and-answer periods as the moderator will allow. The result is that most sales meetings overdo the initial subjects on the agenda and barely touch on those items scheduled late in the program. The last subjects on the agenda get short shrift, if they are addressed at all, because everyone must run to catch a plane or get back to the office or because the hotel needs the room for another meeting.

Four Tricks for Keeping a Meeting on Schedule

How does a manager get the meeting to run on schedule, giving enough time to each subject, but not overkilling any item?

1. Let the speakers know that the time constraints are serious. Well before the meeting, in the cover letter or memo to the speaker, let him or her know how much time is allotted for that speaker's subject. Ask the speaker to time the planned remarks in advance. Tell the speaker to please indicate whether more time will be necessary. This puts the speakers on notice that there is every intention to abide by the established schedule.

2. Appoint a good, no-nonsense moderator who will keep the meeting on track. Managers shouldn't take on this job unless they've

had the experience for it. It's one that might be assigned to a very senior manager if he or she will accept it. The authority of the senior person's position will help keep the meeting on track.

3. Don't allow digressions. There's always at least one salesperson in the crowd who will be willing to take up hours of everyone's time to discuss an obscure point relevant only to him or her. Don't let it happen at this meeting. It's never nice to humiliate anyone in front of an audience, but the person can be told very plainly that discussion is closed on that one issue. Offer to discuss the matter privately. If one person goes on and on, unwilling to let any point rest until it's dead of exhaustion, take that person aside during the break and let him or her know that the meeting is being disrupted. Ask the person to be more considerate of colleagues' time.

4. Fudge a little when making up a schedule. Allow 35 minutes for a topic that can be covered in half an hour. These extra few minutes will easily be soaked up by items that run over.

THE TELECONFERENCE

Many companies are keeping their salespeople out of the office altogether, communicating with them via fax, voice mail, laptop computers, and so forth. This trend is covered in more detail in Chapter 10.

The home-based sales force creates a problem in regard to meetings. The large national-type meetings and training sessions are still held, and the active sales manager can still meet individually with members of the sales crew, but the local get-togethers during which the team met to exchange ideas and information (and lies) become inconvenient or impractical.

Their loss is regrettable, because the manager can learn things about how the field sales force feels about certain subjects. Individual salespeople may not be as vocal or direct when one-on-one with the sales manager as they would be during a joint meeting. Joint meetings also build camaraderie and team spirit, two important intangible assets fast slipping away from many sales forces.

Managers who can't meet with sales crew members as often as they wish should experiment with teleconferencing. These are situations in which every member of the sales team gets on a telephone hookup with the manager. The conferences are not a substitute for the more traditional sales meeting, but they are better than nothing.

Five Instances When Teleconferences Are Appropriate

Teleconferences are particularly useful under the following circumstances:

1. When important sales information must be relayed fast, such as a dramatic price change. A teleconference is better than a fax or voice mail because the manager can interact with the sales crew on how best to announce the new pricing to customers and clients.
2. When there's a problem to be resolved and the manager wishes to consult with every member of the sales team.
3. When misinformation about the company needs to be corrected.
4. When the manager is interested in obtaining up-to-date field intelligence. ("What has been the impact of our competitor's new model?")
5. When company policies change.

13 Tips for Making a Teleconference a Success

The following tips are useful for getting the most out of a teleconference:

1. Set a specific time and date. Send out an announcement confirming the schedule.

2. Have a specific agenda. Problem-solving agendas often get the best response. (How should we respond to this new competitor who is cutting prices?) Send copies of the agenda along with the notice.
3. Inform everyone that during the conference their complete attention will be required. They will be expected to be at their telephones in areas where they won't be interrupted.
4. Inform everyone that they will be expected to actively participate during the conference. No silent "heavy breathers."
5. Have the local phone company take care of making the connections.
6. Have a pad and pencil handy. You'll want to take notes. If possible, record the conference. You may not remember everything said. Be sure to let team members know they are being recorded.
7. Check to make sure everyone is on the line. Begin with an overview of the conference call subject matter.
8. Act as referee when several salespeople start to speak at once. Decide who goes first and who follows. Cut off those who love to hear themselves speak.
9. Make sure everyone is heard. Draw out those who have been silent. ("Diane, what do you think about Joe's suggested course of action?")
10. Verbally summarize the important observations. Make sure everyone understands what has been said.
11. Don't make decisions unless you are convinced. You may wish to digest what you have been told.
12. Commit to some action, even if it's only a review of what was said. The crew wants to feel the conference call had a positive effect. Obtain commitments in return.
13. Send out a written summary of the conference to everyone who was on the line.

Some Final Thoughts on Sales Meetings

The meeting has run smoothly, valuable information has been transferred, it's actually finishing on time, and it's almost over. What's to be done now? First, acknowledge the suggestions that were made at the meeting. Follow up on those items that are worthwhile. One of the purposes of a meeting is to bring attention to new ideas. Give the person who made the suggestion proper credit. Next, give a verbal summary of the meeting's results. Remember when an official minutes-taker was suggested earlier in the chapter? Have this person provide a written summary for all attendees. Lastly, go back to your office and dissect the meeting. What worked and what didn't? What could be improved? What should be left out of the next meeting? Managers who follow all those steps will have meetings so popular they'll have to hold them in the Roman Colosseum.

Chapter Fourteen
How to Run Trade Shows and Conventions

Brief History of Trade Shows

Trade shows are one of the oldest ways to market a product. They began at least five hundred years ago back in the Middle Ages when merchants gathered in town squares to sell their products. By the fifteenth century, shows in Germany were so large they attracted buyers from all over Europe. The old method of show and sell is still working. Today there are more than one thousand international trade shows and hundreds of shows throughout the United States.

Making a Big Splash at a Trade Show

Companies spend a great deal of money to exhibit at trade shows. For many companies it is their single largest marketing expense. It's important to receive proper value for the money spent. That value comes in the form of sales opportunities.

Why Managers Must Prepare for Trade Show Management

Almost every sales manager will be required to manage a trade show sometime during his or her career. The success or failure of that show can affect the future promotion possibilities of that manager. The trade show is an arena where managerial skills, or the lack of them, come sharply into focus over the year—and it can certainly affect the manager's chances for future promotion.

Eight Typical Costs Associated with Trade Shows

Trade shows can be confusing. There are so many details to remember, so many things to coordinate, and such a bewildering array of expenses to approve. At first glance everyone associated with a trade show seems to have his or her hand out. Here are just some of the costs you can anticipate:

1. Booth space. A good-sized booth in a prime location at a major show can cost the company more than six figures. The cost for space at regional shows is much smaller. Local shows have almost minimal costs.

2. The cost of the booth itself. Designing good-looking booths that will attract visitors has become a major industry. Some of these booths are more ornate than the Taj Mahal. (And more expensive to build.) Look for the company to spend another six figures for a jazzy, eye-catching booth. A single booth is not likely to suffice for the different kinds of trade shows around the country. Many companies have big, spectacular booths for the national shows and smaller booths for regional shows. There are also local shows with "tabletop" exhibits, meaning that no booth is allowed at all. In these shows the exhibitors display their products on tables provided by the show's promoter.

3. Booth storage, transportation, and setup. Where is the booth kept between shows? It's stored somewhere, and the company pays

a storage fee. When it's showtime the booths are shipped across country, and that isn't cheap either. When a booth arrives at the show, it must be set up by professionals. A company can use its own people to actually erect the booth, but the carpeting, the electrical wiring, the lights, the telephone, additional carpentry, the movement of material from the loading dock to the booth site, all must be handled by the convention facilities' union personnel. Their rates are not inexpensive. It's foolish for a company to try to do the work on its own.

For tabletop shows the company pays for the rental of the tables, the table coverings, the drapes in back of the booth, the sign identifying the company, and so forth

4. Equipment transportation and setup. What products will be displayed at the show? The manager must arrange for the transportation and setup of the company's product line. Company personnel can be used to set up the equipment, but any electrical wiring needed will be installed by the convention facility's union personnel. There's always a charge for every outlet.

5. The people to man the booth. The company will be bringing in salespeople, equipment demonstrators, and perhaps even technical personnel from other parts of the country to assist in manning the booth. Their salaries, travel expenses, hotel and meal expenses while in the convention city are part of the trade show cost. Another cost, more difficult to measure, is the loss of production because the sales crew will be away from their territories during the show.

6. Advertising, giveaways, and sales literature. To have a successful show, prospects and customers must be made aware that the company is participating. The location of the booth must be widely circulated. The company should do some advertising to announce these details. Direct mail usually works best for this. Make sure the salespeople will devote some time to informing customers, ensuring that the company draws a big enough crowd. Giveaways, such as pens, bags, pins, and so forth, can be used to build booth traffic. There must be plenty of sales literature, and the prospects should be encouraged to take it.

7. Special traffic builders. Some trade show participants use pretty female models, magicians, mimes, professional actors, celebrities, prizes, and gimmicks of all kinds to attract attention to their booths. These traffic builders can be costly, but they can also do a heck of a job luring people into the booth.

8. Entertainment. Many companies have hospitality suites to entertain important clients. Others throw cocktail parties in the ballrooms of first-class hotels, complete with live bands, good food, and free-flowing liquor. Some have breakfasts for their customers and prospects; others offer dinner. These parties can cost tens of thousands of dollars. Often there is a good deal of private entertaining when salespeople take important clients for drinks or dinner, or both, during the time of the trade show. Some companies have elaborate receptions or tours of the convention city or riverboat cruises.

Why Companies Exhibit at Trade Shows: The Return on Money Spent

With all these expenses, and others that are less direct, why do companies exhibit at trade shows? What can managers expect to get for the expenses they incur? There is one overriding reason: *to make sales*. The purpose of the trade shows is to generate leads, and those leads should result in sales. Keep this goal in mind when you're managing a trade show. In Europe, some companies generate half their annual sales volume through trade shows. Here, some managers expect a *ten to one return* on every dollar spent for a trade show.

Seven More Reasons Why Companies Participate in Trade Shows

There are other less tangible reasons why companies participate in shows. Here are some of them:

1. Because the competition will be at the show. The exhibits at the competitors' booths can give the company a preview of other product lines and pricing structures.
2. Because not being there would cause talk about the company in the industry. There might be suggestions that the company is experiencing difficulty.
3. To conduct market research. What better time to find out what new ideas are circulating in the industry?
4. To recruit new sales agents. All the old pros who know the industry will be there.
5. To get industry reaction to a new product. The company's customers and good prospects will be there. What better opportunity is available? A product under development can be shown, under wraps, to these very customers.
6. Because the customers expect the company to be there.
7. Because the company wants to support the industry's trade association, which has a financial stake in the show.

These reasons seem varied, but they all amount to the same thing: The company is at the show to make sales.

THE ECONOMY OF TRADE SHOWS

Despite the cost of the shows, the cost per *contact* at a show can be surprisingly small. We all recognize that the cost for making direct calls on prospects and customers has risen dramatically in the past few years. The costs vary by industry, but they can be as high as several hundred dollars per direct call by a sales rep. The computer industry estimates that it costs $452.60 to make a direct sales call. The petroleum and coal products industry estimates direct sales costs at about $100.* In a well-attended trade show, the cost per contact can be as low as $10. That's quite a difference.

**Sales and Marketing Management,* 11/86.

The Key to a Successful Trade Show

The spiraling cost for a trade show means that it's vitally important to take advantage of the opportunity the show offers to generate leads and make sales. The key to a successful show is organization. There's no such thing as too much advance planning. Even a small tabletop show can't be taken for granted. Many a big sale was conceived at a small show.

The 22 Planning Steps Necessary to Make Trade Show Participation a Success

Here are some of the planning steps necessary for a successful show regardless of the industry:

1. Start planning well in advance of the show. Don't expect everything to automatically come together in the last few weeks. Use the convention promoter's staff to help with details.

2. Give some thought regarding what will be used to encourage show attendees to stop at the booth. Most companies use a combination of preshow ads and also promote through their direct representatives. Send prospects information on the show very early on. Tell them what you'll be presenting. Use industry journals and direct mail to get your story out. Invite a few special customers to stop by the booth to pick up a gift. Phone calls a few days before the show never do any harm. Make sure that special guests receive tickets.

3. If this is a trade show in combination with an association meeting, remember that the attendees will be spending much of their time at association functions. Get an advance copy of the association program. Schedule company events so that there's no conflict. If there must be a conflict, arrange company events during association sessions that won't be popular.

4. Establish a checklist for everything needed at the show. Did someone arrange for the shipment of all the demo equipment? The booth and other displays? The sales literature? The giveaways? Has

contact been established with the convention facility's manager to coordinate the logistics? Are there enough personnel to man the booth? Have enough outlets been ordered from the show's electrical service? Have plants and flowers been arranged to dress up the booth? Are booth people going to arrive far enough in advance to put up the booth properly?

5. Remember to check over all equipment and products well in advance of the show. There's nothing so defeating to the sales process as to have service personnel still tinkering with demonstration equipment after the show opens its doors. Keep the service technicians on hand in case any equipment breaks down during the show. If it does, shut that exhibit down and do repairs after the show closes for the day.

6. Establish show objectives. What is the goal set for this exhibit? Are orders the key? For what dollar value? Are leads wanted? How many? Setting these kinds of goals helps determine a show's success and enables managers to compare one show with another.

7. Some companies offer seminars during trade shows. This technique can be effective if the product or service is technical or requires customer education. Make sure that the prospects know when these seminars will be held, and be absolutely certain that enough company people attend to support the educational effort. The seminars can backfire if prospects assume that the product shown is too complicated.

8. Choose carefully the people who will be manning the booth. Their attendance should be based on ability and skills best suited to a trade show environment, not proximity to the trade show city. The company has spent a great deal of money on the trade show itself. Trying to save a few pennies on air fares is not the best economy. (More about training for the show later.)

9. If the company employs "traffic stoppers," such as magicians, sketch artists, actors, and so forth, for the booth, make sure these temporary people know where to direct prospects who have questions about products or the company. (It's a mistake to have these temporary employees try to dispense detailed product information or pricing.)

10. Be sure that printed invitations are available for specific events. Divide crowds when necessary. Some guests might be invited to a company-run cocktail party, others to the tour of the city. The invitations also serve as a reminder of where and when the events will be held.

11. Appoint a booth manager who's in charge of the work schedules of the people who are manning the booth. This maintains booth discipline and prevents everyone from taking a break at the same time. A booth that is overcrowded with company personnel makes prospects pass by. The booth manager should also be responsible for the sales literature and the working condition of all demonstration equipment in the booth.

12. Employ a booth receptionist who can direct prospects to various salespeople. This receptionist should be in charge of the leads. Many trade shows now provide embossed identification cards for attendees and imprinters that can capture this information on lead forms.

13. If the company wishes important customers and prospects to visit with senior company management during the trade show, establish specific schedules for the meetings. Neither the customer nor the senior managers will be kept waiting.

14. If there's a telephone at the booth, don't allow the salespeople to use it for ordinary sales messages and to conduct territory business. There are plenty of public phones available in most exhibit halls.

15. If giveaways, such as pens, shopping bags, and so forth, are offered, have enough supplies on hand to last the entire show. It's embarrassing to run out.

16. Show specials, such as better pricing, more favorable terms, quantity discount, and so forth, are a good way to obtain orders during the show. The show special also encourages customers to stop by the booth at every show to get the details of this year's deal.

17. Prize drawings are hokey and counterproductive! Many companies try to use drawings to generate leads. They display something at the booth that will be given away at the show's end to

some lucky attendee who's filled out a card with name and company affiliation. Everyone passing by the booth fills out the forms, including salespeople from competing companies. There's no quality to this kind of list, only quantity. Instead of obtaining the names of prospects who are interested in the company products, they get the names of people who want something for nothing. Besides, a full list of show attendees is usually available from the trade show promoters.

18. Use printed invitations for any cocktail party or reception that is planned. The invitations should include the time and location of the affair. The show attendees are often bombarded with invitations to various functions. The printed invitation is a good way to remind customers of the company's party.

19. If the company has a not-quite-ready-for-release product that management wishes to expose to a very select group of customers and prospects for their reactions, do not keep this product at the booth where the competitors will also see it. Show it in private at the hospitality suite or in the rooms of a senior executive.

20. Booth location is very important in attracting traffic. Trade show promoters give location preference to companies who have been in the show for the longest term and who sign up earliest for next year's show. All trade shows have a period when the company can sign up for next year's show. If you know that the company will be participating, don't wait. Sign up a full year ahead of time. The company will be rewarded with a better choice of space.

21. One of the values of trade shows is the opportunity they offer to check up on all the competition. Be sure that someone from the company is assigned to visit each competitor's booth and collect literature. *Don't play James Bond!* Managers should always identify themselves and their company affiliation before asking for information. If a competitor has been cooperative, invite him or her back to the booth and be just as gracious.

22. After the show is over, have a Monday morning quarterbacking session. What worked well? What could have been done better? What improvements are needed for the next show?

Preparing Sales Reps for Trade Shows

The behavior of the sales personnel who participate in trade shows can do more than anything else to determine the show's success or failure. The best way to ensure a "good" show is to call a sales meeting shortly before the show begins. All salespeople who will be manning the booth should attend. The meeting should be conducted by the booth manager. Here are some of the subjects that should be covered.

The 11 "Musts" for Sales Personnel Working a Trade Show Booth

1. The show schedule and the schedules of the individuals who will be on duty should be provided. Provide printed copies of the hours everyone will be working. The only thing worse than an undermanned booth is one in which the company sales personnel are falling all over themselves. (Trade shows are fatiguing, standing-on-your-feet sessions. Two-hour "watches" are best.)

2. A well-groomed personal appearance. If the booth people are put into blazers or other identical uniforms, that solves the personal appearance problem. If uniforms aren't desirable, review the kind of clothing that is appropriate for this kind of show and establish some kind of dress code.

3. Information on the game plan. Exactly what is the company trying to accomplish at this show? Explain the procedure for recording leads and sales. Consider offering a bonus for the person who develops the most qualified leads. Keep daily totals to stimulate interest in the contest. A bonus or prize might also be offered to the group that provides the most leads or sales. This develops a team competitive spirit.

4. Details on the products that will be displayed. Go over every product that will be in the booth. Make sure the salespeople are familiar with the benefits and features of each. Review demonstration techniques. This procedure is particularly important with new

products. The sales literature should also be reviewed. Just what kind of packet is going to be given to booth visitors? Does it contain the kind of information that the prospects want?

5. Specifics on pricing. Is everyone familiar with the pricing that will be quoted at the show? Do they all know about show specials? Discounts? Will the company be selling the demo equipment on the floor at a reduced price so there's no need to pack it up and take it home? Make it easy for booth people to give prospects fast, correct answers by providing a "cheat sheet" with all show pricing.

6. A clue about anticipated attendance. What kind of prospect can be expected to visit the booth? Develop a profile of booth visitors. Are important customers expected who deserve special treatment? Is there a key prospect who needs a customized demonstration?

7. A review of demonstration techniques. Demos should be planned to attract people into the booth and to sell them once they're there. However, demos during trade shows must often be shorter and more concise because of the many distractions. During the preshow meeting make sure that everyone's demo is modified for the trade show environment. Hands-on training is necessary to ensure that the salespeople look as professional as possible. If everyone isn't familiar with all the equipment in the booth, appoint "specialists" for particular models.

8. A warning about rude behavior. There are a number of things *not* to do at a trade show. Review them all with sales personnel. It's impolite for booth people to ignore visitors, use the booth telephone to conduct private business, to eat in the booth, or to talk to one another when prospects are waiting.

9. The company line on what to tell the competition. Competitors will be scouting the booth looking for the same sort of information company personnel are seeking from them. Instruct the sales crew regarding what to tell the competition. Booth personnel should be courteous, willing to part with sales literature, and openly discuss published information such as suggested list pricing on equipment, and so forth.

They should not reveal such things as dealer pricing, costs, terms, delivery schedules, items on back order, anticipated new products that haven't been released, customers, prospects, and so forth.

10. The schedule of hospitality suite and company functions. The salespeople should know when the hospitality suite is open, when and where the cocktail party will be held, and who they should invite. If they're setting up meetings with senior company management, they should know the times when these managers will be available.

11. When to be available for booth knockdown. After the trade show is over there's still the chore of knocking down the booth and packing everything up. Make sure the staff understands their responsibilities in this area. Otherwise there'll be some quick get-aways out of town, and the booth manager may be stuck with the job.

Leads: The "Product" of a Trade Show

The "product" of a trade show is the leads it produces. That's why a lead card is vital. The information needed is obvious. Who came by the booth and what were their areas of interest? In the hurly-burly of a show, sometimes salespeople neglect to get enough information from a prospect unless they're prompted by a lead card that asks all the right questions. The shows using embossed identification cards and imprinters usually supply lead forms as well, but a custom-designed lead form can exactly fit the needs of your company. The right kind of form can also be used for follow-up action.

The Ten Essential Points to Cover in a Trade Show Lead Card

Here are some of the things to consider when designing a trade show lead card for your company:

1. The name of the trade show or exhibit where these leads are being used.
2. The prospect's name, his or her title, and the name of the company, including the division the person is in. (It's also desirable to record the names of others in the prospect's organization who are involved in the decision process.)
3. The date the prospect stopped by.
4. The product or products in which the person was interested.
5. The possible application(s) for these products.
6. The degree of the prospect's interest (red-hot, keen, average, mild, just curious, or a "literature collector").
7. The decision time frame. Will the prospect definitely be buying this kind of product from someone? When?
8. Necessary follow-up action. What's needed next? A demo? A personal visit? A proposal? A letter of quotation? A tour of a user's facility? A phone call? Literature? How urgent is this action?
9. The name of the person who took the lead. This is important if the performance of trade show personnel is to be evaluated. It's also vital if there are contests for the most leads or sales resulting from a show. (The manager can also go back to the salesperson if it's impossible to read the writing on the lead form.)
10. Comments. No matter how well a form is designed, there is always some bit of information that needs additional explanation.

A Sample Lead Form

On the following page is a sample of a lead form that meets these criteria (Exhibit 14–1). Of course, the best lead form is one designed to meet the specific needs of the manager's company.

Exhibit 14–1
Trade Show Lead Form

1996 Business Equipment Show
Name____________________ Title________________Date____________
Company name___________________________Division____________
Product interest____________________Application__________________
Degree of interest: Keen______ Good______ Fair______ Poor______
Decision time-frame__________________Follow-up__________________
Comments____
Salesperson____

The Importance of an Immediate Review of Lead Cards

Now that you have all these glorious leads well recorded on custom-designed lead forms, what is to be done with them? A good procedure is to review them all immediately. Some executives review the lead cards every evening after the show closes. They sort out the ones that seem the most urgent and require immediate follow-up. Because the review is immediate, they're in a position to question the salesperson who filled out the lead card while the show is still in progress.

Distributing Trade Show Leads

The next step is to distribute copies of the leads to the proper salespeople. If this is a national show, the home office usually takes care of this chore. The area manager would handle lead distribution from a local show.

A Sample Trade Show Follow-up Letter

It's important to write the prospects and thank them for stopping for the booth. Both a cover letter and pertinent literature should be included. Here's a sample of such a cover letter (Exhibit 14–2).

EXHIBIT 14–2
SAMPLE TRADE SHOW FOLLOW-UP LETTER

Dear Visitor:

Thanks for stopping by our booth at the recent Business Equipment Show. We appreciate your interest in our new line of automatic letter openers.

The Regal model you saw opens 10,000 standard or legal size envelopes per hour. The Emperor model operates at an even faster speed. Both models have the best record for "uptime" in the industry. I've enclosed literature on these models.

We can arrange an in-house demonstration of these slitters using your material. First, I'd like to make a survey of your operation so I can recommend the model best suited for your company. I'll call you next Monday to arrange a time for this survey.

This mailing should be sent as soon after the show as possible. A thank-you letter sent out several months after the trade show is over demonstrates that at the least the company is disorganized, and at the most it is not very interested in the prospect's business.

POSTSHOW STRATEGY

One section of the lead form can be used to record exactly what literature and other material is sent or delivered to the prospects. If the customer only requested literature, include a reply card that allows the prospect to ask for an in-person contact. Better yet, call the prospect and ask if more information is needed.

If the prospect is telephoned, the salesperson calling should record the discussion and when the call was made. Note that the lead form has an area where this kind of notation can be made.

When the trade show lead is followed up with a personal call, copies of the lead form should go to management. This will help the manager keep on top of the sales effort being made to these prospects. If the progress isn't fast enough, or the job not thorough enough, management should follow up personally.

The Trade Show Payoff

There's a results section on the lead form. This is the payoff box that records if a sale was made and for what amount. This section is important. It tells management if the show has paid off for the company. With this kind of report, managers can match the results of one trade show against another. If the show budget is trimmed, there's enough hard information to determine which shows to keep and which to drop.

A Summary on Trade Shows

Trade show exhibits are expensive to stage, but then can reach a great many prospects and customers in a relatively short period of time. The cost per prospect reached makes the shows effective. The key to a successful show is organization before the show, a clear-cut idea of what the company wishes to accomplish from the show, and extensive follow-up when the show is over.

Demonstrating the organizational ability to efficiently run a trade show exhibit can be a manager's ticket to the next promotion. They offer two opportunities: To help build sales right now and to help managers reach that next rung up the ladder.

Chapter Fifteen

How to Deal with Subpar Performers

Sales Performance Is Easy to Measure

One of the advantages (and curses) of being in sales is that performance is so simple to measure. Salespeople live and die by their numbers. The month's sales figures tell the sales manager just how well, or poorly, everyone is doing. Managers of administrative personnel don't have it nearly so easy. It's more difficult to determine just how many pieces of paper a clerk shuffled during the same period. So the subpar sales performer is easy to identify. The year's percentage of sales against quota seems to tell the whole story. (It doesn't really, but we'll cover that later.)

The Ten Early-Warning Signs of Poor Performance

Many managers wish there were ways to sniff out subpar performers early on, before the numbers go off the bottom of the page, before the territory lies in shambles, before customers are lost, and before the entire region's chances at quota are destroyed. This is difficult, because good, solid salespeople can suddenly become subpar performers. Are there any early-warning signs, any red flags for the manager to heed? Fortunately, there are quite a few. Here are some of the most obvious:

1. The salesperson constantly complains that quota in his or her territory is not attainable. Managers should be alert when they hear that tune sung over and over. They're getting good, reliable information. It's what they call a "self-fulfilling prophecy." If a person doesn't believe goals can be reached, they won't be reached. Incidentally, don't worry too much about the salesperson who constantly complains that quota will be difficult to achieve. There's nothing wrong in worrying about meeting objectives. In fact, it's almost a salesperson's *obligation* to scream about quota.

2. The salesperson doesn't believe any sales plan will work. No matter how much detail the manager goes into to prove how numbers can be reached, this person doesn't buy the pitch. The job seems impossible to this hombre.

3. The person doesn't fulfill assignments. The manager tells this person to make four calls a day; he or she makes three. The manager asks for a list of the territory's ten best prospects by Monday morning; eight are turned in—on Tuesday.

4. The person misses a lot of work. A plague of minor illnesses is circulating in this salesperson's territory and he or she catches every disease that's passed around. There are colds, headaches, back problems, even trips to the doctor for a dislocated earlobe. The salesperson also comes down with more injuries than an NFL quarterback. There are back conditions, neck dislocations, bruised ribs, perhaps impacted nasal hair. The real problem is that this salesperson no longer enjoys the job. Any excuse is used to be away from doing it.

5. The salesperson is full of alibis and excuses. Everything that's ever gone wrong is the fault of others. Why isn't quota being met? The competitors have better equipment and lower prices. Why was last month so bad? Market conditions stink. Why wasn't that big

prospect closed? The buyers won't buy anything because there's nothing in the budget. What about next month? Okefenokee Swamp has more industry potential than exists in this salesperson's territory.

6. The salesperson gets things wrong. The manager is told that competition got a deal at a special price. A quick check reveals that the pricing wasn't that unusual. The manager is told that a prospect wants a thousand pieces of something and will make a decision in a week. A visit shows that the prospect has made a preliminary inquiry about a hundred pieces and at this point does not know if they'll buy anything from anyone. The salesperson isn't necessarily lying. He or she may just have lost all concentration. In a way, lying would be preferable. This salesperson doesn't care enough about the job to check the facts.

7. The salesperson avoids the manager, avoids the office, and even avoids the other salespeople who are his or her peers. This person is always in a hurry to leave, especially if the manager wants to have a private, heart-to-heart talk about performance. He or she shows up late for meetings, is the first to leave when the meeting is finished, and generally can never be found when wanted. Often the manager must play "track-down" to locate this salesperson, calling customers, home, and other hangouts. This person is avoiding a confrontation. He or she doesn't want to hear anything the manager has to say because the salesperson expects it to be a notice of termination.

8. The salesperson has no zest, no enthusiasm, no energy, no ideas, no enterprise. He or she even manages to dampen the enthusiasm of others.

9. The salesperson readily agrees to any management ideas or plans even though it's obvious there is no mental acceptance of the plan. This should rightly infuriate every manager. By saying yes without really agreeing, the employee has discounted his direct superior.

10. The salesperson openly talks about other job offers. The person wants the manager to know that the business world is clamoring of his or her services.

What to Do with a Classic Nonperformer

Any manager who has a salesperson who fits into most of these categories should get rid of him or her fast. This is a classic subpar performer, and he or she should be chucked out the door.

Classic Nonperformance Is Rare; Subpar Performance Isn't

Unfortunately, circumstances are almost never clear-cut enough to define a classic nonperformer. What is most likely is that a manager is stuck with certain staff members who display only one or two of these symptoms. Some of these staff members can not only be saved but can also be changed into superstars.

How to Begin Changing Poor Performance

How can managers change a subpar performer into a superstar? They begin by *stopping*. What do they stop doing? They stop merely complaining about poor performance and they do something to fix it.

Every Manager's Four Primary Responsibilities Regarding the Performance of Staff Members

Managers have four primary responsibilities regarding the performance of staff members. These responsibilities are:

1. Set the standards by which staff members are measured. (How are they going to know what kind of job they're doing unless the manager tells them what kind of job is expected?)
2. Measure the quality and quantity of the results that staff members are attaining.
3. Convey the results to staff members so they know how well or poorly they have performed.

4. Show staff members exactly how they can improve their performances.

Why Managers Can't Complain About Poor Performance

If a manager is working with people who are making an effort, are trying as hard as they know how, but the results aren't satisfactory, that manager shouldn't complain. Perhaps the standards weren't set high enough. Perhaps the manager didn't clearly explain to the staff what was expected. Or maybe it was explained and the staff didn't buy it. In this case, *the manager didn't get a signoff on what was achievable.* The manager failed to do a good enough internal selling job. As Shakespeare would have put it if he were a sales manager, "The fault, dear Brutus, is not in our stars, but in ourselves." That means managers who are getting bad results have only themselves to blame.

The First Rule in Dealing with Subpar Performers

The first rule for managers in dealing with subpar performers is to examine their programs, their way of assigning goals and tasks. Handing out quotas at the beginning of every fiscal year is not nearly enough. Neither is harassment when quotas aren't being met. (Harassment is nothing more than background noise that prevents people from doing their jobs well.)

Setting Higher Expectations: The Gateway to Improved Performance

Managers can improve the performance of staff members by having higher expectations for them, by trusting them, by giving them responsibilities. (A salesperson who isn't allowed to handle a particularly large account in the territory won't ever feel capable of covering the big accounts.) By raising levels of expectation for staff members, they raise their own sights and set higher goals for themselves. Managers should force their people to extend themselves. The manager's belief in staff members must be genuine. They must give their people more challenging assignments, they must *know* their staff members can do more, they must help their people tap their own resources.

Raising Potential

Very few people work at their full potential. Some believe that most people work at less than 50 percent of their capacity. Think of what the area's sales record would look like if each person's output could be raised to just 75 percent of capacity. The sales figures would soar!

How to Get More Output from Salespeople

How do managers get increased output from staff members? Many managers concentrate on getting their worst performers up to minimally acceptable standards. They're not worried about getting their people up to 75 percent of capacity; they'd be thrilled and delighted if they could get only a few people on staff moving along at 50 percent.

Managers who feel this way, not the underachievers who make them want to gnaw the monthly sales computer printouts, have the attitude problem. People do the level of work expected of them. If little is expected, little is delivered.

How to Encourage Staff Members to Set Higher Standards for Themselves

Expressing confidence in staff members is the surest way to develop confidence. Believe what you say. Support their efforts through training, sales tools, better working conditions, encouragement, respect for their abilities.

Expectations for people must be high, but they must be attainable. Don't take a beginning mountain climber and ask him to tackle Mount Everest. However, he might be pointed toward some rather steep local hills. When goals are reached, this encourages the person to try to repeat the pattern. Confidence can be incubated like microbes in a laboratory culture. The more success attained, the more confidence breeds and multiplies.

Make expectations specific. Saying that a 30 percent increase in sales for the next quarter is wanted may seem specific, but it is not. The salesperson believes that he or she is doing the best job possible now. Unless the manager offers clear-cut guidelines on exactly how the 30 percent increase will be achieved, that manager is just tossing numbers in the air.

A Sample Dialogue with a Salesperson on a Performance Issue

The following is a sample dialogue a manager might have with a salesperson on the performance issue:

Manager: "Frank, your closing ratio is excellent, but your sales volume is disappointing. How do you explain that?"

Frank: "I don't know."

Manager: "Could it be the number of presentations you're making? I noticed you're averaging only four presentations a week."

Frank: "It's hard to get more presentations. Everybody's on vacation this time of year."

Manager: "I agree that it's hard, but it's not impossible. What if you set your sights on just one more presentation every week? Do you think you could reach that goal?"

Frank: "It would be tough. I'd have to start earlier and do some telephoning at night."

Manager: "That sounds like a good plan. It's just what I would have suggested. Then you think you can do it?"

Frank: "I guess so."

Manager: "Then let's set that as a goal for the next quarter. You get those five presentations a week and with your ability to close, your sales figures should improve by 25 percent. Come into my office next Monday and give me a progress report."

What the Dialogue Demonstrated

In this dialogue the manager began by praising the salesperson for something the person did well, making presentations. He tried to improve the person's performance by building on this skill. Notice that the manager hasn't just established arbitrary goals, he's obtained the salesperson's agreement that those goals are attainable. He's also eased the pressure on the salesperson by making presentations, not sales, the central issue. The manager has also set an early date to check on the progress of the mutually agreed-upon program. If the salesperson hasn't achieved the objective, the manager can take additional action.

Setting Incremental Goals: A Nine-Step Program

Setting incremental goals is a particularly good technique to follow when breaking in a new salesperson. If the company's product has a long selling cycle, it's difficult to track the progress of recent additions to the staff. In some cases, it could be a year or more before management has any idea if a new salesperson is a winner or loser. One way to help judge performance is to set intermediate goals, using a structured sales cycle to move the buyer through incremental levels of commitment. These levels of commitment or action target dates could be the following:

1. Reach the decision makers at target company.
2. Make initial presentation.
3. Make survey of prospect's current method of doing business. Uncover areas where your company could improve prospect's operation.
4. Reach agreement with prospect on objectives to be achieved.
5. Demo proposed solution to prospect.
6. Take prospect on tour of customer sites where the company solved similar problem.

7. Get agreement from customer that the company has answers to certain problems.
8. Make proposal.
9. Close sale.

This is a rather generic and simplistic timetable, but it shows the principle of incremental commitment. In a real-life situation, there could be twice as many steps in the timetable, with agreement required at many different levels and departments within the prospect company. You can rate the salesperson's performance on his or her ability to achieve these intermediate levels of buyer commitment.

Spending Time Improving Performance Where It Will Show the Best Results

When evaluating performance it's important to remember that sales team members will drive themselves differently. Some will be high achievers, most will be average performers, and a few will never get off the floor.

If blessed with high achievers, give them plenty of latitude and leave them alone, except for numerous strokes that show that the job they're doing is appreciated.

Some low achievers will never be motivated to try harder; time spent trying is wasted. The best management skill in the world won't salvage the person who won't work. These people should be replaced once they're recognized.

Sales results can be improved most by spending time and giving attention to the middle group, the average performers. Concentrate management efforts here. This area will provide the best return on your investment. Do the things all good managers do. Train people well. Coach them. Show them by example. Advise them. Cheer them on. Help them plan. Set standards for them that are high, but achievable. Review their results. Praise their accomplishments.

A Five-Step Program That Will Improve Staff Performance by 25 Percent

What's the best way to get people to perform above that average 50 percent level to the 75 percent figure that would make the area's numbers look so good? There's a five-step program that's simple, but it works:

1. Give staff members strong incentives. (There's nothing wrong with money, but there could be many other things too, such as recognition, plenty of praise, chance for promotion, and so forth.)
2. Set high standards and give them interesting challenges.
3. Believe in them.
4. Give everyone the same treatment.
5. Be a good, effective manager. (There's nothing so depressing and energy-sapping as working for a manager who doesn't know how to do the job.)

Burnout

Dealing with a salesperson who had been a good, or even superior, performer, but whose numbers have fallen off dramatically is a problem that many managers find difficult to solve. Some managers call this problem "burnout." Like most labels, it is inadequate.

Why Performances Fall Off

A falloff of performance could be caused by many different circumstances. These factors could be one or more of the following:

1. Personal problems
2. Lack of motivation
3. Fatigue (lack of excitement is one of the major causes of fatigue)
4. A grudge held against someone in the company

5. Disgruntlement over being passed over for promotion
6. A new philosophical outlook
7. A host of other reasons

Confronting Subpar Performers

Many managers are reluctant to confront the old pro who has gone stale. They remember that this salesperson made healthy contributions in the past, and they hope against hope that somehow things will get turned around to the way they used to be. These managers are ignoring their responsibilities, not only to their regions and their companies, but to the salesperson who is having the difficulty. For what usually happens is that the managers give these salespeople plenty of rope until the district's or region's numbers are affected, then they let the person go.

Eliminating Probable Causes for Subpar Performance

The manager who must solve a problem of a veteran gone sour can eliminate some probable causes. For example, the manager needn't be concerned about the salesperson's ability. The veteran's ability to sell has been demonstrated in the past. Product or industry knowledge can also usually be eliminated. (Although in some cases an old pro's product knowledge can become obsolete.) The causes usually lie elsewhere.

Treading on Dangerous Ground: Intruding into the Private Life of an Employee to Determine Causes for Subpar Performance

Managers have no right to intrude into the private lives of the people who report to them, but they do have a right and obligation to inquire about whether something in the person's life has changed so radically that performance is affected. For example, a divorce can so absorb a person's thoughts and energy that no quality time is left for the job.

If a salesperson admits to a personal problem that affects job performance, it's awfully tempting for the manager to play parent or try to provide a homemade brand of amateur psychology. Avoid this temptation. Most managers are not qualified to give this kind of guidance and advice. Be a friend, as well as a good manager, and suggest that the affected salesperson get professional help. (It can only be a suggestion. The manager really can't make demands.) If the company's medical insurance covers this kind of help, assist the person with the claims. Do everything possible to try to salvage a once-productive salesperson who is going through a trying time.

Some Less Obvious Reasons for Burnout

Often the reasons why a veteran salesperson suddenly stops performing are less evident. There is no "smoking gun," except the monthly sales figures, and they are lousy. Veterans go sour for many reasons. Perhaps the person is just tired of doing what he or she has been doing for so many years. The exhaustion is more mental than physical. They're tired of talking about the same product to the same prospects. They're tired of the last-minute rush to make quota. They're tired of solving all the problems that exist in any territory.

Some Quick-Fix Solutions for Burnout

One way to help resolve this problem is to offer the salesperson a new, challenging assignment. Perhaps it is a new territory. Changing territories has revived many "exhausted" salespeople. Perhaps it is asking the salesperson to take on the responsibility of introducing a new product into the district. This can create new excitement into the career of an experienced salesperson who has become jaded. Perhaps the person can be temporarily assigned to train beginning salespeople. In the process of helping others master the basics, the burned-out salesperson relearns those methods that created the success that he or she enjoyed over the years.

Going Back to Basics: A Six-Step Solution to Burnout

If these kinds of changes aren't possible, then the best tactic is to treat the non-performing old pro like a beginner or trainee. Give the person the same sort of close supervision that would be given to any new salesperson starting without previous experience. Many managers are reluctant to do this, or perhaps too embarrassed to do it, even though a career may be salvaged in the process. What exactly should be done? Get out the manual for breaking in trainees. Use the standard drill.

1. Monitor activities closely. Know where the salesperson is every hour of the day.
2. Set up quotas for the number of calls, demos, proposals, and so forth.
3. Interrogate the person about the sales report. What happened on this particular call? What's the next step? What help is needed?
4. Go with the person on important sales calls. Occasionally take the lead role. Critique calls.
5. Set up weekly and monthly performance goals.
6. Review the person's demos and proposals to make sure they are up to the company's standard.

Why treat a veteran like a raw recruit? Because going back to basics is always a good idea. It is the best idea when dealing with a veteran who is giving a subpar performance. Just the act of putting in hours in the territory, standing in front of the right number of prospects, making the prescribed number of presentations, will have a positive effect on business.

In the major leagues, when a batter's average begins to drop, the coaches study the batting stance, the swing, the balance. In short, the coaches make the player go back to the basics.

The Cure for Sales Lethargy

Never discount lethargy as the cause of a sales problem. The best cure for sales lethargy is activity, a show of confidence on the part of the manager, and a flow of orders. Nothing achieves this better than going back to basics. Success may rekindle the competitive spirit that the veteran had demonstrated in the past.

What Actions Not to Take When Faced with Subpar Performance

Is there anything that shouldn't be done when faced with subpar performance? Yes. Avoid issuing threats and ultimatums. "Get your numbers up next month, or lose your job," may be dramatic, but it isn't an effective motivator.

Almost all salespeople are keenly aware of the importance of achieving quota performance. They all know they're in a numbers game. The first thing that most salespeople do when threatened with job loss is to go home and dust off the old resumé. Let's face it, sales ability is a transferable skill. If the job with your company doesn't seem secure, it's easy for the veteran salesperson to find another somewhere else.

What to Do When Disappointed in Results

How should the manager behave when disappointed in someone's sales figures? The disappointment should be communicated. Then follow up by suggesting solutions to the problem. For example:

"I'm disappointed in your results over the last quarter, Mary, because I know you can do much better than that. Let's talk about ways to get your numbers up to where they belong."

This manager doesn't like the sales figures, but hasn't threatened the sales rep. He demonstrates that he wants to work with the rep to achieve desired objectives. The rep working for this manager is likely to go all-out to see that the objectives are met. She isn't always looking up to see if she can spot the sword that's hanging over her head.

When Termination Is Necessary

There are times when nothing the manager tries works. The beginner who seemed so promising is just not cut out for sales, or the veteran cannot conquer certain personal problems that prevent good performance. The manager must do something to rectify the situation, because the poor performance in this one territory is dragging down the results in the entire region or district. A change must be made.

The Legal Side of Termination

A few years ago companies could just fire someone and hire somebody else to take their place. Those were the innocent years when people still believed in the tooth fairy, elves, and the ghost of Christmas past. Today, we live in a litigious society with more lawyers than microbes per square inch of inhabitable space. Anyone fired without specified cause is likely to sue the company for unjust dismissal. If the person belongs to a minority, discrimination can be claimed. (Women, despite their numerical superiority, are considered a minority.)

Putting an Employee on Probation

All of this means that subpar performance by anyone on the staff must be documented. It also lengthens the dismissal process. Earlier in the chapter we said that giving poor performers a warning was a bad idea. It is if there is hope for those persons and the company wishes to keep them. If management has given up on improvement and wishes to make a change, a warning should be given, preferably in writing (Exhibit 15–1).

In this warning, state what the performance has been over the period in question and exactly what performance is expected over the next several months.

In effect, the person has just been put on probation. One of the results this warning may achieve is to cause the person to quit or at least have the foresight to start looking for another job. (If someone leaves voluntarily, that usually takes care of the legal problems.) If the person hangs on by the fingernails, refusing to let go, and performance is not improved, the company is on firmer legal ground if legal action is taken. The reasons have been documented for why the person was dismissed.

How to Handle an Employee Termination

If the probationary period passes with no improvement, hold a dismissal meeting. This can be a tough chore, and repetition doesn't make it any easier. Avoid any kind of recriminations. Just state the facts that the person did not perform up to expected standards. Give the person *immediate walking papers*. Don't keep lame ducks around the office. Of course, provide the kind of severance pay that is consistent with the company's policy. Ask that materials such as demo equipment be returned. Give receipts for these things. Don't try to offer advice or counsel. "I don't think you're cut out for sales," comes across as pompous and presumptuous.

A Sample Termination Letter

Give the person a dismissal letter. On page 298 is a sample of such a letter (Exhibit 15–2).

These few paragraphs are not a substitute for seeing a lawyer or consulting the personnel department when faced with this situation. Get legal advice on dismissal procedures that are appropriate in your state.

Exhibit 15–1
Progressive Counseling or Progressive Discipline

FROM: Name: ______________________ Date: ______________________

Position: ______________________ Department: ______________________

RE: Employee: ______________________

Position: ______________________

1. I have made the following observation of this employee's conduct/performance.
2. I have informed this employee of the following standards that will be expected from him/her in the future, by (date) ______________.
3. These standards are important because of the following impact on the work environment:
4. I have informed this employee of the following consequences if he/she fails to follow the above standards:
5. These matters will be reviewed within ______________ days.

____
SUPERVISOR Date

I have read and received a copy of the above statement.

I do/do not wish to submit written comments of my own about this matter.

____
EMPLOYEE Date

____
DEPARTMENT HEAD Date

Routing: ❑ Supervisor ❑ Department Head ❑ Personnel File

EXHIBIT 15–2
TERMINATION NOTICE

EMPLOYEE NAME ______________________________

Last First Middle

CURRENT ADDRESS ______________________________

Street

____

City State Zip Code

SOCIAL SECURITY NUMBER ______________________________

LAST DATE EMPLOYEE WORKED ______________________________

EXPLANATION IN SUPERVISOR'S WORDS OF THE REASON FOR EMPLOYEE LEAVING THE POSITION

____

____

WAS EMPLOYEE PAID ANY ADDITIONAL COMPENSATION? ______________________________

IF SO, AMOUNT OF COMPENSATION ______________________________

TYPE OF COMPENSATION ______________________________

TYPE OF TERMINATION:

VOLUNTARY	*INVOLUNTARY*
____ NEW JOB	____ LAYOFF
____ MEDICAL	____ RETIREMENT
____ OTHER ______________	____ UNABLE TO PERFORM
	____ OTHER ______________

Exhibit 15–2 (continued)

CHECKLIST:				
	_____	TRAVEL ADVANCE	_____	LOANS
	_____	SAMPLES OUT	_____	AIR TRAVEL CARD
	_____	TELEPHONE CREDIT CARD	_____	OTHER CREDIT CARDS
	_____	COMPANY CAR	_____	PRODUCT PURCHASED
	_____	VACATION PAY DUE (AMOUNT_____)	_____	FINAL CHECK PREPARED (AMOUNT_____)

I understand that my employment with ______________ is terminable "at will," and in consideration for any severance pay or continued health insurance benefits to which I am not necessarily entitled to receive, I agree to relinquish all civil actions arising out of my termination of employment.

EMPLOYEE SIGNATURE ____

SUPERVISOR'S SIGNATURE____

ADMINISTRATIVE MANAGER'S SIGNATURE________________________________

EMPLOYEE UNAVAILABLE TO SIGN, COPY MAILED ON______________________

Date

Chapter Summary

In summary, managers are responsible for the performance of the staff members who report to them. They can have a positive effect on this performance by believing in their people and holding high expectations for them.

Managers should stimulate and excite staff members by setting challenging goals.

Managers should spend the bulk of their time with the people on staff who will benefit the most from close attention. These will inevitably be the average achievers, who may be working at only 50 percent of their potential.

Don't write off an old veteran salesperson who may be going through a tough time until the situation has been examined.

There is no such thing as burnout. There is only fatigue and boredom, and these two maladies can be corrected.

Work hard to get a one-time superperformer back on track. This can pay better dividends than training someone entirely new.

Use encouragement and praise rather than intimidation and threats to motivate people to perform better. This tactic works much better.

Most of all, managers should perform their management tasks well if they want to surround themselves with a cast of good performers.

Performance quality is like pure mountain water. It trickles from the top, picking up speed as it moves downhill.

Chapter Sixteen

How to Sell Through Dealers, Distributors, and Manufacturers

Three Different Distributing Systems

Manufacturers use many different methods for bringing their products to market. They're always looking for the most cost-effective way to distribute their goods. Today, dealers, distributors, and manufacturers' reps are getting more attention than ever before because selling directly to end-user customers has become so expensive.

Why Indirect Marketing Channels Are Important

Exact marketing costs are difficult to forecast. One of the advantages of using indirect networks such as dealers, distributors, and manufacturers' reps is that marketing costs can be fixed because the manufacturer pays these agents a set percentage for moving product.

The Advantages of Direct Marketing

For years most manufacturing companies relied on salaried and commissioned sales forces who approached customers and prospects directly, selling the company's products. Obviously, this method provides the most control over the market. If salespeople are on the payroll or full-time commissioned representatives, they can be told exactly what to do and when to do it. One hundred percent of the sales force's time is spent representing the company.

The Disadvantages of Direct Marketing

Direct marketing is the most expensive system of distribution. Payrolls are larger, the expenses of making direct calls are increasing every year, and employee fringe benefits packages add, on the average, another 30 percent to total wage expenses.

Marketing Trends

The costs of selling are becoming so large that many companies are dismantling their direct sales forces and beginning to use intermediaries, that is, dealers, distributors, or manufacturers' reps, to bring their products and services to market.

The Advantages of Using Indirect-Marketing Channels

The advantages of using any one, or a combination, of these networks is that costs are easier to control. The manufacturer knows exactly what the selling cost of the product is. A direct sales force is still maintained, but it is much smaller because the salespeople are now calling only on those companies who are actually calling on the end-users.

Dealers often take on service, installation, training, and maintenance requirements for a manufacturer, saving the vendor these expenses as well. (Most often distributors and manufacturers' reps do not take on any service responsibility.)

The Disadvantages of Indirect-Marketing Channels

There are disadvantages to using an indirect distribution system. The most prominent disadvantage is the loss of control over the marketplace. The manufacturer cannot direct any one of these independent business entities to spend a specific amount of time with the manufacturer's product. Quotas can be imposed and the loss of the line threatened if sales aren't up to snuff, but it's not the same as having a direct sales force out there. Another problem is the loss of contact with the end-user customer. Because others are doing the selling, the manufacturer doesn't know exactly who's using the product and sometimes loses sight of how it's being used. Still, the lure of controlling sales costs has caused many manufacturers to use one or more of these indirect selling channels. In the cases of dealers and distributors, they actually become the customer for the manufacturer.

How Dealers Function

Exactly what are dealers and how do they function? Dealers are independent businesspeople who usually operate within a local geographic area and specialize in a specific industry. They can be large businesses, operating in several states with sales volumes in the tens of millions, or they can be mom-and-pop storefronts serving only a few city blocks. The dealer is expected to maintain an inventory of the manufacturer's product. The dealer buys a product from a manufacturer at wholesale, attaches a profit margin to the cost, and sells it to the end-user. Service, maintenance, and any training the product requires often are the dealer's responsibility.

How Dealers Sell

The dealer will maintain an outside sales force to sell the product or use advertising to bring customers to showrooms. Some dealers do both. The method favored depends on the product and the tradition of how it's sold. Automobiles are sold through dealers who most often sell through showrooms. Office equipment dealers most often sell through outside sales forces.

Product Exclusivity and Dealers

Some dealers will carry one manufacturer's products exclusively, while others will carry competing lines. In turn, the manufacturers sometimes offer dealers an exclusive for a geographic area, while others will sign up as many dealers as they can. Obviously the dealers prefer products they can have on an exclusive basis, while manufacturers prefer dealers who handle only their line. Mutual interests are often served by assigning dealers sales quotas and offering product on an exclusive basis within a specific area, just as long as those sales objectives are met.

The Objectives When Selling Products Through a Dealer Organization

The manager who calls on dealers for a manufacturer has two basic selling chores. The first job is to load up the dealer with as much inventory as his credit limit will stand so this dealer won't have the money, space, or time to consider competing lines. The second job is to make sure the dealer is reaching as many prospects for the product as possible through advertising or through the activities of the dealer's outside salespeople. The idea is to keep the inventory moving into the dealer's showroom and back out the door to the end-user customer. It's the revolving-door theory: The faster that door is spinning, the better the job the manager is doing.

One Big Problem with Selling Through Dealers

One problem with selling to dealers is that many are small businesspeople with limited credit lines. Getting a nice order from a dealer is one thing, convincing the credit department to ship it is another.

Required Sales Support for a Dealer Network

In many industries, dealers who own the business started as service technicians or are entrepreneurs with little business experience. They are familiar with the maintenance requirements for a product, but are not experienced in sales techniques. Often, they need heavy support and advice from the manufacturer's manager on how to get the product to market. The manager becomes a sales consultant to the dealer, helping with the advertising, training the dealer's salespeople, working on promotions, setting up the showroom, and so forth. These tasks are important if the manager wants the inventory that has been moved into the dealer's operation back out the door so more goods can be sold.

Ten Characteristics That Make for a Good Dealer

The most essential element in moving merchandise through dealers is establishing a good dealer network initially. What's a "good" dealer? Here are some of the basic things to look for:

1. A good dealer is a dealer who's established in the local community, who knows the industries to which the company's products are sold, and who has an established customer base.
2. A good dealer is a dealer with adequate credit lines. If the credit department won't take the paper, a sale hasn't been made.

3. A good dealer is a dealer who can service the product after it's been sold. The company's reputation is on the line if the product isn't maintained properly.
4. A good dealer is a dealer with a good outside sales force or nice showroom that will attract prospects. It's even better if the dealer has both.
5. A good dealer is a dealer who understands how to sell the product and is willing to dedicate time and people to it.
6. A good dealer is a dealer who is a good business person, who prices the product to produce a profit, who takes advantage of special promotions, who uses the advertising allowance the company gives, who will not antagonize other company dealers with rapacious business practices, and who will be there for years to come.
7. A good dealer is a dealer who isn't carrying all the competitors' products. In some industries, dealers always carry two or three competing lines, but too many lines means a division of attention, less floor or inventory space for your product, less open credit availability for your product, and a lack of commitment to make your product a success.
8. A good dealer is a dealer who has the respect of other dealers in the same industry.
9. A good dealer is a dealer with a positive attitude toward the company and its products, who considers the dealership part of the company's "family," who offers suggestions on product improvement, who won't desert the company over an incident or misunderstanding.
10. A good dealer is a dealer who is intent on satisfying the customers he or she sells. That dealer can be counted on to produce repeat business.

Where to Find Good Dealers

Where are good dealers found? Locating the best dealers isn't difficult, because most already possess reputations in the industry and, by definition, are known in the areas where they do business. In addition, most dealers within industries maintain national associations that willingly provide their membership listings. For example, most dealers who sell office equipment are members of the National Office Machine Dealers Association (NOMDA). Those who sell office supplies are members of the National Office Products Association (NOPA).

One way to meet prospective dealers is to take a booth at the association's national conventions. Many vendors take booth space at these shows. They're good places to see what the competition has to offer and show off the company's products as well. In addition to the national shows, many associations have local or regional shows—less expense to enter, but more limited in scope.

How to Recruit Good Dealers

Recruiting good new dealers is difficult. It's relatively easy to sign up marginal operations, but those dealers with a consistent record of success are like goldmines with well-known locations—everyone wants to stake a claim. If the dealers are well established and satisfied with their current product lines, why should they want to take on another company that's an unknown entity? They're good businesspeople, so they understand that a new line requires an extra effort to get started. This effort could be used for current products that they know are successful. Besides, the manufacturer–dealer relationship is almost like a marriage. It doesn't matter what promises you make when you come courting. The dealer still wonders just what kind of lifetime partner you are going to be.

The Irresistible Enticement for a Dealer

The best, and sometimes irresistible, enticement for a dealer is the offer of a product line with a strong competitive advantage. When the Japanese car companies decided to bring out luxury automobiles, they had no problem signing up dealers, despite making strong demands. The car dealer that wanted to take on the Honda-manufactured Legend, the Nissan-made Infiniti, or the Toyota-produced Lexus had to set up a separate agency with a distinctive showroom, signs, and a dedicated sales force. Why did the automobile dealers, who already carried many different lines, accede to these costly demands? They recognized that the Japanese luxury cars would be much less expensive than the comparable European models and represented an opportunity to make exceptional profits.

Good Profit Margins Never Scare Dealers Away

The second advantage needed to attract strong dealers is a good profit margin on the products the dealer is asked to sell. Dealers recognize that they have a cost of sales. There must be enough margin in the product to allow them to hire a sales force, maintain a showroom, service the equipment, and so forth. Margins vary according to industry. Managers anxious to recruit dealers must be certain that their margins are competitive with industry standards.

The dealers with outside sales forces demand higher margins than dealers using advertising to bring prospects into showrooms because their cost of sale is higher.

Dealer Attitudes Toward Price Cutting

Dealers don't like price cutting because it slices into profit margins. That's why a dealer is not likely to take on a product if it's sold through wholesalers or other types of mass-merchandise distributors. Because of low overhead and bulk buying, these outfits sell products at costs far below most dealers' breakeven point. Excessive price cutting by other dealers is also not welcome. A few dealers, or even one, who are lowballing on every sale can ruin a market. Other dealers, the stable ones who are there year after year, will just walk away and devote their time to products that are profitable.

Establishing Sales Prices

Manufacturers are not allowed to set the actual selling price the dealers charge for the product. That's price fixing, which is frowned upon by Uncle Sam. The manufacturer can make recommendations (suggested selling price) and can educate the dealers regarding the kind of profit they'll need to stay in business. The wisest thing the manufacturer can do is be very selective about the kind of dealer who is recruited in the first place.

Product and Profitability: The Real Keys to a Good Dealer Network

Superior products and excellent profit margins will atone for many other sins. If the public is clamoring for the product, it's easy to find dealers who are aching to sell it no matter how they are treated.

A Ten-Point Program Designed to Attract Dealers and Establish a Good Dealer Network

If the company's product is average, with a host of competitors, other strategies must be used to attract good dealers. What are these strategies?

1. Service. The dealers want fast delivery on products because they'll lose sales if they don't get it. They want a courteous order department, knowledgeable salespeople who call on them, and reasonable follow-up when an order goes astray.

2. Support. They want attractive literature, good training aids, advertising layouts, help in launching new products, suggestions on how to set up product displays in the showroom, sales promotion ideas, assistance with the actual sale to end-users, and lots of hand-holding.

3. An understanding credit department. Most dealers are small businesspeople living on a tightrope that is tied only at one end. If their credit limit has been reached, they'll understand if the company won't ship them more goods. But don't allow credit people to hold up orders for spare parts to exert pressure on the dealer to pay up outstanding balances. The company may get paid on that one invoice, but that dealer may be lost as a customer.

4. A genuine interest in the dealer's business. The company should want the dealers to make a reasonable profit—heck, hope they get rich. Don't load the dealer up with excessive inventories, sell him obsolete goods without telling him they're closeouts, or suggest business practices that would cause the dealer to lose money.

5. A reliable product. Dealers love products that don't require excessive maintenance. Servicing a product two or three times within a warranty period can take all the profit out of a sale.

6. An orderly dealer organization. One of the best ways to attract new dealers is to be selective about the kind of dealers already on the books. When a dealer signs up with the company, he doesn't want to see another dealer selling the same products on every corner. Neither does he want to be associated with an organization whose dealers have a reputation for price cutting or general craziness.

7. Exclusiveness. One of the easiest ways to attract a dealer is by offering that dealer sole selling right for a specific geographic area. Be careful when dangling this particular carrot. Make sure the dealer selected to represent the company will deliver the business that area deserves.

8. Honesty. Don't lie to dealers. Don't hold up their credits, don't load them up with merchandise and then drop the wholesale price, don't mislead them.

9. Loyalty. Don't abandon a good dealer just because there is an opportunity to sign up a bigger dealer across the street. Dealers within an industry talk to one another. They know which manufacturers have a reputation for standing behind their dealers.

10. Fairness. Treat all the dealers the same, regardless of size.

Manufacturers who offer all these things, no matter what the product, will find that dealers will be breaking down their door, anxious to sign on the dotted line.

A Sample Dealer Agreement

Dealer and manufacturer sign an agreement outlining the responsibilities and obligations of both parties. This kind of agreement is a good idea because it tells both parties what to expect of one another. A sample dealer agreement is shown in Exhibit 16–1.

In many cases the dealer's industry association will have a standardized agreement form they recommend to their member dealers. If they do, the company can save the legal expense of hiring lawyers to draft a custom agreement. The topnotch dealers in that industry normally will not sign a contract that has not been approved by their trade association.

Exhibit 16–1
Able Corporation Dealer Agreement

THIS AGREEMENT made the ______ day of ______, 19___, between ABLE CORPORATION and _________, an individual, _________, a partnership, and _____________, a _______________________ corporation.
State of Incorporation

____

Address City/State Zip Code

____

Telephone (including area code)

("Dealer")

1. Able appoints Dealer as a nonexclusive authorized dealer for the sale, leasing, rental, and servicing of the Able machines set forth on the schedule(s) attached hereto and accessories, parts, and supplies therefore (the "Products") to end-users in the area set forth in the schedule(s) attached hereto and identified by geographic boundaries (the "Territory") commencing on the date this Agreement is executed by Able. Since this grant is nonexclusive, Able may set up other dealers. The dealership created by this Agreement shall continue in effect until terminated by Able or Dealer in accordance with the terms of this Agreement. Able shall have the right to eliminate any of the Products from its product line at any time upon thirty (30) days prior written notice. Able and Dealer agree to act in a fair and equitable manner to each other and to end-users of the Products.

(Plus another three or four pages of gobbledygook.)

How Distributors Function

Distributors are still another marketing vehicle, and these vehicles range from jet planes to kiddy cars. Who are distributors and how do they differ from dealers? For one thing, distributors are usually larger business organizations than are dealers. Often distributors buy from the manufacturer in bulk and sell to dealers in small quantities. In these instances, a distributor is a reseller selling to another reseller. Distributors don't require the profit margins that dealers do because they don't normally invest much time to make the sale. What the distributor does require is volume.

The Changing Role of Distributors

In the past few years, the word "distributor" has become more encompassing to include any network for dispensing goods, services, and/or information. A large television network, for example, *distributes* entertainment programming to its network affiliates.

In many industries, distributors have, in effect, become giant retailers. Their operations have changed the face of consumer merchandising and impacted the traditional relationship between manufacturers and resellers. This subject is covered in more detail in the next chapter.

Why Manufacturers Need Distributors

Why do manufacturers need distributors when they can sell directly to dealers? The distributors perform many valuable services. One major contribution they make is to handle the small orders that may be a bother or unprofitable for the manufacturer to process. Another service they often render is to provide credit to small businesses that the manufacturer may not consider creditworthy. Usually they are able to process orders faster than the manufacturer because quick service is the main thrust of their business.

How Distributors Sell

Distributors normally don't do any selling to develop need. They work to exploit needs that have already been developed. Outside salespeople are sometimes employed, but many distributors do without them. They use catalogs, telephone salespeople, sharp pricing, quick deliveries, and service to reach customers who already have indicated an interest in the manufacturer's product.

How to Attract a Good Distributor: Four Requirements

The first requirement in attracting a good distributor is to have a recognized product that people want to buy. Without the known product, forget about enlisting a first-rate distributor. Remember, they are not business missionaries. They don't sow new seed, but harvest crops that have already been planted.

Taking on a new product means a considerable investment for a distributor because they buy in such large quantities. They don't like to gamble with unknowns.

The second requirement is a quantity discount schedule that will allow the distributor the chance to make a few percentage points by buying in bulk and selling in small quantities. They must buy for the lowest price you offer if they are to be competitive.

The third requirement is to limit the number of distributors for the product. While there may be dozens of dealers in one major metropolitan area, a single distributor per region may be enough. Remember, the distributor must maintain volume to be successful.

The fourth requirement is a good discount for cash or fast payment. Financially healthy distributors try to take advantage of their cash or prompt-payment discounts and will often use these discounts as their profit margin on big deals.

Are Distributors Really Useful?

A company that offers these four things can attract distributors. The question is, are they really needed to move product? They are the traditional "middlemen" that everyone seems to be trying to eliminate these days. Are they still useful?

Well, middlemen can brace up the center, helping the company get from start to finish. Distributors can be useful in reaching market segments that might not be profitable for the company to tackle directly. They buy in quantity and try to use the muscle that big customers always have. They're forever demanding better pricing, better discounts, sweeter promotions, and so forth. Used correctly they can be valuable sales tools.

How Manufacturers' Representatives Function

A manufacturer's rep is someone who is contracted with to sell the company's products on a straight-commission basis. That sounds exactly like the definition for a commissioned salesperson, so what's the difference? The difference is that the manufacturer's rep is a fully independent person, or firm, and may represent many different companies. A large repping outfit may carry 15 or 20 lines.

The Profile for a Manufacturer's Rep

There is no profile for the average repping company because there is no such thing as an average rep. Some are one-man bands operated by a single person using a spare bedroom in the house as an office. Others have luxurious suites in prestigious buildings, employ large sales staffs, and represent several dozen lines. Some are engineering-oriented and offer technical support to their customers. Others couldn't identify the business end of a screwdriver. Some are better than gold when it comes to bringing in orders. Others can't get the lead out of their posteriors.

How Manufacturers' Reps Are Compensated

There are some similarities in the way repping outfits work. As a rule, manufacturers' reps are responsible for all their sales expenses. They're paid strictly on the basis of results. Often they're paid only after the customer pays the invoice, so the company using a repping outfit is never out-of-pocket. Repping outfits normally don't purchase products for inventory. They obtain orders on the company's behalf and turn them in for shipping and invoicing. If demo equipment is needed, they're usually expected to pay for it. If the relationship is severed, sometimes they're allowed to return demo equipment for a refund. They seldom service equipment.

The Advantages of Using a Repping Outfit

Because the manufacturer has few up-front costs, repping outfits are one of the least expensive ways to build a sales network. They're also a quick way into a market because a good repping outfit is likely to be established in a specific geographic area. They have contacts with local customers that can be exploited to produce fast results.

The Disadvantages of Using a Repping Outfit

Why doesn't everyone use repping companies? They certainly seem like the ideal solution to controlling sales costs.

Unfortunately, using manufacturers' reps is one of the most frustrating ways to increase sales. Some managers believe that if a rep network is organized and one out of five reps is doing a reasonably good job for the company, you've beaten the odds. Does that mean that manufacturers' reps are ineffective salespeople? Not at all. Some are excellent and will do a better job for the company than would be possible with a team of skilled direct representatives. *Some* will. Others will not. The result is that sales coverage will be spotty—terrific in some areas, almost nonexistent in others.

One of the big problems in using manufacturers' reps is that their time and attention is fragmented by the number of vendors and products they represent. The sales literature in the average rep's briefcase outweighs a diesel locomotive. Their standard sales pitch tends to be, "What do you need today?" not, "I've got something you want to buy." They seldom have the time or inclination for creative selling. They may not even have enough time to thoroughly learn the products they represent.

Reps are sometimes difficult to control because they are independent businesspeople. They can't be directed to spend a certain amount of time on the company line, or to target a specific prospect. Some reps are cynical, feeling if they do too good a job in the area the company may make it a direct operation. (They have a lot of historical evidence to support this fear. Many companies have assigned reps a territory when there was missionary work to be done, then made that territory a direct sales branch after it was established.)

Mixing Reps with Direct Salespeople

Still, manufacturers' reps are an inexpensive way to enter a market. Those with industry contacts can generate sales faster than you could be hiring direct people. Some companies use direct salespeople in larger metropolitan areas and reps in smaller towns and cities.

Five Ways to Find Good Manufacturers' Reps

Repping outfits capable of doing the job for a specific product can be found in the following ways:

1. Advertise in the local newspapers under sales-help wanted.
2. Make inquiries with the purchasing agents of large local companies.
3. Ask friendly sales managers working for companies with allied products.
4. Scan the Yellow Pages of local phone directories for the names of companies selling products to your targeted industry.
5. Place notices in one of several newsletters catering to manufacturers' reps.

Chapter Summary

The three systems of indirect distribution—dealers, distributors, and manufacturers' reps—can be effective in controlling sales costs while getting the company's product out into the marketplace. They are sales tools, just as are advertising, brochures, direct-mail campaigns, and so forth. Like all tools, their effectiveness depends on how they are used. They are not mutually exclusive. Many companies use a combination of dealers, distributors, and manufacturers' reps. How, and even if, a manager uses these kinds of organizations depends on company objectives, how much money is targeted for marketing, and how much control of end-user markets the company must maintain.

Chapter Seventeen

Shifting Sales Channels and the Phenomenon of Mass Distribution

Definition of a Sales Channel

Let's begin with a definition: A sales channel is nothing more than a distribution network through which goods or services are moved. If a computer manufacturer offers its products to end-user customers through direct-mail catalogs, that is the channel or vehicle of distribution it has chosen. (Dell Computer, a mail-order computer firm, did just that. Started in 1984 with $1,000 by a University of Texas student, its first-year revenues were $6 million. In 1993 the company posted sales of $2 billion.)

Suppliers make deliberate choices concerning which channels will be the best vehicles (move the most product at the highest margins) for their goods or services based on two factors:

1. The kind of products they're trying to sell.
2. The profile of the channel:
    a. Who it reaches
    b. How it distributes product

c. Its market niche
d. Its pricing policies

Not every channel is suitable for every product. For example, a telemarketing organization would not be a good channel choice for Russian ermine coats.

Why Sales Channels Are Important

Channel distribution is a subject that would appear to be more appropriate to a book on marketing rather than sales, so why is it included here? One reason, of course, is that penetrating a channel and convincing those within it to carry the company's product or service is very much a sales function. Marketing may develop the strategies, but sales has to carry them out.

The other reason is that the sands are shifting; that is, the makeup of many sales channels is rapidly changing. Sales managers who aren't alert to possible changes within their favorite channel may find that they've lost the primary method for moving the company's products or services.

Using Multiple Channels to Distribute Products

Distribution isn't an either–or proposition. No supplier is stuck with one particular distribution method except through ignorance or apathy. Many suppliers will offer their products through several channels simultaneously. For example, a clothing manufacturer might offer one line of merchandise through upscale retail shops and another, less expensive, lineup through discounters.

There should be some distinction between the products offered through multiple channels. In many instances, the supplier makes only minor cosmetic changes in the products offered to each channel to give both the appearance of exclusiveness. Different brand names, labels, skin design, options, packaging distinctions, and so forth, help blur the fact that the products are essentially the same. A Lexus ES300 is essentially a Toyota Camry with a different grill and a few more luxury appointments.

Ten Typical Sales Channels

Each sales channel is plugged into a different prospect and customer base, although their "constituencies" often overlap. Each channel demands different requirements of their suppliers. Some of the more typical channels to move products and services include:

1. Dealers. The dealer buys a product from the manufacturer and resells it to the end-user. How dealers sell and how to sell to dealers was covered in the previous chapter.

2. Distributors. Distributors traditionally buy products from manufacturers and resell them to dealers and retailers. They also carry inventory, and their "value-added" is often quick turnaround on orders. Traditional distributors were covered in the previous chapter. This chapter deals with the new breed of distributor.

3. Mail order. An old standby distribution network and still chugging along nicely, thank you. The sharp demise in general merchandise mail-order catalog outfits has been balanced by the emergence of direct-mail outfits appealing to niche markets. Some surprisingly sophisticated products, such as computers, are moved through this channel.

4. Traditional retailers. This channel includes department stores, national chains, and other types of shops that cater to retail customers. Their value-added includes the number of physical plants where customers can buy goods, attractive display of high-style merchandise, personal service, enjoy liberal return policies, and so forth.

5. Mass merchants. So-called mass merchants are a different breed of retailer. They include the warehouse clubs, off-price stores, buying clubs, deep discounters, and so forth. Their appeal is price,

offering products at a discount from suggested list with a minimum of services. Often, the surroundings are deliberately stark to suggest a "no-frills" approach. Their appeal to suppliers is the ability to move large quantities of goods and services. Their purchasing power is so enormous, that these merchants have become eight-hundred-pound gorillas as far as suppliers are concerned. More about them later.

6. Manufacturer's reps and independent agents. These are salespeople, not direct employees of the company, who work on straight commission to move a product or service. Information on manufacturers' reps was included in the previous chapter.

7. Salaried and/or commissioned sales forces who are in direct contact with end-user prospects and customers. This is still the most popular channel of all and likely will continue to be, because it gives companies the most control over results.

8. Home shopping networks and the Internet. Although they are quite different from one another, these two "electronic" sales channels are lumped together here because their potential has still not been realized. They both offer the opportunity to reach an incredible number of prospects in a short time. (There are 40 million international users of the Internet network, and the list grows larger every day.) They both have been the subject of much hype. They both have severe limitations. Marketing via the Internet and home shopping networks is reviewed in Chapter 10.

9. Telemarketing. This is another old distribution standby, but one in ill repute because this channel is so often associated with boiler rooms and bucket shops out to swindle customers. As the cost of making a direct sales call increases, however, many companies are using telemarketing as a less expensive way to contact prospects and customers.

10. Packagers and integrators. Packagers buy goods and services from several different suppliers and add value by tying them together for resale to an end-user. This channel is sometimes neglected by suppliers.

The Six Basic Rules for Moving Product into Any Channel

Each sales channel may appeal to similar prospects and customers, but each reaches these customers in a different manner. Their strategies are different, and each one makes different demands on their suppliers. (They don't do business at a Federated department store the way they do business at Wal-Mart.)

Sales campaigns must be tailored to fit the specific requirements of a sales channel, but there are some basic rules that apply to all. They are:

1. Be able to talk their language. Understand how the other channel works and the basic requirements of the distributors operating within that channel. For example, if your company wishes to sell through a direct-mail company, the packaging for the product you offer them had better be able to endure the bouncing around it will receive in the delivery process. A mass merchant, on the other hand, may require that the package itself be an advertising piece that attractively illustrates the product so it can be used for "stacking" in-store displays.

2. Be aware of other profit margin expectations of that channel. Upscale retailers, for example, require on the average an additional 3 percent profit margin than other types of retailers because of their relatively high cost of doing business in shopping malls, their liberal return policies, and so forth. Some companies develop specific product models and suggested price points to meet the profit margin demands of their distributors.

3. Understand the limitations the channel imposes. If you want an upscale department store chain to carry the company's product, that same model can't be offered to mass merchants. The department store won't be able to compete on price. Some companies get around this constraint by offering one model to the upscale department stores and another model, with cosmetic changes, to discounters.

4. Set suggested price points that meet the reseller's margin requirements. They have to be suggestions only, and the distributor

won't adhere to them if the product isn't moving well, but price points are necessary to maintain stability in a market.

5. Learn and provide the level of support the channel demands. Will your company have to set up 800-HELP lines to give buyers instruction on the use of purchased equipment? Will warranty repair depots be needed?

6. Create demand for the company's product or service that the channel can use to stimulate sales. Creating demand means commitment to advertising programs, public relations campaigns, and so forth. Every sales channel wants their selling job to be as easy as possible. If the product has been "presold" by the supplier, there's a much better chance that the distributor will want to carry it.

Shifting Distribution Channels

Nothing lasts forever, including favorite sales channels. Sales and marketing managers who have become comfortable with existing channels for moving their products and services had better become aware of a recent phenomenon. A change is occurring in the replacement of distribution channels with others just as dramatic and significant as the change when Cro-Magnon Man replaced Neanderthal. For example, traditional office equipment dealers and independent office supply stores are fast fading away as they are replaced by superstores such as Office Depot, Staples, and Office Max. A small, independent dealer can't match the purchasing power of a national merchandiser. That dealer's prices have to be higher, and former customers will go elsewhere.

The same thing is happening in other areas of retailing. Warehouse clubs, price clubs, deep discounters, and so-called mass merchants are replacing more traditional sales channels. The arrival of a Wal-Mart store in town usually decimates the local merchant population. Mom-and-pop stores aren't the only ones affected. Wal-Mart often knocks off regional distributors as well. It has become increasingly difficult for small- and medium-sized companies to compete against these distribution behemoths and survive.

Retailing is only one of the areas affected. Similar "channel realignment" is happening in banking, pharmaceuticals, entertainment, and even transportation.

The Impact of Channel Realignment on Suppliers

Why is this change important? Obviously, it is of high concern to the old-line office equipment dealers who are being forced out of business. That is unfortunate, but in our tough, competitive marketplace the inefficient and the obsolete are whistled to the sidelines, nevermore to get back in the game. That is the nature of business.

Shifting channels are also significant to suppliers. Here's why:

To stay with our first example, office machine manufacturers who relied primarily on old-line office equipment dealers to move product found their sales volumes steadily declining as their favorite channel faded. The dealers couldn't compete with the discounters, which meant that their suppliers couldn't compete with those manufacturers who are "plugged in" to Staples, Office Depot, and so forth, the new mass-merchant network.

The manufacturers who distribute through the old channels now begin to "adjust" for lower sales volume by cutting corners, perhaps trying to squeeze an extra year out of an obsolete model that should be replaced, reducing advertising expenditures, and so forth, all of which only makes their resellers less competitive and accelerates their decline. Here is the lesson: *If the supplier doesn't make adjustments to the new distribution reality, it becomes caught in a quicksand that swallows the rescuers along with the original victims.*

11 Warning Signs to Determine If Your Sales Channels Are in Trouble

Can you get a good night's sleep secure in the knowledge that your sales channels are in good shape? Will they, for the foreseeable future, support the flow of products you wish to move in the marketplace? If you're not sure, here are 11 warning signs that point to a channel in trouble:

1. Your customers (resellers) complain about new competition. There's a new store the size of three football fields down the street that's just "killing" them. As proof they show you the outfit's flier, advertising prices they can't meet.
2. There's a longer time period between orders from your channel resellers. For example, instead of ordering every month, they order every six weeks or every other month. Sell-through isn't happening.
3. Resellers begin to ask to return merchandise they can't sell because of the new competition.
4. Resellers ask for price reductions or rebates on goods already purchased to make them more competitive for sale. (This is known as "inventory balancing." It's a quick fix, but no solution to the larger problem.)
5. Resellers will no longer order for inventory, but only buy products that have been presold. They're not interested in quantity discounts, promotions, "baker's dozens," or any deal that requires them to buy product for the shelf.
6. More and more of your resellers request extended terms of payment. Even then, some of them are late paying their bills. A few default.
7. Several resellers ask you if you know anyone who would like to buy their business. Failing that, they ask if there are openings with your company.
8. There are not enough attendees at the national trade show or convention to get up a pinochle game. Resellers who normally support the show can't afford the travel expense. Some of the exhibitors have also pulled out. On the last day of the show you could shoot a cannonball down the main aisle without fear of striking a single reseller.
9. Several prominent resellers who have been landmark companies close their doors.

10. The resellers talk about taking on other lines, entering other areas of business, or taking the business elsewhere. They're really seeking "pockets" where the competition isn't quite so tough. (An idle dream. Those pockets and backwaters don't exist anymore. With modern communications, efficient suppliers can "reach out and touch anyone.")
11. Some resellers actually purchase a few items for resale from the distributor they complain about. (This one is really the kiss of death, because it dramatically illustrates just how noncompetitive the channel has become.)

If any of the above signs seem familiar, you had better begin scouting around for new channels. You can start playing taps over the current one.

Four Reasons Why Sales Channels Fail

Why do some sales channels fail while other just become more prosperous every year? Here are some of the salient reasons:

1. The channel is locked into a way of doing business that has become noncompetitive. Department store chains expanded rapidly into shopping mall locations in the sixties, seventies, and early eighties. They are locked into these high-rent, high-upkeep facilities with long-term leases that include paying the mall operators a percentage of sales. Their cost of business is much higher. They can't compete with discounters who have purchased or leased space in small strip shopping centers.

Check out any major department store. They aren't offering the same type of merchandise they handled a few years ago. Product after product has disappeared. The electronics department is gone. Furniture is fading. Other departments have been abandoned.

2. The individual resellers in the channel are too small. Small is good in emerging markets, where versatility and flexibility matter. Large is better in mature markets because of the buying power of giant distributors, advertising muscle, and so forth.

3. The resellers' value-added is no longer quite so valuable in the eyes of end-user customers. Office equipment dealers relied on personal service, that is, providing demonstrations, operating instructions, site delivery, repair, and so forth, to justify their higher prices. The marketplace preferred a lower price.

4. The channel is complacent. A new competitive distributing network arrives and no one takes notice until the market has been captured.

Distributors' New Muscle

For a long time, suppliers ran the show. They dictated to the distributors what could be sold and the price they could sell it for. If the reseller got out of line, the flow of products would dry up faster than an Arizona creek bed in August. The loss of one reseller really didn't mean anything to the supplier. It could easily be replaced. Resellers were careful to do as they were told.

All that is changing. Distributors of goods and services are gaining an edge over producers of goods and services. The buying and selling power of these new distribution networks is clearly a new major marketing force. They control the market, and suppliers had better dance to their tune. The carrot they dangle before manufacturers is *sales volume* and simplicity in marketing. Make a few sales calls, and quota for the year is accomplished. Why market through a thousand resellers when you can get the same, or even better, sales volume moving your product through several giant chains? (Before answering, remember the cautionary advice about putting all your eggs in one basket.)

How Distribution Giants Function

Distribution is the entire system of delivering products or services to customers. This is a valuable and necessary service. Our networks are responsible for the great diversity of products available to consumers. (One of the most painful areas of the Soviet Union's conversion to capitalism is that they have no distribution networks in place through which goods and services can flow. The lack of these channels complicates the task for anyone who wants to do business in the country.)

There's a recent management philosophy that preaches "smaller is better," but it doesn't apply to distribution. Companies that control the channels of distribution of goods, services, and information are becoming ever larger and more aggressive. That's because new communications and computer technologies allow giant distributors efficiently to operate large, national networks.

Their financial and marketing muscle gives them a significant negotiating advantage over their suppliers. For example, Office Depot sells one out of every eight fax machines purchased in the United States. Every fax machine manufacturer wants to plug into this network.

When a manufacturer wishes to bring a product to market, often it must now do so through one of these giant distributors. There are no reasonable alternatives. That means the distributor can dictate tough terms. In some instances, they don't even take ownership of the goods they distribute, leaving the manufacturers with this financial responsibility.

The distributor offers the traditional services related to the sale of a product, including advertising, display, marketing, shipping, billing, product demonstration, inventory, aftersale service, and repair.

"Value-added is shifting from the point of production to the point of sale," says Dwight Gertz, a vice president for Mercer Management Consulting. In other words, the buck (profit) now stops with the distributor. It is the supplier (manufacturer) of goods and services who gets squeezed.

Distribution Niches

Distributors carve out market niches for themselves and drive out their competitors. Home Depot and Home Base have taken their toll on the independent hardware store. They are gobbling up a $127-

billion-dollar-a-year industry. The independent store had better be located in a town too small to attract one of these giants.

Hardware stores aren't the only small businesses in trouble. Large, regional banks are currently going through a merger mania, specifically to strengthen their distribution of financial services. In a few years the independent bank will disappear, crushed by regional financial service outlets offering a cornucopia of services the independent bank can't match.

If you're a supplier whose current sales channel is the local hardware store or the independent banker, or a dozen other assorted industries, you had better be casting around for alternatives to move your company's products.

How to Sell to the New National Distributors: A Ten-Point Program

First, a word of warning: Giant distributors often eat small- and medium-sized suppliers alive. You'll be considered snack food. This is because these distributors are capable of taking up so much of the supplier's production capacity, the supplier becomes a virtual captive that must comply with the distributor's demands (which, of course, are escalated at each negotiation). Profits get squeezed a bit more each year.

On the plus side, mass merchants have given many small- and medium-sized companies a springboard into volume marketing. Often, there's no need for the supplier to set up a national sales organization. These mass merchants can move all the product the supplier can manufacture. There have been many instances of hole-in-the-wall outfits expanding tenfold because of their association with a giant distributor.

If you still feel a crack at this channel is worthwhile, here's how to go about getting it:

1. Don't use an independent agent or manufacturer's rep to make the contact with a mass merchant. Approach the distributor directly. Most won't even make an appointment with indepen-

dent reps because they want the commission that reps normally earn sliced from their price for the product.

2. Have a complete program in place and be prepared to present it. It isn't enough just to give an inspired sales pitch about the product and pricing. The distributor will want to know everything about your company's policies concerning:
   a. National advertising
   b. Cooperative advertising
   c. Sales support
   d. Rebates
   e. Returns
   f. Training
   g. Warranty (how long, how inclusive, and where performed)
   h. Exclusiveness
   i. Out-of-warranty service
   j. Help lines

   In addition they'll want to know about production capability, packaging, in-store displays, warehousing, shipping, and so forth.
3. Come in with an offer containing your lowest possible price and expect that number to be the opening point for negotiations. Expect mind games. Many of these distributors locate their buyers and purchasing agents in sparse surroundings to symbolize how "lean and mean" they operate.
4. Be prepared to defend your pricing. The distributor may want access to your cost figures.
5. Be prepared to change the way you run your company. The distributor may require improvements in your production, quality control, inventory levels, and so forth.
6. If agreement is reached, be prepared to be tossed out fast if the product doesn't move. Shelf space is sacred to a mass merchant. They can't afford to waste it on a slow-moving product.

7. Expect the distributor to demand price reductions or rebates on products already sold to them if these products prove to be slow movers. Their attitude toward slow movers is to slash the price and move them out.
8. Mass merchants want as much margin as possible, but expect them to ignore suggested price points if the products your company provides prove to be slow movers. This can be dangerous if your company is trying to move products through several sales channels.
9. Expect the distributors to demand to be able to return unsold goods, no matter what the terms of original sale.
10. Expect to operate at lower profit margins than you originally intended.

If these points seem negative, you can also expect moving more product than ever before if it is a good fit with this channel.

Are the New Distribution Channels Set in Concrete?

The emergence of new sales channels that are now swallowing old distribution networks doesn't mean that they will triumph forever. Some will stumble. Here's what inevitably happens when a few distributors dominate a channel:

1. Senior management wants to squeeze out more profit from every sale. They add more margin, making them less competitive.
2. They become ever more demanding of their suppliers, causing the suppliers to seek alternatives.
3. In the effort to increase sales volume to maintain growth, they begin to expand into marginal areas, again squeezing profits.
4. They, in turn, become complacent.

5. Despite advanced communications technology, their "empires" become unwieldy.

The Reaction Against Mass-Merchant Distributors

Is there a manufacturer's outlet shopping center near your town, perhaps in the hinterlands, 15 or 20 miles outside the main line, where brand-name manufacturers run their own off-price shops? These outlets are cropping up all over the country, and they are in direct response to the new marketing clout of mass merchants. Manufacturers aren't stupid. They recognize the tremendous life-and-death power of giant distributors. They don't like putting the futures of their companies completely in the hands of these merchants. What many are doing in response is beginning to sell their own products through their own stores.

Technically, these outlets sell out-of-season merchandise or factory seconds at reduced prices. The centers are supposed to be located in a remote area where they won't compete with the distributor. Actually, they've become an ace-in-the-hole for manufacturers, a channel for moving product should the relationship with the mass merchant sour. They represent an effort by suppliers to take back control of the sales process. Expect to see more of them, and expect to find them ever closer to the center of the action.

Chapter Summary

A sales channel is a distribution network through which goods and services are moved. The makeup of many sales channels is changing as never before. Some channels are fading; others are moving products at a dizzying pace. The most important change is the growing power of distributors over manufacturers. The movers of product have become more important than the makers of product.

Sales managers who aren't alert to possible changes within their distribution networks may find that they've lost a method for moving the company's goods or services.

Chapter Eighteen

How to Use Advertising Effectively

Local Advertising

Many companies, recognizing that there are geographical differences between regions, give area sales managers control over a certain amount of advertising budget that is to be spent locally. Usually, none of this advertising is of the "institutional" variety—that is, promotion the company image—but rather the kind of advertising that's designed to directly produce sales, or at least inquiries, on a near-term basis.

The Local Advertising World

The advertising the field manager is likely to encounter is not the "slick," high-production-value type, chock-full of willowy blondes and half-mad art directors. Local advertising is the more mundane quarter-page newspaper ad, the 30-second radio spot, or the direct-mail campaign aimed at area businesses.

Advertising to Satisfy Demand

There's a field of opinion that holds that advertising can shape and mold the wants of consumers. These people believe that advertising can literally create demand. Others feel that consumers control their own behavior, that they are highly selective, taking what they like and ignoring the rest. Local advertisers may as well accept the second theory. Even if it is possible to create demand, most local budgets won't be large enough to attempt this approach. Try to access demand that already exists, usually demand that can't otherwise be reached. The famous ad man Fairfax Cone said, "Advertising is what you do when you can't go see somebody."

The First Management Consideration About Advertising

The first thing managers must consider about advertising is what they expect to get out of it. The simple answer is that most want to use advertising to sell more goods or services. It's simple, but it's too easy. If an advertising program is to be successful, specific goals must be developed.

Six Questions Managers Must Ask Before Developing an Advertising Program

Before developing an advertising program the manager must understand the product, the situation it faces, and the other marketing tools at the company's disposal. The following questions should be asked:

1. What kind of companies or groups of consumers are targeted with this advertising?
2. What kind of ads should be run and what information should be included in these ads?
3. What media will be used? Newspapers? Radio? Television? Direct mail? Magazines?

4. What kind of budget is available for the job?
5. How do the local ads tie in with the company's national advertising program?
6. What yardsticks shall be used to measure the success or failure of the advertising?

The answers to these questions help the manager write the advertising program.

The Big Question of the Advertising Budget

The question to tackle first is the one of budget. How much does the manager have to spend? At higher levels in the company, preparing the advertising budget is a complicated process. Senior management works hard to develop optimum ad budgets, not wanting to spend too much or too little. They use complicated formulas, charts, diagrams, computer models—all showing the rate of return for every advertising dollar invested.

In the field, ad budget preparation is likely to be less taxing. In some companies, ad budgets are handed to managers in sealed envelopes. They can spend so much on local advertising and no more. Case closed.

Three Ways of Calculating an Advertising Budget

When managers are asked to submit their own advertising budgets, the figures are likely to be based on one of three different justifications. These are:

1. A percentage of past sales
2. A percentage of anticipated sales
3. A percentage of a combination of past and anticipated sales

How the Calculations Work

Here's how these systems work. If last year's sales were $1 million and the company will allow the manager to spend 3 percent of last year's sales on local advertising, the advertising budget is $30,000. Budgets based on anticipated sales, or a combination, would be calculated in the same way.

The Problem with Using a Percentage of Sales to Develop an Ad Budget

One problem with using anticipated sales to calculate ad budgets is that if the manager falls short of meeting first-half projections, the ad money is likely to be cut in midyear. That could present the manager with an even bigger problem of reaching quota in the second half because the promotional funds will have been withdrawn.

When Using a Percentage of Anticipated Sales for Budget Preparation Works to the Advantage of the Manager

One advantage of using anticipated sales as justification for an ad budget is that when managers project a sales increase, more ad money becomes available. There's more advertising to make the sales projection become a reality.

Other Kinds of Ad Budget Calculations

There are other kinds of budgets, such as zero-based budgets, in which all programs are created from the ground up every year. In these budgets this year's calculation has no relationship to last year's results. Field managers are unlikely to be involved in this kind of budget preparation.

How to Develop an Ad Budget That Top Management Won't Shoot Down

There are three basic keys to developing an ad budget that top management will approve. These are:

1. Develop an exact figure as to how much money is needed.
2. Be able to demonstrate how that figure was calculated.
3. Have a specific plan on how the money will be spent.

Be as detailed as possible. Use month-by-month calculations.

A Sample Advertising Budget

Exhibit 18–1 on page 338 shows a sample branch budget that is likely to pass muster in the home office.

Notice that this budget uses the past year's sales to arrive at the total local advertising figure. Also notice that the one constant figure is for Yellow Pages advertising. The size and cost of the Yellow Pages ad is usually contracted for a full year. The plan shows how much will be spent, month-by-month, and what media will be used. The concentration of spending is in the months that have proven to be the "buying seasons."

Where Advertising Money Is Best Spent: Advertising Media

Once there is budget approval, how is it spent? There are a number of advertising vehicles out there, and they're all happy to take the company's money. Of course, the prime objective is to use advertising where it will do the most good, that is, have the best chance to increase business. The question is, how does the manager know in advance what the wise advertising purchase will be?

Let's take a look at the different media choices.

Exhibit 18–1
Ad Budget

BRANCH'S LAST YEAR'S SALES	$1,600,000
LOCAL ADVERTISING ALLOWANCE	3%
THIS YEAR'S AD BUDGET	$ 48,000

Monthly Budget

Month	*Media*	*Amount*	*Total*
January	Yellow Pages	$ 250	
	Newspaper	$1250	
	Direct mail	$ 500	
			$2,000
February	Yellow Pages	$ 250	
	Newspaper	$1250	
	Direct mail	$ 500	
			$2,000
March	Yellow Pages	$ 250	
	Newspaper	$2250	
	Radio	$2250	
			$5,000
April	Yellow Pages	$ 250	
	Newspaper	$2250	
	Radio	$2500	
	Direct mail	$1000	
			$6,000
May	Yellow Pages	$ 250	
	Newspaper	$2250	
	Radio	$2500	
			$5,000
June	Yellow Pages	$ 250	
	Newspaper	$1750	
			$2,000
July	Yellow Pages	$ 250	
	Newspaper	$1250	
	Direct mail	$ 500	
			$2,000

Exhibit 18–1 (continued)

Month	*Media*	*Amount*	*Total*
August	Yellow Pages	$ 250	
	Newspaper	$1250	
	Direct mail	$ 500	
			$2,000
September	Yellow Pages	$ 250	
	Newspaper	$2250	
	Radio	$2500	
			$5,000
October	Yellow Pages	$ 250	
	Newspaper	$2250	
	Radio	$3500	
	Direct mail	$2000	
			$8,000
November	Yellow Pages	$ 250	
	Newspaper	$2250	
	Radio	$2500	
	Direct mail	$2000	
			$7,000
December	Yellow Pages	$ 250	
	Newspaper	$1750	
			$2,000
		Grand Total	$48,000

Newspapers and Magazines

Except maybe for smoke signals, newspapers were here first. They are the old reliables. There are daily newspapers, Sunday papers, weekly newspapers, giveaways, national dailies such as the *Wall Street Journal,* and special-interest papers. Some are prestigious publications and others are sleazy rags. They all accept advertising, and they're all filled with ads. Do people look at those ads? According to McGraw-Hill, only 16 percent of newspaper readers ever read a *full-page ad*. As television takes a greater hold on all of us, there are fewer newspaper readers every day. So why even consider advertising in a newspaper?

THE ADVANTAGES OF NEWSPAPER ADVERTISING

Advertisers choose newspapers because that's where some shoppers look when they're in the market to buy something. For example, grocery shoppers are conditioned to look in certain days' issues of their local newspapers for stores offering food bargains. Someone in the market for a home will look in the Sunday real estate section. In other words, the newspaper is a shopping guide. Retailers, who are the primary users of newspaper advertising, use them because they can pick a paper whose circulation closely matches their marketing area. Newspapers offer territory flexibility. They are the only mass media some retailers use. If the company's product is one that is carried by retailers and shopped by end-users, then newspapers are a good media buy.

THE DISADVANTAGES OF NEWSPAPER ADVERTISING

What's wrong with newspaper advertising? The newspapers themselves have a short life. Technically, they're current for 24 hours. Actually, most papers receive 20 to 30 minutes of attention, *and it's not close attention*. Material is scanned rather than read. An ad competes not only with other ads but also with the substantive stuff put in the paper to attract readers. Whole sections of the paper are passed over without even being opened.

THE COST OF NEWSPAPER ADVERTISING

The cost for your ad depends on the paper's circulation, the size of the ad, and when and where it is run. Most papers quote their rates in *lines*. Billing is by the column-inch (14 lines), but cost is calculated in lines. The more lines purchased, the lower the rate that can be obtained. The least expensive rates are available through a contact with the paper. That's why planning and budgeting are so important. It's possible to cut a better deal with the local paper when you are able to guarantee it so much business for the forthcoming year.

Line rates don't tell the whole story about the true cost of newspaper advertising. What is important is how many readers will be delivered for the money charged. This figure is given as CPM (cost per thousand). An ad will cost more in the Sunday edition than will ads run on weekdays. Special advertising sections and neighborhood sections also have different rate structures.

Positioning a Newspaper Advertisement

Where the ad is positioned in the paper depends on what is being sold. An ad for running shoes would attract the most interest in the sports section. An ad for women's clothes would do best in the fashion section. There are many refinements to this positioning. The ads for personal computers will run in both the business and sports sections. Why the sports section? Because most personal computer buyers are men, and men are the principal readers of sports news.

Designing a Newspaper Ad

Managers who don't know how to design an ad should leave the job for the professionals. If the company is big enough, they'll have an advertising department or an independent ad agency to help an area manager. The ad department will have sample ads, approved for company use nationwide. They can also provide layouts, artwork, logos, and so forth. If this material isn't available, use the resources of the newspaper running the ad. They have professionals who can design an appealing ad. Newspapers want to do a good job because if the ad doesn't pull, the manager won't use the paper anymore.

Five Design Tips That Help a Newspaper Ad Look Professional

Those managers who feel driven to design their own ads should consider the following to give the ad a professional appearance:

1. Don't try to cram everything into the ad. Deliver the message in "bullets." White space is very appealing. People are drawn to it to find out what the few words do say.
2. Consider a border for any ad running less that a full page. The smaller the ad, the larger the border.
3. Use large type. The message is important. Shout it out.
4. Consider reversing. That means using a black background and white letters. Reversing can look good on small ads, and partial reversing is okay on larger ads. Full reversing of a large ad can look messy.
5. Don't split the ad into two equal halves. It lessens the impact.

Repetition: The Key to a Successful Newspaper Ad Campaign

No matter how well an ad is written, no mater how good the layout, don't be surprised if it doesn't draw too well the first time it is run. A one-time ad can have a dramatic effect for a well-known retailer advertising a really special sale. But that retailer has probably built a reputation over years of merchandising to the community. Most ads require repetition to be effective. Those managers who run two column-inches one time in a weekday edition of a local paper to "see how it draws," might as well save their company's money. Unless the offer is spectacular, the ad won't draw. That's why planning is so important in newspaper advertising. Work with the space salesperson to develop a complete program of ads over the entire year.

The Advantages of Magazine Advertising

Magazine readers generally have higher incomes than newspaper readers do. They make good vehicles for high-ticket items. Another advantage is that the quality of printing is superior to newspapers. Many magazines use slick paper and four-color printing, which help show off a product very well. A third advantage is that many magazines are nationally distributed. While there are a few national newspapers—such as the *Wall Street Journal* and *U.S.A. Today*—most are local publications.

Recently, special-interest magazines have gained the enthusiasm of advertisers. They target specific markets better than any other media choice. What better place to advertise skiing equipment than in a magazine devoted to the sport?

The Disadvantages of Magazine Advertising

Magazine advertising requires more lead time, more advance preparation, and, usually, a bigger budget. The national publications and even the special-interest magazines are good for "image building," but often are not the best choice for creating sales in the near term.

Magazine Ad Preparation

Magazine advertising requires that ads have fairly high production values to get attention. Normally, an advertiser wouldn't want to consider a magazine ad unless it was professionally prepared. Don't count on the magazine for any production help. Use the company's in-house advertising department or a professional agency if planning a magazine campaign.

Magazine Advertising Costs

Magazines use two criteria for their advertising rates. The first is the size of their subscription list. The bigger the list, the higher the cost to advertise in that magazine. The second criterion is the kind of reader who is on that subscription list. Advertisers must pay a premium if the magazine can deliver so many readers who fit certain economic groups or lifestyle patterns that the advertiser seeks to reach.

Yellow Pages Advertising

Advertising in the local classified phone directory is almost always the responsibility of the field manager in the area. Headquarters may decide what kind of ad is run, but the local manager will normally have a voice in the decision over the size of the ad and how many different places in the directory the company's name will appear.

A Yellow Pages listing is almost mandatory for some industries. If the company is not in it, some customers may wonder why. Hard merchandise and services get the best results from Yellow Pages advertising. Intangibles don't fare nearly as well.

What a Yellow Pages Ad Should Accomplish

Yellow Pages readers are always shoppers. They have already decided they want something. The decision they want to reach is not if they will buy, but rather who they will buy from. In these circumstances the purpose of the ad is not to sell concepts or promote the company image; *the purpose is to kill the competition.* (Don't buy it from that jerk, buy it from me.) This is the place to pull out the shotgun and shoot off both barrels.

The Four Kinds of Yellow Pages Ads

There are four kinds of ads that can be purchased in the Yellow Pages directory. They are:

1. The basic listing. Normally this is free. Payments start when the listing is in **boldface** or the company wants listings in more than one category.
2. Space ads running from one-half to two inches high and a column wide.
3. Display ads running from one-quarter of a column to one-quarter of a page.
4. Trademark listings. This bands together dealers of a brand name. One example might be all the Sony tape recorder dealers. One offshoot of the trademark listing is the category listing, for example, listing all the Italian restaurants in the area.

Buying Ads in the Yellow Pages

Yellow Pages space salespeople have a reputation for talking fast and selling hard. The largest ad they can sell is usually a quarter of a page, but they may try to sell space in various categories and in "foreign" (out of the area) directories. Some of these additional listings may benefit the company and others may not. Spend the Yellow Pages ad money in the areas where the company draws its business.

Since the breakup of AT&T, Yellow Pages directories have bred like rabbits. Some of these new directories are good buys and others are distributed only to a few local warehouses. Be certain that the directory being used by the company is being widely distributed to potential prospects of the company's product or service. Be a prudent buyer.

Seven Tips on Designing a Yellow Pages Ad

This is a media that requires boldness. Here are some guidelines:

1. Refine the proposition to a few words. There's not much time to capture the reader's attention, so tell the company's story fast.
2. Use big print. It's the best way to catch the reader's eye.

3. Don't try to say too much. Rest the product's case on its few best features.
4. List the phone number prominently. After all, that's what this medium is all about.
5. Use borders, the bolder the better.
6. Forget about photographs. They don't reproduce well on yellow newsprint.
7. Don't try to be too clever or too subtle. State the company's case plainly.

What to Do When the Phone Rings

The most important step to take with Yellow Pages advertising is to train those employees handling the calls to respond correctly to the phone inquiries the ads will generate. Most of these people will be calling the company for the first time. Be sure they get courteous, friendly, and businesslike treatment.

Radio: Back from the Dead

Those who predicted the death of radio a few years ago were dead wrong. Radio is growing. It's becoming what is called a "portable" medium. People carry radios everywhere and listen to them at work and during recreation. Just about every worker driving to and from his or her job listens to the car radio on both journeys.

Why Advertisers Like Radio

The stations are able to "shape" and define their audiences by the type of programming they offer and the kinds of personalities they use. The station playing rock music will have a different audience from the station with talk and all-news shows. As with the special-interest magazines, advertisers are able to define their markets.

Five Decisions That Must Be Made When Buying Radio Time

The radio time buyer has a wide variety of choices. Network buys or sponsoring programs will usually be the responsibility of the company's advertising department under the direction of the Director of Marketing. Local and area managers can get involved in the purchase of *spot* advertising, which is a position between programs. That still leaves the manager with a number of decisions to make. Some of these decisions are:

1. What station will be used? This will depend on the kind of audience the company wishes to reach. The format of the station shapes the audience.

2. What time of the day will the advertisement be on the air? More radios are turned on during two specific time periods. These are the early morning hours between 6 A.M. and 10 A.M. and the late afternoon between 4 P.M. and 7 P.M. Why is the audience so large during these time periods? That's when people are in their cars driving to and from work.

3. Will the ads be run on an AM or FM station? The latter is the best buy if the product is geared toward a young audience.

4. What days of the week will the ad be run? The day as well as the time and kind of programming shape the audience.

5. How much is the company prepared to pay? Radio advertising, all advertising really, charges on the basis of the audience it delivers.

The Strength of Radio

The strength of radio lies in its ability to deliver a message frequently. It's fairly inexpensive to repeat a message over and over. Radio is also effective at reaching specific groups, as long as the categories are broad. For example, young people and working stiffs are two groups proven to be frequent radio listeners.

The most important characteristic of radio for the field sales manager is that it has become a local medium. Stations feature local news, rhapsodize about the local sports teams, and employ local personalities. The radio station has become an integral part of the local community. Using radio advertising can help the company become part of the community.

Radio's Disadvantages

One of radio's disadvantages is that once the advertising message is given, it's lost, disappearing into the ozone. A reader can go back to take a second look at a newspaper ad. Not so with radio. The message disintegrates. Another problem with radio is the sheer volume of commercials it delivers. The company's message can get lost among the blizzard of ads broadcast during prime listening periods.

How to Use Radio

Radio isn't any good for complicated messages. Keep the radio story simple. That's also the reason why the advertiser should try to get only one idea across at a time. Use repetition to get the story across. Develop a simple theme and repeat it again and again.

Still, radio can be the best advertising buy in that it delivers the most "bang" for the buck. It's a mass medium with some degree of audience selectivity. If the company provides the budget to support it, radio should be included in local advertising plans.

Buying Radio Time

When buying radio time the important thing to understand is that the rates are negotiable. The radio time salesperson will have a rate card to look at, but these rates have not been chiseled in concrete. Deals can be made. Consider the rate card as absolutely the most the company is expected to pay, and a point from which to work down. During the prime listening hours, there may not be enough leverage to negotiate special pricing. During less attractive hours, anything goes. The bigger the commitment the company is prepared to make, the more leverage possible when negotiating. Shop around for the best deal and let the time salespeople know that the rates are being shopped.

Ten Tips for Writing Radio Scripts

If the company has an in-house advertising department or a relationship with an outside agency, perhaps there are prepared scripts that can be used for local radio ad campaigns. If not, consider using the resources of the local station. Their writers usually can help shape the pitch. If driven to prepare the message yourself, there are a few rules to follow. These rules are:

1. Keep the message simple. Use short, direct sentences.
2. Don't try to be funny unless there's a genuine gift for humor. There's nothing worse than the attempt at humor that falls flat.
3. Use professional announcers to tell the story. Don't use the company's money to underwrite your debut as a performer. Keep your family out of it too. The purpose of the advertising is to sell goods, not build your ego.
4. The key to a successful ad is repetition. Repeat the product name, the price, the phone number, the company name. It can't be done often enough. If there's not enough money to repeat the ad many times, radio is not the vehicle for the company.
5. Don't confuse the audience with too much information. Don't talk about a whole host of products in one ad. If price is mentioned, keep it to a single price.
6. Avoid trite superlatives such as "wonderful," "best," "quality," "great," and so forth.

7. Avoid words that sound like other words. Remember, the message disappears into the ozone. Don't leave the audience wondering exactly what was said.
8. Be sincere. Nothing sells better than meaning what is said.
9. Don't try to cram too much information into a single ad. Everyone has heard the commercials in which the announcer spoke too rapidly. How much of the message was retained?
10. Don't use comparisons with the competitor. Why give them air time?

The Advantages of Television Advertising

Television's primary advantage is that it delivers a large audience. National television is the place to advertise products used by large segments of the population. This is the medium for toothpaste, mouthwash, and nationally distributed cookies. Another of television's advantages is that it gives the seller an opportunity to actually show the product. Drama can be used when devising scripts. People can be shown not only using the product but also loving it. Being on the tube gives a product a kind of legitimacy. Some people feel that if a product has been shown on television it must be good.

The Disadvantages of Television Advertising

The expense of advertising on television is so large that the product must have broad appeal to make the cost worthwhile. Even local television programs in major markets can reach hundreds of thousands of viewers. The ability to select specific kinds of audiences is not as great as with radio. It's a broad-brush medium. The continual drumroll of advertising on television has hardened some viewers against it. Ad production costs are another factor. The slick commercials shown on national television cost as much as some movies did a few years ago. Even the spot ad on the 2:00 A.M. horror show may be more than the company can afford if the spot is to be played often enough to be effective.

TELEVISION ADVERTISING ALTERNATIVES

Local cable channels do have lower spot time costs. These channels deliver a fair number of viewers in defined geographic areas. Some provide national coverage. The television "shopping clubs" have proven remarkably successful, making fortunes for some promoters and moving product for many different vendors. Cable is an alternative worth pursuing, providing the product the company offers is one that has broad-based appeal suitable for this medium.

THE ADVANTAGES OF DIRECT-MAIL ADVERTISING

Direct mail is one of the most effective ways to target a specific group of prospects. Mailing lists can be purchased for doctors, lawyers, or Indian chiefs. It's possible to pick the kind of industries that are prospects for the company's products and even to identify the names of individuals within those companies for direct-mail campaigns. Mail can be directed to different parts of the country, different ethnic groups, various political persuasions, and so forth. It is the most personal form of advertising because the message can be slanted to the type of individual receiving the mailing. It fits very well into a localized advertising program or a national campaign.

THE DISADVANTAGES OF DIRECT-MAIL ADVERTISING

Direct mail is expensive, and the sheer bulk of mail being received by buyers every day works against direct-mail effectiveness. Many clever advertising pieces are relegated to the "circular file." Managers who wish to get full value for their direct-mail advertising dollar should be careful how it is used.

Five Situations When Direct Mail Can Be Effective

Here are the times when direct mail can be effective:

1. When the company wants to deliver a message to a specific marketing area or class of prospect. Direct mail can pinpoint better than any other medium.
2. When the company wants to sell something directly to end-users without third-party involvement.
3. When the company wants to create a friendly atmosphere for a salesperson's follow-up call.
4. When the company or an area manager wants to restrict an offer to a localized area.
5. When the message to be delivered is complex or requires detail. Lengthy explanations are possible in direct-mail campaigns.

How to Conduct a Direct-Mail Campaign: Obtaining the Mailing List

The first thing that's necessary for a successful direct-mail campaign is a mailing list that's current. These lists may come from company compilations of customers, prospects, and suspects. It's also possible to purchase lists from mailing-list brokers.

The Yellow Pages of telephone directories contain the names of companies offering mailing lists for sale. Most of these companies are brokers; they buy the lists from other sources. Lists are relatively inexpensive; it's possible to purchase a list for about $60 per thousand names. They can be bought by area, by kind of company, by job title, and by a combination of all three. They come on printout sheets, on adhesive labels, and on floppy disks.

Generally, lists are sold on the basis of one-time use. How will the company who sold the list know if it's used a second time? They've sprinkled the list with the names of bogus companies. A few copies of every mailing go directly to the list company. The company that tries an unauthorized mailing of the list gets a bill for a second use, and maybe even a lawsuit.

Many list brokers provide a complete service, stuffing, stamping, and delivering mail to the post office. Often their work is cheaper and faster than doing the job in house.

The Three Parts of a Direct-Mail Package

Once a good list is purchased it's time to make up the mailing package. These packages usually consist of three parts. They are:

1. The offer letter
2. The description or picture of the product being offered
3. The return piece (the action you want the recipient to take)

It's hard to say which piece is of the package most important, but it's probably the offer letter.

Seven Tips on Writing a Direct-Mail Piece

Here are some guidelines when writing a direct-mail piece:

1. The offer is everything. What kind of a deal is the company making to the reader? Get it out in the open in the first paragraph or two and make the offer irresistible.
2. Keep the paragraphs short. The direct-mail piece will never be confused with a Russian novel.
3. Keep the text chummy and personal. A formal-type letter may turn off the reader.
4. Don't worry about the length. If it takes five pages to tell the company's story, use them.
5. Add a postscript. Even people who don't finish the letter will read the postscript. Personalize the letter.

6. Address it to a specific individual in the company that is being targeted.
7. Prove any claims with testimonials, third-party studies, independent reports, and so forth.

The Value of the Product Brochure

When the offer letter is satisfactory, it's necessary to develop an attractive rendering of the product the company is trying to sell. If the company has a classy brochure, fine. If not, use a graphics specialist to make something up. Don't chintz here. Use the best material to create the most attractive presentation possible.

The Direct-Mail Response Form

The offer letter and the product rendering are designed to motivate the reader to do something. Make it easy for him or her to do. That's where the third part of the mailing package comes in. If the idea of the mailing is to stimulate the reader to order something, include an order blank that's simple to fill out. If the purpose is to arouse the reader's curiosity and perhaps request a product demo, include a return card that can be completed with a check mark. Do everything possible to get the response desired.

Two Ways to Increase Direct-Mail Response

In many cases a "good" response to a mailing is a 1 or 2 percent return. That means that 98 to 99 percent of the letters will be thrown away. There are a couple of ways to improve this percentage:

1. Conduct test mailings before embarking on a big mailing program. Experiment with different lists, different offer letters, different brochures until a formula is found that works. Then do the mass mailing.

2. Follow up on the direct-mail piece with phone calls, making the same appeal in the phone call that was made in the mailing.

CUTTING DIRECT-MAIL COSTS

Costs can be cut by using third-class mail. Before going ahead with a third-class mailing, get the sorting and other requirements from the local postmaster.

COOPERATIVE ADVERTISING: WHAT IT IS

Cooperative advertising is a program by which manufacturers pay part of local dealers' or distributors' advertising costs. The amounts are usually related to the dollar value of the products the dealer purchases for resale. For example, if the manufacturer offers 3 percent co-op money and the dealer buys $100,000 in goods, he accumulates a $3,000 co-op ad allowance. The money usually has strings attached. Often the dealer must put up matching funds, and there are restrictions on where, when, and how the advertising can be used.

THE ADVANTAGES OF COOPERATIVE ADVERTISING

The big advantage of co-op advertising is that it allows the manufacturer to stretch the ad budget. The local dealer must kick in a like amount. Local advertisers get better rate schedules from newspapers and are able to purchase the ad space at more attractive pricing.

THE DISADVANTAGE OF COOPERATIVE ADVERTISING

The disadvantage is the co-op ads are often not carefully controlled and the quality of the ads can deteriorate. The company image can suffer as a result. One solution to the quality problem is to provide local dealers with finished-copy ads, including space for the dealer name, address, phone number, and perhaps price.

The Internet and the World Wide Web

Two new advertising media with exciting possibilities are the Internet and its commercial section, the World Wide Web. These media are explored in Chapter 10.

Chapter Summary

Managing an ad budget and milking the most out of it is an excellent way for an area field manager to learn how advertising works. It is an introduction to marketing. For the senior manager it is a vital skill.

There are many advertising vehicles from which to choose. There is no single best choice. Advertising money well spent can have an important impact on company sales. Making poor advertising choices is just throwing money away.

Chapter Nineteen
Benefits of Sales Force Automation

A "Gift" from Technology

Sales force automation (SFA) is a hot topic. At this writing, it's a billion dollar industry with a 30 percent annual growth rate. Companies large, small, and many in between have climbed aboard the bandwagon. (One reason is that SFA fits neatly into the popular concept of "reengineering," that is, streamlining the corporation to compete in the next millennium.)

Some users are ecstatic over what SFA has done for their organizations. They regard it as a gift from technology. Others have looked this gift horse in the mouth and found a few rotten teeth. This second group claims that the systems they've installed have cost a ton of money, turned existing systems topsy-turvy, and required weeks of additional training without producing any noticeable benefits.

What Sales Force Automation Is Not

So what is this controversial new "management tool"? First, the good news for salespeople and sales managers: Your function is safe. The sales process itself has not been automated. Making a sale still requires prospecting, uncovering need, demonstrating, making a proposition, and asking for the order. These are all warm-body interactions. Silicon chips don't qualify.

An Explanation of Sales Force Automation

Stripped of the technical jargon, SFA is basically computer software that can help companies get more productivity out of their sales forces. How? By giving the field sales force, their managers, and company customers better and more timely information. The key word here is *information*. Data—never before obtainable with manual methods: data about territories, about customers, about prospects, about potential business, about performance, and more—becomes available through the power of personal computers to massage numbers. The sales process can more easily be tracked, measured, coordinated, and managed. When the hype is put to bed, SFA offers the benefit of the here and now. Everyone in the organization has current information. The caveat is that companies *must do their homework before installing systems.*

A List of 16 Popular Sales Force Automation Programs

What sales functions, exactly, can be automated? Here are just a few of the automated software programs available:

1. Lead tracking and management. Every contact made with a customer or prospect by anyone in the company can be recorded.
2. Territory alignment. Designing territories that are aligned for optimum travel time by sales reps.

3. Sales reporting and forecasting. Recording near-term sales potential with percentage likelihood and timing of close.
4. System and product configuration. Integrating company product configuration around the requirements and applications of the prospect.
5. Literature fulfillment. Automatic sending of product brochures, spec sheets, publicity releases to customers, prospects, and field sales personnel.
6. Proposal preparation. Automatic preparation by the system of uniform proposals, quotations, and other offers.
7. Presentation kits. Using laptop computers, CD players, overhead projectors, and so forth, as tools in product presentations to prospects and customers.
8. Task assignments. Using a central communications facility to "download" tasks to field reps' laptop computers.
9. Expense reporting. Reps send in expense report claims from laptops.
10. Rep performance analysis. Electronic call reports and lead results make it easier to evaluate reps' performance.
11. Competitive intelligence, pricing, and strategies. Electronic call reports include data on competitive activity. Lost-order reports track competitive pricing strategies.
12. Account order and credit status. Customer order situation and current credit status can be called up on-line.
13. Inventory availability. Inventory status of any product is available on line, as are production and shipping schedules.
14. Product specifications. Complete information on any product is available on electronic "marketing encyclopedias."
15. Customer complaint follow-up. Customer complaints can be tracked until resolution.
16. Standard customer correspondence. System generates boilerplate letters for sales staff members.

Each of the described applications offers the sales manager something different, but the programs do not stand apart as separate and distinct entities. They interact and "trade" information with one another. Information supplied to satisfy one function will be used to support another. Call report information from field reps, for example, might generate lead-tracking data.

A Typical Sales Automation Application

Still a bit hazy on what SFA accomplishes? Let's "walk through" a relatively simple automated system. In the model system, a company has field reps equipped with laptop computers and a telemarketing group operating at a central location. Here's how the system works:

1. The company uses the in-house telemarketing crew to generate sales leads.
2. The leads are sent electronically to a corporate communications center.
3. The communications center forwards the leads to the field sales reps' laptop computers. The reps, hopefully, act on the leads.
4. Results achieved from the leads is forwarded back to management via the reps' laptops. Management has the opportunity to ensure that all leads are properly handled.

That's a simple lead management and tracking program. Once installed, it could provide the building block for a more sophisticated system. For example:

1: The reps have "electronic price books" in their laptops. These include specifications and various configurations. Any price changes are made electronically by the corporate communications center to reps' laptops as required. Every price book is always up-to-date. "Stale" pricing is eliminated.*

---

*A refinement of the electronic price book is the marketing encyclopedia on CD-ROM. This is an electronic representation of all the company's products, including a overview, specifications, applications, video clips giving a short demonstration of the products, testimonials of satisfied users, and so forth. These encyclopedias could be used to give prospects product presentations.

2. The sales reps' laptops include software that helps the reps prepare quotes and proposals from "templates" known to be effective.
3. The sales reps' call reports detail the number of sales resulting from leads. This information is sent electronically by the reps' laptops to the corporate office.
4. Reps' electronic call reports also detail orders received from customers and other prospects.
5. Forecasts, outstanding quotes, proposals, and other contact information are forwarded.
6. Reports generated by the information received from the sales reps allow sales management to evaluate the quality of the leads, the efficiency of individual sales reps in managing their territories and closing sales, the accuracy of forecasts, and so forth.

In the above system, information derived from one operation is used to support other applications. The result is more timely data for both managers and field reps.

Eight Advantages of a Typical Sales Automation Application

The SFA system just described offers the company a number of advantages. They include:

1. Leads are delivered to the field while they are still current.
2. Management can ensure that leads are handled in a timely manner.
3. Management can determine whether the lead generation program is producing results.
4. Management can determine the effectiveness of the sales crew.
5. Pricing mistakes are reduced because everyone's price book is always up-to-date.
6. Quotations and proposals are uniform.

7. Managers receive current information on field activity.
8. The same data related to prospects and customers are available to all interested parties. Dial up a customer record and the identical screen is called up on every computer. If the company has both inside and outside sales reps contacting accounts, both groups are now reading from the same page.

Five Benefits of Sales Automation

Notice something? The above were all a list of features. Every salesperson knows the real key to making the sale is not by reciting the features but by listing the benefits. A well-planned SFA system can produce the following benefits:

1. Revenue growth is improved. (If the sales force can reach prospects faster, they will make more sales.)
2. The cost for making a sale is lowered.
3. Customer satisfaction is increased. (The company is reacting more quickly to their needs.)
4. More "intimacy" is created between an organization and its customers.
5. Information is more evenly disseminated throughout the organization.

Territory Balancing

Here's another popular application to help explain what makes SFA such a hot button with so many sales managers. This one is called territory balancing.

Setting up or realigning territories is one of those tasks that drives sales managers nuts. Most sales managers want to be fair with individual members of the sales team. Their primary goal when setting up or realigning territories is to create boundaries that give every salesperson an equal shot at the brass ring (potential busi-

EXHIBIT 19–1
TELESALES MANAGEMENT IN ACTION WITH TELETRAK

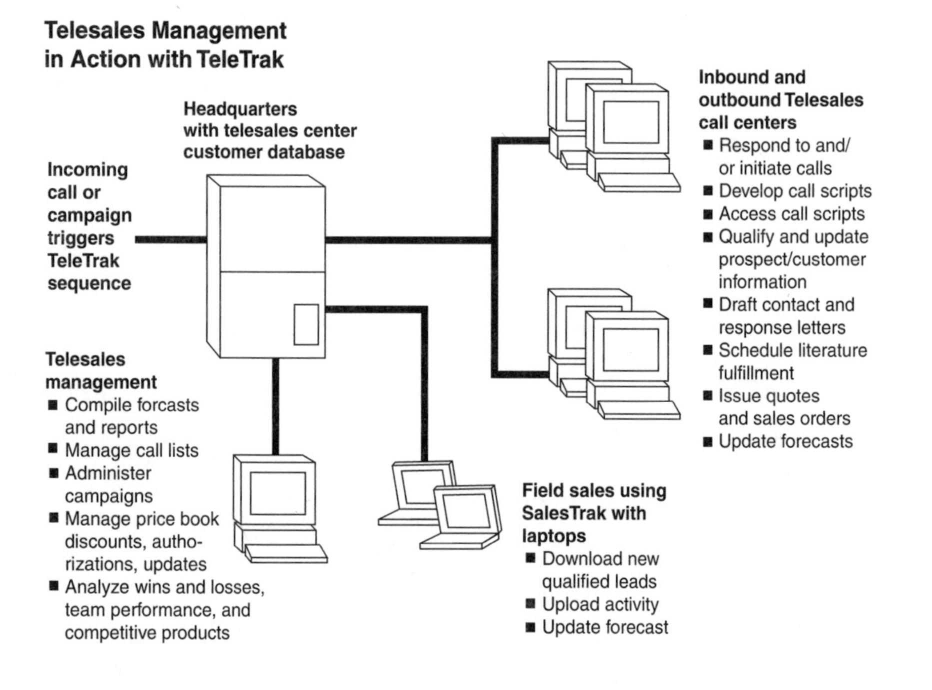

(Display courtesy of Aurum Software, Santa Clara, CA)

ness). That's why, in many companies, one salesperson will have a territory consisting of twelve blocks of Manhattan and another, with a similar quota, will cover ten upper-midwestern states.

It would appear relatively simple to segment territories based on actual sales, business potential, or a combination of the two, but the devil is in the details. Geographical and administrative considerations become vexing. For example, it's simpler to end a territory at a state or county line, or to define a region by a natural boundary such as the Mississippi River.

The problems are compounded when sales managers also try to factor in *calling efficiency*. Compact territories are always a good idea because the sales reps can spend more time in front of prospects and less time to-and-fro. It might be more efficient for a sales rep based out of Portland, Oregon, to call on an account in Vancouver, Washington, just over the state line, than it would for a rep based in Seattle to travel 170 miles to make the call.

When the requirement for calling efficiency is added, the territory boundaries inevitably change. This in turn creates imbalances in business potential. One rep gets half the Fortune 500, while another's biggest prospect is a Salvation Army thrift shop. Each attempted "fix" or balance has consequences that are difficult to discern in advance. The manager armed only with a few maps, a customer list, and a business guide often feels the urge to drop the project and do something productive, like going out and making a few sales calls. Calling efficiency becomes one complication too many when setting up territories.

Enter software programs called "Territory Optimization Technology." These programs use the client company's own data and parameters to balance territories any way the company wishes. Here's what they offer:

1. They take into account the total business in a territory, the potential, and the cost to cover that territory *based on the estimated driving time between calls*.
2. They allow sales managers to "trade" dollar-volume equality for improved geographical proximity. Territories are developed that require salespeople to spend less time deadheading between calls.
3. When changes are made, say a dozen zip codes are reassigned from one salesperson to another, the programs inform the manager of the ramifications of that change. How much in sales volume one rep gains and the other loses is apparent.
4. New territory "maps" are printed by the system.
5. The programs design territories that are more compact, allowing for better call efficiency.

EXHIBIT 19–2

BEFORE OPTALIGN OPTIMIZATION

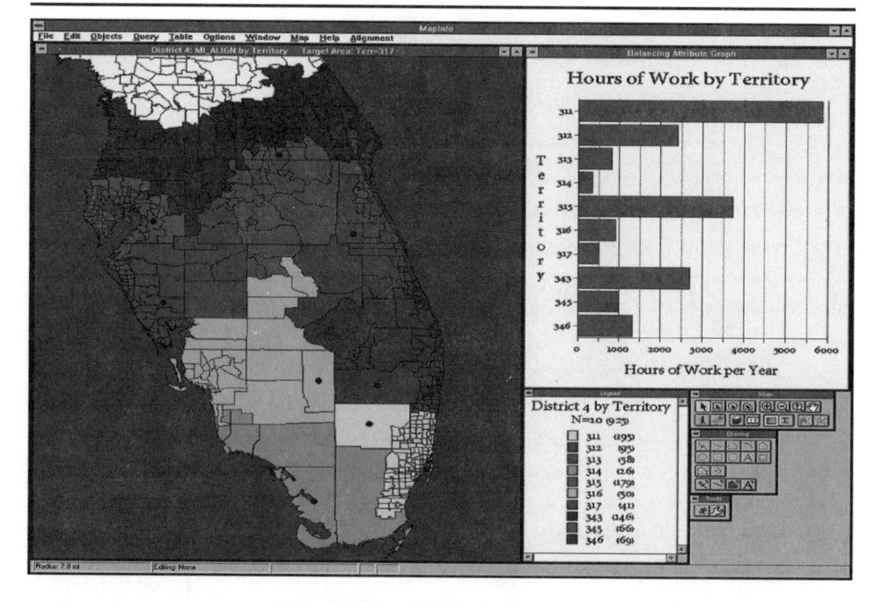

AFTER OPTALIGN OPTIMIZATION

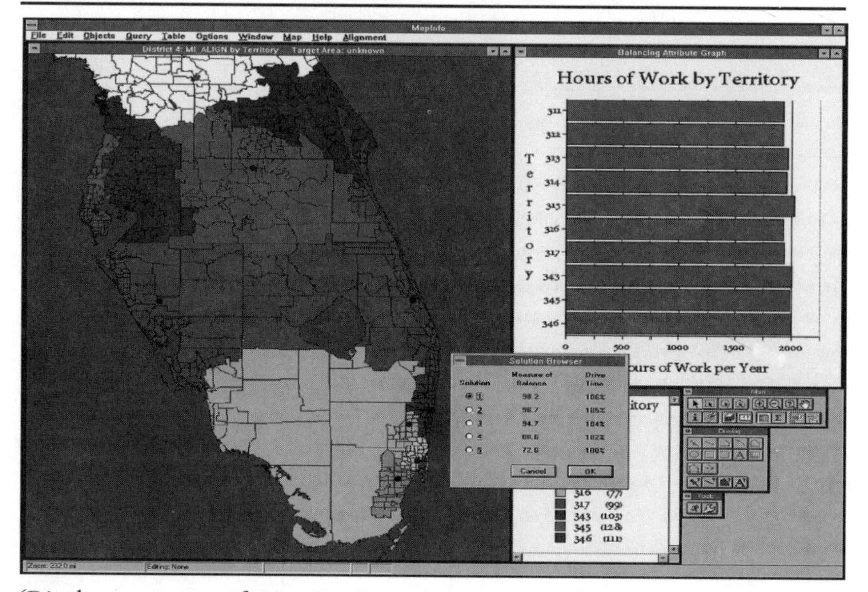

(Display courtesy of Metron, Inc., Reston, VA—the original map distinguishes territories by color)

6. Information is provided about every sales unit within the newly created territories.
7. The programs suggest where the territory's "center" should be located. This is particularly helpful in multistate territories. When a new rep is required, the sales manager knows where the rep should be positioned (which tells the manager where to recruit).
8. Territory guides are automatically created for each salesperson.
9. Additional realignment is relatively easy if the created territories don't work out or new factors are added.

This kind of information, plus additional available data, allows the sales manager to make the most appropriate compromises when balancing territories. Byproducts are better and faster reports, such as:

- Assignment reports
- Summary reports
- Gain/loss reports

A Possible Fly in the Territory-Optimization Ointment

Territory optimization sounds great. Managers who use computers to design "optimum" territories should, however, keep one thing in mind: the human factor. Numbers never tell the whole story. A manager may have a salesperson on staff who has spent years cracking a lucrative account. It isn't fair to take that account away just because the salesperson must travel 40 minutes out of the way to reach it. Do that often enough and the territories may be "optimized," but morale will be minimized. The point is that there are always special relationships between customers and salespeople and special considerations that should be taken into account when setting up territories. For computers, these factors are irrelevant. For managers, they are vital.

Why Sales Force Automation Is Possible

While it would be theoretically possible for managers to manually do what SFA programs perform, no sales manager who wants to get out from behind the desk and into the field would ever have the time. Three technological factors account for the proliferation of sales automation software. They are:

1. The advancement in computer technology that gives computers number-crunching capability.
2. The advancement in communications systems.
3. The availability, and relatively low cost, of laptop computers.

Sales automation programs, such as the previously described one for territory optimization, require powerful processing capability. New communications systems make it easier to link a field sales force and customers to the home office. Laptops are mobile computing devices. They have become the communication links, the military outposts, through which information is received and orders transmitted.

How Not to Install Sales Automation Systems

Do the benefits of SFA sound good? A word of caution before steaming ahead: Those companies who begin by buying laptops for their field sales forces and then, after the fact, call in an SFA software company to write a few "nifty" programs are doomed to failure. They won't see any clear results because they don't have a clear idea of the results they want to see. Without proper training, the sales force won't use the laptops. The company will be stuck with expensive boat anchors.

The First Ten Baby Steps Toward Installing a Sales Automation System

The way to begin an SFA project is by deciding what information the company wants to get out of the system. Work backward. Output required determines input. Hardware comes later. Do your homework. The success factors include:

1. Commitment by senior management. This is listed in first place because if senior management is not solidly behind the project, stop right here. The sales manager's time is better spent making a few more sales calls.
2. A sense of urgency. Set a timetable, keep the timetable short, and make the timetable come true.
3. Work with an SFA software vendor with a good track record. Better yet, find a vendor who understands your industry.
4. Sales and marketing must share the same "vision" of the project. Division here is guaranteed chaos.
5. Keep control of the project in sales and marketing. Sure, data processing and/or MIS should be involved, but if they call the tune the system will function according to their convenience.
6. Designate someone who has responsibility for the project. Without a strong leader, the project will flounder.
7. Assess the readiness of company employees to implement the system. (Can the company salespeople use laptops? Heck, can they operate a QWERTY keyboard?)
8. The system should be tested before initiating a national rollout. The time to fine-tune is before everyone on the sales force is involved.
9. Educate, educate, educate. Most experts believe that 30 percent of the total SFA budget should be spent on training.

10. Set up benchmarks and a method for measuring success.

Sales Force Automation and the Customer

For the past several years, many companies have concentrated on cost reduction, which is what downsizing is all about. In the next few years, that focus will shift to profit through revenue growth. (More money coming in the front door and less money going out the back.) One key to improving profits is something called *customer asset management*. That's a fancy phrase for getting and keeping more customers.

Most businesses lose between 15 and 35 percent of their existing customers every year. (It's a corporate form of hemophilia.) Any company seeking to increase sales from last year to this must first make up the loss of those customers who have bled away. It's no great revelation to point out that repeat sales are the most profitable sales. According to the *Harvard Business Review,* reducing customer defections by as little as 5 percent can improve profits by 25 to 80 percent. So methods for retaining customers has become a focus for many organizations.

So what's new? Every company tries to obtain new customers, and once in the fold, they try to please them. How can sales automation help keep customers satisfied? The answer lies in the reason why customers leave their suppliers. What makes them stray? No, it isn't because they're a fickle bunch. Most customers stray because of perceived indifference. They felt they weren't appreciated. (Fewer than 9 percent leave because they were dissatisfied with the supplier's price.)

Everyone in sales management has experienced some of the ways in which indifference toward a customer is often manifested:

- The salesperson is out chasing new business and doesn't give existing accounts enough attention.
- When the customer calls to make an inquiry, a clerk on the other end of the phone doesn't recognize the name.

- Two different company contacts tell the customer two completely different stories related to a shipping or inventory situation.
- A pricing error can't seem to get corrected no matter what.
- Credit takes the attitude that each new order the customer places is a blatant attempt at armed robbery.

For sales managers who claim that things couldn't happen that way in their companies, try "mystery shopping." That is, have someone pretend to be a prospect and place an order with the company. Learn what it's like to be your company's customer. The exercise will help managers determine how easy, or how difficult, it is to deal with their organizations. They'll see how the mechanics work, how knowledgeable the staff is, and if the administrative procedures help or hinder the sales process.

Any of the above situations seem familiar? What sales automation can do to correct them is to make sure that everyone who could possibly come in contact with a customer has the same information about the account.

- The technical-support person phoned about a problem could call up that customer's record on a computer screen and learn what the customer has purchased, when it was purchased, and the application it was used for.
- Both credit and sales could have access to accounts receivable records to help determine if credit limits are strained.
- The sales manager could check the electronic call reports to make sure the customer has been adequately serviced.
- Small problems could be red-flagged before they became major concerns.
- The clerk who processes the customer's orders could have an electronic record of the pricing schedules given that customer.
- The salesperson could check the customer's ordering history to see if a near-term purchase is possible.

- The customer feels more comfortable when contacting the supplier because everyone contacted seems to be familiar with the account. Comfortable customers are long-lasting customers. *Organizations and individuals want to do business with those who are easy to do business with.*

Review of the Six Sales Force Automation Benefits

A good SFA system can deliver the following benefits:

1. More time spent by salespeople in front of prospects and customers. This is accomplished by optimizing territories, which means less travel time between calls, improved organization, reduction in paperwork requirements, and so forth. (If the number of calls per day per rep can be increased, sales will be increased. Every sales manager understands this equation.)

2. Better customer and prospect records. Sales automation systems can track the number of calls to a customer and service reports, record what that customer has purchased and when the purchases were made, and even predict likely reorder dates. All this information makes the salesperson better prepared for the call.

3. Improved customer service. The well-informed salesperson is in a position to provide better service. This, of course, leads to happier customers.

4. Better-informed sales managers. The manager with a sales automation system can more easily track the activities of each sales rep, determine how much time is spent with existing customers as opposed to courting new accounts, measure the productivity of that rep, and determine just where the rep needs help.

5. Companywide access to customer information. Customer records are easier to review at every management level.

6. An integration of sales and marketing functions. The information developed from sales automation packages is exactly what marketing wants to know.

Six Disadvantages of Sales Force Automation

With these substantial advantages, why isn't every company rushing to install sales automation systems? A great many are; just look at the way the industry is growing. There are, however, some caveats that those investigating these systems should heed.

1. Cost. Everybody on the system needs a laptop computer, which translates to at least $2,000 per rep. A sophisticated communications network is also required, and the software isn't cheap either. Most of these costs are on the front end. Industry studies suggest that 50 percent of the cost for a sales automation system comes in the first year.

2. Unreasonable expectations. When sales automation systems first appeared, promises were made that they would improve sales volume by 10 to 30 percent. In most companies, these kinds of gains weren't experienced.

3. Sales managers can become so reliant on sales automation programs as to allow the systems to become substitutes for their personal judgment. Technology is baloney if you try to substitute it for face-to-face communications.

4. Training required. A grizzled sales staff that may include a few computer phobics is not going to quickly embrace the use of computers. Expect many calls for help, regardless of the care and training during implementation.

5. Lukewarm senior management. Unless the sales automation system is part of a larger corporate information package, senior management may not be enthusiastic about endorsing it. Without their support, expect others to snipe away.

6. Possible problems in implementation. Any new system will have its glitches. If the program hasn't been "sold" to the sales team, the glitches will be exaggerated.

Can You Put a Number on Sales Force Automation Benefits?

All the advantages of sales automation sound wonderful, but can they be quantified? That's what the bottom-liners in senior management want to know. What's it going to cost, and what will it deliver? Will an automation system improve sales? If so, by how much?

The advantages of better and more timely information do probably translate to greater sales volume at better profit margins. The improvement, however, may not be enough to pop the champagne corks.

In the early 1990s, many companies installing SFA systems were burned by expectations of large increases in sales volume. In addition, early software also did not provide the kind of information senior management requires, such as customer, competitive, and marketplace data.

This leads to a general truth about any kind of information automation: *Automation itself usually does not save money.* That's a heresy to some and an article of faith to others. Installation of SFA probably won't result in lower costs for running the sales operation, and it may be difficult to prove that more sales volume resulted.

What most automation systems do is to make more information available to more people on a more timely basis. It's a tool. It's up to management to use that tool to make the operation efficient.

15 Things Needed to Implement a Sales Force Automation System

1. A clear set of goals. Don't bother about any further steps until this one is resolved. The first step in establishing goals is to develop a clear understanding of the company's current operation. How can you know where you want to go unless you know where you are?

2. A computer-literate sales crews. They must be able to use desktop or laptop computers, preferably the latter. That doesn't mean that salespeople who don't know how to use a computer can't be trained. This training will, however, take additional time. It may be difficult to provide both basic computer skills and training to use the sales automation software at the same time.

3. A commitment from management. Company senior-level executives must be solidly behind the installation of the system.

4. A clear definition of what other company departments want the system to accomplish. Get consensus on the goals. There's an old data-processing maxim to the effect that "output determines input." Determining what the company wants out of a system determines what goes into it.

5. A firm budget. Calculate what the system is worth to the company.

6. A set of priorities. Obtaining everything on the sales manager's wish list may not be practical or even politically astute. Managers should decide which functions of a sales automation system are the most important to them. Discuss the issues with others in the company. (Don't be surprised if there are substantial differences of opinion within the company regarding what the priorities should be.)

7. A thorough investigation of sales automation software packages. Learn what is out there. Even if your company's situation requires complete customization, knowing what's available can stimulate ideas regarding what the company needs. Seek a sales automation software vendor with a track record of serving your company's industry. You may think your company is unique, but there are common problems shared with other related companies. If possible, work with experts who understand industry problems.

8. A consultation with the field sales reps. Make that "many consultations." What would they like to get out of a sales automation system? What would get them excited? What are they prepared to live with in terms of additional data-input requirements? It is a good idea to have several field reps present at priority meetings.

9. Somebody in charge. Give someone in the company clear authority to decide on the parameters of the system and the responsibility to install it. Make it someone who is a master at internal selling.

10. A realistic timetable for implementation. Then add a fudge factor. Depend upon it, there will be confusion. If you allow for it, there will be fewer tense times.

11. Dual systems kept in place during the implementation period. Just in case, have a back-up system for the inevitable SNAFUs.

12. A nondefensive attitude toward criticism. Expect gripes. Sales automation is revolutionary and not everyone will like it, but some of the complaints may be legitimate.

13. A building-block system installed function by function. If it is too feature-rich in the beginning, that translates to confusion. People won't use what confuses them.

14. A training program—the most important plank in the implementation program. Deliver the training in several short sessions. Let sales crew members absorb one aspect of the system before exposing them to another.

15. The patience of Job. You're going to need it.

A Final Caution on Sales Force Automation

Smart managers realize that salespeople need to spend their time in front of customers and prospects. They don't saddle their crews with duties and procedures that won't contribute to sales. When installing SFA systems, make sure that field salespeople aren't burdened with additional administrative tasks that steal productive time. Don't ask for information that isn't absolutely vital. (Information is useful only if it is used.) Don't allow administrators, data-processing, and MIS types to dictate the parameters of the system. They will turn your sales crew into clerks.

Chapter Summary

Sales automation consists of a series of software programs that can deliver better and more timely information, via computers, to managers about the status of accounts, prospects, the sales crew, competition, and a whole lot more. It offers substantial benefits to companies who set realistic goals. An SFA system requires careful planning and plenty of training to be successful.

In the past, extravagant claims were made for SFA, claims that were not borne out by experience. An SFA system *may not* result in an immediate increase of 30 percent in sales volume. It *will* give the manager a clearer picture of what is going on in the field.

Chapter Twenty
MANAGING FOR THE FUTURE

THE QUESTION THAT STAYS WITH MANAGERS THROUGHOUT THEIR CAREERS

There is one question that should occur to every manager within the first hour of accepting their first sales management position. It is, Where do I go from here? The question is appropriate because many managers are asked to make a financial sacrifice in exchange for the title on their calling cards. Others find that the few dollars more they earn as first-time managers aren't worth the extra workload and the added responsibility. These managers are betting on the future, looking toward the next leg up for their payoff. Company senior management understands and approves of this ambition. They often regard beginning field management jobs as a proving ground, a natural selection process that would make Darwin proud.

The question of the next step isn't for junior managers alone. It is one that should be in the back, and sometimes in the front, of every manger's mind throughout their business careers. The first requirement is adaptation from being good sales performers to being good managers. At higher levels the key to further promotion lies in absorbing critical sales management techniques.

The 11 Yardsticks That Determine If a Manager Is Ready for Another Promotion

When does senior management consider a manager ready for that second promotion and a third step up? Most managers probably consider themselves candidates for another jump right now. They *know* that they're ready. What are the yardsticks senior management applies to help them determine what is already apparent to the manager? Here are some of the things most senior managers look for, regardless of the industry.

1. Sales is, and always will be, a numbers game. The first requisite is that the manager is handling the current assignment well. The district or region's numbers are being met or exceeded. It's even better if the manager is outperforming many of his or her peers in the company who are in similar or equal positions.

2. Sales expenses for the area of responsibility are within budget, or pretty close to budget. This is a good indication of managerial ability.

3. The sales reports and forecasts are done on time and they are accurate. Senior management automatically considers anyone who turns in accurate numbers a good internal communicator. The accurate forecasters don't give them many unpleasant surprises.

4. The product mix the area moves is pretty much what the company wants to sell. So is the customer mix. The manager is not relying on one or two products or a few major accounts to make the area's numbers. (Want to know why? Because areas with a heavy reliance on a few products or customers are more volatile. If they lose a major account or a pet product becomes outmoded, the entire area takes a nosedive.)

5. The profit margins from the area's sales are in line with the company's requirements. The area is not selling too much product at a discount. (If profits can be kept the same during a down market period, senior management will regard the area manager with awe.)

6. The manager has established a fairly stable sales personnel situation in the area. The people who report to the manager respect his or her ability. There's not a revolving door in the district, with people moving in and out of the company.

7. The area is not experiencing extraordinary bad-debt losses. There's a good base of customers established who pay their bills in a timely manner.

8. The manager is considered reliable. He or she can be counted on to be there when needed. The manager will tackle extra assignments when necessary.

9. The manager is positive and enthusiastic. There's a genuine belief that the job can be done.

10. The manager gives an honest opinion. When there's a problem this manager states it openly, but also offers solutions.

11. The manager has ideas and suggestions for the future. Thoughts are contributed regarding the product line, possible improvements, the way the company sells, ways to beat the competition, and so forth.

Waiting for the Right Opportunity

Managers who possess most of the above traits are automatic candidates for another promotion. (They'll probably make any manager who is endowed with them all president of the company.) That doesn't mean that this manager will automatically get that next leg up. A spot must be open that the manager is qualified to fill. In the corporation version of musical chairs, no one gets to occupy the next seat unless that seat is vacant.

The Problem of Doing Too Good a Job

There's another impediment in the way of that next promotion. It is that same list that makes the manager a candidate for the second set of stripes. This person is doing a wonderful job in the current position! The company wonders how in blazes they're ever going to find someone to replace this paragon. Perhaps they'll worry about it so much that they'll decide to keep the manager right in the spot where the good work is being done. Proficiency at the job can work to keep a manager tied to it.

The Importance of Grooming a Successor

What does a manager qualified for promotion do about the problem of being vital to the position? It is by ensuring there is someone qualified to fill the manager's shoes. How is this accomplished, especially if there are no obvious choices available? *Someone must be trained to take the manager's place.* This idea disturbs some managers, who don't like to have a potential rival on the premises. They view such a person as a threat. Don't be so shortsighted. A manager's security is not based on an absence of rivals but rather the level of performance. (Helen Keller said, "Security is a superstition," and she was right.)

One of the things that will help set a manager apart from other ambitious managers who also are scrapping and politicking for that next promotion is the foresight and ability to train his or her own successor.

When to Begin Training a Successor

The training of a potential replacement begins the minute the manager is settled into a position. It's a mistake to delay it until the manager is getting impatient to move on to bigger and better things. It may be more than a mistake, it may be too late. From the very beginning, evaluate staff members as potential managers. Could they cut the mustard sitting in the manager's chair?

How to Evaluate Staff Members as Potential Candidates for Promotion

What characteristics should a manager look for that may indicate if staff members have the stuff to move up? Raw sales ability is not enough, even though it is the criterion most often used. Many very effective salespeople could never be good managers. Couldn't the same list of attributes that makes a manager a good candidate for a second promotion be used as a general guide for management potential? Yes, to a degree. But many of the items on the list are related to performance in a manager's role. The same yardstick can't be used for someone who's never been in that spot.

Eight Characteristics That Identify the Potential Manager

The things to keep a beady eye on are those traits known from experience that show some leadership ability. What are these characteristics?

1. A person who is well organized.
2. A person who has a good sales record.
3. A person who is enthusiastic.
4. A person who is ambitious.
5. A person who is knowledgeable about the product line.
6. A person who is respected by others in the office (as opposed to just liked).
7. A person who is trustworthy.
8. A person who desperately wants the manager's job. (Ambition is a terrific qualifier. The person who wants the job the most will work the hardest to keep it.)

How to Groom Someone for Management

How, exactly, is a person "groomed" to become a manager? Begin by dispensing responsibility in small doses. A manager might ask the person to take care of the details relating to a sales meeting. This includes finding the site, arranging for the room, sending out the notice, and perhaps working on the agenda, including speaking on several topics.

Another responsibility that might be given this person would be to take the lead role in any new products the company offers. The management candidate could be the one designated to be the first in the office to learn how to operate the new product, the best way to demo it, and the applications that will help sell the product. He or she would then pass along this information to the others on the staff.

A third responsibility might be to ask the person to work with another salesperson who appears to be floundering. A similar idea might be to make the person the sales trainer for the rookies on the staff.

Still another thought might be to give the person minor decision-making responsibility during the manager's absence.

Make Sure the Management Candidate Is Willing

When dispensing these responsibilities, the manager must determine how well they are received by the person being groomed. If the person laps them up and begs for more, there's a potential manager on the staff. If the responsibility is accepted reluctantly, or with grumbling, or, worse yet, handled poorly, then perhaps the manager had better look elsewhere.

Bringing Along a Management Candidate Slowly

When dispensing extra assignments, don't pile on so much responsibility that the person's personal sales and income suffers. That will breed resentment, or withdrawal. The best situation is when the manager is able to compensate the person for any extra effort. This compensation could be in the form of an override on a trainee's sales, or maybe some of the commissions from a vacant territory, or a prime house account, or a bigger expense budget, or a better-grade company car, or whatever.

Avoiding the Appearance of Favoritism

One thing managers must avoid is the appearance of favoritism. Make the person you're grooming work hard for each plum received. In fact, this person should be putting out more effort than anyone else on the staff, excepting the manager. While giving out additional responsibility, never appoint the managerial candidate as a straw boss, giving direction to the sales staff in the manager's absence—unless he or she has actually been appointed an assistant manager. The staff, or any other staff, will not easily take direction from someone they regard as one of their peers.

Using Competition for a Managerial Position to Improve Overall Performance

One of the best situations a manager can be blessed with is having several potential managers on staff. Let natural competitiveness take over and watch them work their tails off for position. At least this situation is good as long as the competition continues. Once a choice has been made, the manager loses those who have not been selected. In fact, avoid making a choice unless it is absolutely necessary. Groom both candidates as a possible successor until circumstances force a choice. That's what senior management does all the time to stimulate competition among area sales managers. It works, doesn't it?

"Advertising" the Candidate for Management

The manager's grooming job isn't going to do any good unless senior management learns that there is a managerial candidate on staff. They learn about the candidate from the manager seeking promotion. This educational job is accomplished via the employee evaluation form if the company uses it. A more effective, short-term method is to praise the person's abilities whenever the opportunity arises. "Ed really has his territory organized. I can always count on him to do a good job" is one not-too-subtle way to get the message across. It's possible to be even more direct and say, "Ed is ready for more responsibility. He's chomping at the bit." The same message can be delivered via memo.

Arrange for the boss to be exposed to the candidate the next time he or she is in town. Have the candidate pick up the boss at the airport or make an important call with him or provide the background on an important sales project. Appointing someone as a project leader is a good way to bring attention to that person.

Management Candidates Reflect on Their Sponsors

Of course, only candidates who would make good managers must be selected. Don't use "grooming" in the cosmetic sense to just give someone the appearance of a leader. Even if the manager who made the recommendation has moved on to something better, his or her reputation suffers if a loser has been picked. If managers anxious for promotion don't have good candidates for replacement on staff, they shouldn't try to manufacture one from straw.

In the first place, the tactic probably wouldn't work. The person selected probably would not withstand senior management inspection, and the manager making the recommendation would get a reputation for poor judgment. Another problem is that it could prevent a really qualified person in another area from moving up.

Polishing Leadership Skills in Management Candidates

Part of the grooming process is coaching the person selected in managerial skills. If there are rough spots, see that they are polished. Emphasize leadership. Go over the nitty-gritty details of management that every manager has been required to master. Discuss the value of motivation. Convince the person of the importance of paperwork if these tasks are currently being ignored. Be a confidant, a teacher. Most important, let the person know that the boss is on his or her side.

Confiding in a Management Candidate

Should the person know what's going on, that there are great expectations for the future? The manager should let him or her know as much as practicable without making specific promises that may not be possible to keep. Unless a promotion can be guaranteed, don't offer one. However, every manager uses possibilities as a motivator for better performance. Managers should use the possibility of promotion as a carrot to get this performance while building their own bridges to the next management level.

Embracing Change

There is no question that the trend toward corporate downsizing and reengineering has put more pressure on sales managers at every level. Performance will always be the key by which most sales managers are measured. There are, however, other factors that will contribute to individual success—or possible outplacement. Of these factors, none is more important than an open and inquisitive attitude. Senior management may reconstruct the sales function, redefine lines of authority, set new standards, or ask the manager to do twice the job with half the staff. Today's managers must not only be flexible to these innovations, they must embrace change. Nothing is more important to success.

What Else Managers Need to Know to Advance to Senior Management

When everything is in place, when the area is performing at better-than-expected levels, when area reports are eagerly anticipated in the home office, when planning is first-rate, when the manager is respected, when all the managerial skills have been mastered, when senior management recognizes these skills, when a replacement has been trained, when peers have been outdone, then a manager is ready to move on. And this kind of manager will move on.

The second level of management won't be nearly as difficult to master. The skills necessary from now on will be a refinement of the things already learned. They may be more intensified, and at every level the stakes become higher—but now the manager know everything necessary to go all the way to the top. Good luck and keep climbing!

Chapter Twenty-One

How to Survive the Very First Managerial Assignment

Why Salespeople Are Promoted to Management

Most salespeople are promoted to management positions because they know how to sell. Consistently beating quota doesn't necessarily endow a person with management skills, but it's the best criterion available. Unlike some other management positions, sales managers must have had some practical experience in the field before they are ready to lead other salespeople.

The Entry Fee into Management

More than one company charges an "entry fee" into management. Often, a beginning sales manager won't make as much money as a successful salesperson running a lucrative territory. This seems unfair, but it isn't. The successful salesperson is performing at company standards. The new sales manager has yet to prove this level of performance.

Four Similarities Between Running a Territory and Managing an Area

Many of the skills salespeople acquire when successfully running a territory are useful to them when they become managers. Some of these skills are

1. Good time management. Effective salespeople are able to budget their time well. This ability is even more important to a manager. There are even more demands on the manager, more choices to make, more details that require attention. Skillful management of time is the path to a senior sales management position.

2. Comprehensive product knowledge. The quota-busting salesperson knows the product line inside-out. This knowledge is also vital to the sales manager. The salesperson uses product knowledge to turn prospects into customers. The manager teaches the sales force to do the same thing.

3. Excellent communication skills. Successful salespeople possess good interpersonal skills. They get their points across and understand what the other person is really trying to say. For a manager, this skill is a basic requirement. The manager communicates at three levels: to staff members, to important customers, and to senior managers within the company.

4. Good organizational ability. The successful salesperson knows where all the important prospects within the territory are located. Their briefcases always have the right literature. Their records are accurate. Their reports are turned in on time. Some salespeople can get by without good organizational skills. The manager cannot. It's a vital part of the job.

The Ten Major Responsibilities of a Sales Manager

What responsibilities can the beginning sales manager expect? Here is a list of the most common, regardless of the industry.

1. Seeing that the area's quota assignment is met. The salesperson has a responsibility for meeting a territory quota assignment. Sales managers have many territories they oversee. It's important that all territories meet quota objectives. Managers are like jugglers keeping many balls in the air. If one ball falls, the performance is a failure.

2. Selecting, training, guiding, monitoring, and motivating a sales staff. This is the task that requires the greatest managerial skill and attention. No matter what the industry, the sales manager is always in the people business.

3. Keeping senior managers informed of the sales situation in the area. This means grinding out an endless string of reports: weekly sales summaries, monthly performance figures, forecasts, expense reports, competitive activity, inventory levels.

4. Responding to management demands. If there's a special action required of the area, the field person in charge is responsible for getting it done. This is the person who puts out local fires.

5. Handling a local budget. The manager is in charge of monitoring staff travel expenses and perhaps office expenses as well.

6. Boosting employee morale. Not the least of a field manager's responsibilities is keeping up the spirits of staff members and seeing that they remain a hard-charging bunch that believes the job can be done.

7. Explaining and defending company policy to staff members. The local manager interprets the actions of the company to local sales employees.

8. Representing the company to the business community. The field sales manager is the company's ambassador to the local community. The local attitude toward the company is largely dependent on how the field sales manager conducts business. They also interpret local business conditions to the company.

9. Replacing nonperformers. Unfortunately, one of the duties of a field manager is to replace staff members who cannot do the job required.

10. Entertaining visiting dignitaries. When senior management visits the local scene, it's up to the local field manager to see that their schedule demands are met.

The Dirty Dozen: 12 Common Mistakes New Managers Make

Most salespeople are promoted to management because they are very good at selling. That doesn't necessarily make them good managers. The most common mistakes of the "greenhorn" manager are as follows:

1. They don't delegate. They want to do everything themselves and are unwilling to trust sales crew members with important tasks and customers.

2. They try to be "one of the guys." The new sales manager has a different responsibility and new authority. It's just not possible to maintain the same relationship with sales team members.

3. They play favorites. They have old chums or drinking buddies who get all the plum assignments. Of course, everyone else on the team feels this is unfair.

4. They take over sales situations. On joint calls, the new manager will "take over" from the salesperson. Not only does the account lose respect for the salesperson, that person hasn't learned anything.

5. They bark out orders rather than motivate. Many new sales managers seem to think that authority is exercised by being stern and never explaining.

6. They apologize for the company. When a new direction is given by senior management, some new sales managers will show the sales crew through word and action that they disagree with it. What they don't realize is that they are part of management now.

7. They keep plum accounts and territories for themselves. This is greed and stupidity at work. Sales managers who behave in this manner won't be trusted by the salespeople who report to them.

8. They take all the credit. If anything good happens in the branch or district, this type of sales manager will let senior management know that it's entirely due to his or her efforts. Staff members had nothing to do with any success.

9. They don't listen. If a salesperson has a problem closing an account or a situation in the territory, no use bringing it to these sales managers. They won't pay any attention.

10. They second-guess their salespeople. Their every conversation begins with "You should have told the prospect this . . . ," or "Why did you say that?" These sales managers aren't trying to teach when they use these tactics. They're merely criticizing.

11. They delay telling senior management about serious problems. By the time senior management finds out, a tiny blaze has become a forest fire, and the new manager is in serious trouble.

12. Their management style is uneven. They will be critical and demanding one moment, jovial and kidding with the crew the next. Salespeople never know which manager, Jekyll or Hyde, will show up on any given day.

Other Management Responsibilities

In some companies a local sales manager may also be responsible for the service and administrative personnel who work in the local sales office. The sales manager may also be responsible for the space where the office is located. This means negotiating leases, getting phone lines installed, buying office machines and supplies, allocating parking space, and a host of administrative tasks. The local sales manager may also be responsible for helping the credit department collect bad debts.

The Phenomenon of Being Promoted in Place

Many times a promotion to management requires a person to take over the very office where he or she had been working as a territory salesperson. One day the person is just another member of the gang, laughing and joking with peers. The next day, the person is running the local show. This phenomenon will occur even more frequently as the costs to relocate people escalate.

Five Advantages of Being Promoted in Place

The new manager whose first assignment is the old office has some definite advantages. These are

1. The territory is familiar. There's no need to learn a geography lesson while the managerial ropes are being mastered. The manager doesn't have to find a place to live. There's no problem with acquiring new friends, getting the kids into a good school, and finding a local dentist. It's much easier to concentrate on the job at hand.

2. The new manager probably knows the strengths and weaknesses of everyone in the office. The manager knows who can be left alone to do the job and who needs close attention.

3. The new manager knows the local market conditions. The person promoted in place knows the area customers and prospects; understands the local economy; is familiar with the competition, the areas of growth, and the business style that fits the community.

4. The new manager is already aware of any specific problems facing the local operation. He or she knows what's working and what needs fixing. There aren't the surprises that frequently face a new boss that comes in from another location.

5. It's easier for managers promoted in place to get off to a flying start because they're taking off from a familiar runway.

Three Disadvantages of Being Promoted in Place

There are also handicaps to being promoted in place. The most significant of these are

1. The people in the office remember the new manager when he or she was just an ordinary salesperson. They may have difficulty accepting the manager in a new role.
2. There may be jealousy and resentment from one or two staff members who believe they deserved the promotion more than the person who got it.
3. Some former colleagues may try to retain the same relationship with the new manager that they had before the promotion. Old friends may expect favored treatment. Others are almost insubordinate.

How to Handle an In-Place Promotion: Five Actions to Take

Managers promoted in place can expect to have their authority challenged just as children test their parent's authority. This challenge is often the new manager's first test. There are several actions to take to handle this situation. These are:

1. Bring former contemporaries into the office for private meetings. Tell them their help is needed to get off to the right start.
2. Ask for suggestions on how the area's goals can be met. They will be flattered, and they may have some good ideas that will improve the performance of the area.
3. Discuss situations in individual territories. Ask what support is needed to meet area quotas. Listen to gripes. Fix the legitimate problems that need fixing.
4. Offer to make the area a breeding ground for future managers. Tell staff members the qualities that identify management potential. These include maturity, leadership, origination, and *cooperation*.
5. Keep all promises made.

Five Things Not to Do When Promoted in Place

Specific actions should be avoided when promoted in place. These are the things that won't work:

1. Don't play favorites with old cronies. Let staff members know there will be no plum assignments or pets based on past relationships. Reward those who deserve rewards.
2. Don't try to be "one of the boys." Many a new manager has tried this approach, and it just doesn't work. That doesn't mean the new manager must be aloof or standoffish, but it's not possible to behave the same way as before and get the respect a leader must have to be effective.
3. Don't begin a managerial assignment by changing everything in sight. Even if changes are needed, there'll be plenty of time for the manager to put a personal stamp on the operation.
4. Don't begin as a martinet, barking out orders, threatening dismissals, and demanding blind obedience. It's not the way to exercise real authority.
5. Don't begin with wholesale firings. Good people will be lost. By the time replacements are trained, the new manager can forget about getting off to a fast start. The home office will wonder if the new manager is out of control.

Training for the New Manager

Large companies may have in-house training programs for middle-management sales managers. Smaller companies allow their managers to attend sales management schools and seminars. Correspondence courses and evening college courses are also available. Certainly, most beginning managers are advised and counseled by the senior managers within the company. This training and guidance is vital to a new manager's continued success. It's up to every manager to see to it that his or her further education is not neglected.

11 Tips for Handling People

The people part of a new manager's responsibility is the part that can be overwhelming. Here are some tips on communicating with employees:

1. Practice creating dialogues, not monologues. Respect opinions different from your own.
2. It's better to underreact rather than overreact. Situations escalate when people match one another in intensity.
3. Rehearse when facing a difficult conversation with an employee. Practice saying exactly the message that must be conveyed.
4. Remember to use the feel-felt-found approach when speaking with staff members. This helps build a bridge to employees. Try to phrase things this way:

   "I know how you *feel*."

   "I *felt* that way myself once."

   "I have *found* that . . ."

5. Don't patronize or discount employees when speaking to them.
6. Be assertive. State views or give directions in a firm but nonaggressive way.
7. Be precise. When an assignment must be carried out, say so in no uncertain terms.
8. Be complimentary. Praise those staff members who deserve it.
9. Be sincere. Don't offer praise if it's not deserved.
10. Deliver company regulations and new programs with a positive attitude. Managers should never announce new policies in a manner that suggests disagreement or disapproval.
11. Don't debate. While it's important to listen to employee views, a meeting with a staff member is not a test of verbal skills.

Six Tips on Working with Senior Management

The new sales manager is under a microscope. The eyes looking through the magnifier are the company's senior managers, wondering if the right person has been promoted. There are actions the new manager can take that will make senior managers more comfortable. These actions are:

1. Report frequently. Nothing is more disquieting to senior managers than silence. They like to know what's going on at all times. Make sure that all required reports are in on time.
2. Be candid. If there's a pending problem, don't sweep it under the rug.
3. Be resourceful. While pending problems should be reported, the manager should suggest solutions to these problems.
4. Be forthright. If there's a management policy that doesn't seem right, say so.
5. Be conciliatory. If senior managers insist on a policy against objections, do the best job possible to make that policy work.
6. Be successful. The other five rules aren't nearly as important as this one. The manager who makes the company's goals for the area year after year is the manager who is promoted.

A Final Word for the New Manager

Within the first two weeks of a new managerial assignment, the new manager will wonder if the title is worth the extra grief. There are so many more demands on the manager's time. Superiors demand to know what's happening in the manager's area of responsibility. Staff members request help with problems. Customers, aware of the manager's new "clout," want special favors. The new paperwork requirements are overwhelming. The new manager's income may even have deteriorated.

The new manager soon learns that authority has its frustrations. Giving direction isn't as simple as it appeared when the manager ran a territory. There's a difference between asking that something be done and getting it done.

But sales management can be rewarding. The rewards are not just in financial terms, though these can be substantial once the manager has advanced to the second rung and beyond. There are rewards in nurturing staff members and watching them grow. There are rewards in having a hand in the company's achieving objectives, and even setting objectives to reach. There are rewards in gaining respect, in commanding, in molding and shaping the direction of a company.

Those rewards may seem a long way distant for the manager just starting out. But they are there and they are attainable. Good luck and get going!

Chapter Twenty-Two

How to Make Ethics and Integrity Valuable Sales Tools

What's right is what feels good afterward.

—Ernest Hemingway

Why an Ethical Code of Conduct Is Necessary

Salesmanship is about establishing trust, and trust is established by behaving in an ethical manner.* The equation is very simple: Want to improve sales performance? Raise the company's ethical standards? The salesperson with a "gift of gab" is overrated. What is more important is whether the prospect *believes* what is being presented. Persuasion begins with credibility.

---

*One of my regrets regarding the first edition of *Desk Book* was the omission of material on ethics. That neglect is corrected here. Nothing is more important to our profession, or more critical to our individual success, then strong ethical conduct. That's why this chapter was saved for last.

How to Establish Trust

The first step toward building trust is by becoming trustworthy. Deserve the trust and you'll get it. The first step in the trust-building process is to establish an ethical code of conduct. Establishing the company's ethical standards is the responsibility of senior management. The leaders of an organization set its moral tone. It is a trickle-down process. It's up to branch, district, regional, and national sales managers to make sure every employee, both veteran and trainee, understands the company's ethical code. They also must abide by it themselves. An ethical code that is ignored by managers whenever they find it inconvenient is soon ignored by every employee in the company.

The Ethical Standards Sales Managers Should Set for Themselves: A 14-Point Program

Sales managers can expect that their sales personnel will profit more through example than by lectures or written notices. In other words, if the manager has high personal ethical standards, so will members of the sales crew. Lip service alone doesn't work. To expect ethical behavior, behave ethically.

It's also a great morale booster to be working for an ethical manager because each member of the sales crew knows that he or she will be treated fairly. Here's a simple code of sales managers' conduct:

1. Be convinced that the best path to success is through being honest and ethical. It's actually the easiest path to success. "Sell" that conviction to members of your sales staff.
2. Be forthright and candid with everybody on the sales team. An atmosphere of secrecy makes staff members suspect there is something to hide. (If you keep secrets from them, they'll keep secrets from you.)

3. Respect confidences. It is not ethical to repeat information given to you in confidence.
4. Don't disparage senior management to the sales team. You are a member of senior management as far as they're concerned.
5. Don't disparage any member of the sales team to senior management. If you have a personnel problem, they'll expect you to deal with it not complain about it.
6. Give sales team members full credit for their accomplishments. Never take credit for a subordinate's work or ideas.
7. Never lie or misrepresent something to a prospect or customer.
8. Never ask a subordinate to lie or misrepresent something to a prospect or customer.
9. Never discuss one employee's performance with another on the same. level.
10. If a salesperson misrepresents something to a prospect or customer while you're on a joint call together, immediately correct the "misunderstanding." Correct it again with the salesperson when you're outside the prospect's office critiquing the call.
11. Keep personal prejudices out of performance evaluations and reports. Base scores strictly on performance and the employee's contribution.
12. Don't "stick" one salesperson with poor accounts or a substandard territory simply because you don't like that employee.
13. Don't give "pets" plum assignments simply because they kiss up to you. In fact, be wary of kisser-uppers. They are often mediocre performers.
14. Bend over backward to make the most tolerant interpretation possible of bonus and contest rules so salespeople recognize that there is a fair chance that their efforts will be rewarded.

Adopting these standards will have an almost magical effect on the sales team. They'll feel more secure, work harder for you, and present you with fewer fires to extinguish. You'll actually be able to spend more time managing your people.

How to Train Salespeople to Conduct Themselves Ethically

Don't expect new salespeople to walk through the door fully aware of the company's ethical standards. They must be taught those standards, and a discussion of the ethical conduct required of sales staff members should be part of every new employee's indoctrination process. The topic should enjoy a place of prominence on the training agenda to ensure that new hires take it seriously. Put the code in writing so there is no confusion over the company's standards.

Any training is a continuous process. Veteran salespeople should be reminded of the company's ethical standards at sales meetings, product-training sessions, and during joint calls with sales managers. Managers should "teach by example" through practicing ethical behavior in their dealings with prospects, customers, and the salespeople on their staffs.

11 Benefits of a Strong Ethical Code

What are the specific benefits of ethical conduct? (A good sales pitch always emphasizes benefits.) Here's what a strong ethical code does for any sales program:

1. It enhances the company's reputation. Prospects contact the company because they've heard it's reliable.
2. It builds customer loyalty. Customers know they won't be "taken" by dealing with the company.
3. It produces high morale among employees. People prefer to work for a company that is highly regarded. Salespeople know that they won't have to compromise their own ethical standards.
4. It creates a positive "we can do anything" attitude among employees.
5. It makes the selling job easier because prospects begin to believe what the salesperson is telling them. ("Hey, she's from Old Reliable Industries. They don't shade the truth over there.")

6. There are fewer problems with customers and few fires to extinguish. More time can be spent selling.
7. Integrity becomes a "value-added" to the product line. Customers are willing to pay extra for it.
8. There's more repeat business. Customers want the company back because they know what to expect.
9. When an honest mistake has been made or when the company has a problem performing as promised, customers are more likely to be patient. They give the company a chance to fix what's wrong.
10. When an existing customer is looking for something new, they're more likely to give an ethical supplier first crack at this new business. They know they'll get an honest appraisal of whether the company can supply this new requirement.
11. Integrity locks out the competition. Satisfied customers don't want to go anywhere else. They know they may get a lower price, but they aren't sure they'll get fair treatment.

That's a long list of benefits and one that can "sell" both management and sales crew alike on the advantages of adopting a strong ethical code.

A Sales Manager's Personal Code of Business Conduct

It's not enough for sales managers or salespeople to abide by the company's code of conduct: they should also establish their own ethical standards. No, this isn't a self-righteous sermon on morality. *Strong ethical standards make it easier to sell.* Establish them for purely selfish reasons.

By business conduct, we mean the practices conducted throughout the sales process, including all the steps from the first approach to the prospect up to the time the customer declares satisfaction that the product or service is as represented.

A Dozen Ethical Rules Applicable to Any Salesperson in Any Company

1. It's okay to wash and polish a car before offering it for sales, but it's not okay to push back the odometer. In other words, put the product in its best possible light, but don't misrepresent yourself, the company, or the product.

2. Do whatever you say you're going to do. That includes the little things such as phoning when you say you're going to phone, being where you say you'll be. Don't make promises easily, but keep the promises you make. (Nothing builds trust more quickly than this kind of conduct.)

3. Turn down an order now and again. If the prospect's intended use for the product or service is not a good one, inform him of this fact early in the game. This isn't heresy. The prospect usually finds out for himself before the sale is consummated, so much time is saved by both parties. It's even worse when the prospect actually buys something that is the wrong product for the application. The salesperson's golden selling hours are wasted trying to make things right. The sales manager makes "quick-fix" visits. The customer is left with a bad taste in the mouth and is frequently lost forever.

4. Develop a sense of personal responsibility toward your customers. They showed confidence and trust in you by buying something from your company based on the claims you made. Repay the compliment by making those claims come true.

5. Inform customers immediately when problems beyond your control occur. Has the production line broken down, causing the plant to be hopelessly behind schedule? If delivery schedules will be affected, tell the customer sooner rather than later. Keep Henry Kissinger's advice in mind: "What must be revealed eventually should be revealed immediately." Customers are much more likely to be patient if you level with them.

6. Buy a lunch or cup of coffee for a customer every now and then, but keep every cent of commission for yourself. Never offer to share a commission or give a kickback to a decision maker in

exchange for an order. This has nothing to do with salesmanship. It's called bribery.

7. Don't knock the competition. Doing so is counterproductive. During presentations concentrate on the positive aspects of your company's capabilities and product line. There's too little time available in front of prospects to waste it talking about the other guy.

8. Represent yourself first, even before the company you work for. This is consistent with good sales practice because the prospect is buying from the representative as well as the organization. The attitude of self-representation resolves any moral dilemmas should senior management request that a local manager or salesperson engage in unethical behavior for the "good of the company." (Unethical behavior never serves a company's long-range interests.)

9. Don't work for or represent companies you don't respect. They'll ask you to do things you know aren't right, and you'll wind up not respecting yourself.

10. Report information, both good and bad, to senior management in a timely manner. Sales managers shouldn't submit rosy projections when they know that sales will be a disaster this month; salespeople should promptly report when a good customer has been lost. Senior management hates surprises most of all.

11. Be respected among your peers. Deal with other managers and salespeople fairly. Don't backbite; never try to take another salesperson's accounts. You have enough on your plate working the territory the company assigned.

12. Don't relax ethical standards just because it's near the end of the month and quota attainment is still beyond the horizon. If it's the wrong thing to do on the first of the month, it's still wrong on the twenty-fifth.

Eight Specific Sales Benefits from a Strong Ethical Code

Does the above code seem difficult to practice? Is it too impractical? Think about the benefits it brings. Here are some specific goodies:

1. More sales, and more sales next year, and more sales the year after that.
2. More effective use of sales time.
3. More friends and deeper, longer-lasting business and personal relationships.
4. Fewer sleepless nights, because there are fewer problems to worry about.
5. Fewer jobs changes. Some managers and salespeople continually switch companies to escape the messes they've made.
6. Increased chances for promotion. Senior management recognizes that things go more smoothly in your areas of responsibility.
7. Impeccable personal reputation.
8. Less prospecting. Customers seek out ethical salespeople and suppliers.

Candor as a Sales Management Tool

Webster's Dictionary defines "candor" as "openness of heart, frankness, sincerity, honesty in expressing oneself." Sounds like dangerous stuff! What place does frankness have in a good sales pitch? If you tell them the truth, they may not buy!

Actually, candor is an excellent sales tool. For one thing, candor is such a rare commodity that prospects and customers will be disarmed by it. A statement such as; "I know that you've tentatively approved our Inter-Galactic Model ZZZ computer for purchase, but for your application, our less expensive Model AAA could do the job at considerably lower cost" will cause a new level of respect for the salesperson making the remark. Here's a salesperson who has the customer's best interests at heart! The customer may even begin to exchange confidences. Hidden agendas and "win-at-any-cost" attitudes get swept away. The company profits by learning what the customer really wants and what they're prepared to pay. The customer profits by learning what your company can efficiently provide and how much it must charge to make a reasonable profit.

So few companies use candor as a sales strategy that it can become a competitive advantage. ("Do business with Old Reliable. They tell it like it is.")

The Internal Benefits of Candor

Another benefit of candor as company policy is that it teaches salespeople to be candid with their managers. That means being candid about sales forecasts, candid about the situations within their territories and candid about the likelihood of closing impending deals. Branch, district, and regional managers in turn are able to provide senior management with more reliable forecasts. Problems are revealed earlier, when action to circumvent them is still possible. Nobody is carrying around a load of dark secrets.

The Candor Litmus Test: Practicing to Be Forthright

Lies of omission don't seem quite as wrong as deliberate misrepresentations. Things that remain unsaid can't be considered fabrications—can they? No successful salesperson is going to be so absurdly forthright as to inform a prospect that there is this single customer in Cedar Rapids, Iowa, who is not completely thrilled and delighted with the product. So sometimes it is difficult to decide what to tell a prospect and what to neglect. One way to decide is to ask the following three simple questions about every pending deal:

1. Does the prospect know all the vital facts? Is there critical information about this proposition that might cause the prospect to change his or her mind if it were revealed?
2. Does company management know all the facts about this pending deal? Is there something about this proposition that might cause the company to change the offer if it were revealed?
3. Is a conscious effort being made, at any level, to conceal important information from either the company or the prospect?

The answers to these questions make it self-evident whether more candor is needed in a specific situation.

Confronting Problems Head-on: How to React When Things Go Wrong

Some companies, and many sales managers, believe in a policy of "judicious neglect." Ignore problems and some of them go away. It's true, some problems do fade away of their own accord. Others begin as tiny sparks, easily stamped out in the beginning, but eventually become raging forest fires that require battalions of firefighters to extinguish.

It's up to sales managers to condition their sales staff members to prevent the nasty conflagrations by stamping out the tiny sparks. That means confronting problems head on. Here's how to do it:

1. When the company has difficulty performing as per agreement, let the customer know immediately. (It's okay to wait for a very *short* period if a contingency plan to handle the problem is being developed. You may wish to present the problem and the solution to deal with it at the same time.) You'll be surprised at how patient customers can be if they know that a problem is getting attention.

2. If a good customer has become dissatisfied with the company's product or service, inform management immediately. This is just common sense and self-survival. Bring in the heavy guns to help salvage a good account. If they fail, the responsibility for the loss is shared.

3. If information passed along in good faith to a prospect turns out to be incorrect, make an immediate amendment. Don't misrepresent the facts by accident or through ignorance.

Seven Reasons Why Knocking the Competition Doesn't Work

It shouldn't take the ethics of a saint to keep from knocking the competition. That's a sales strategy that just doesn't work. Volunteering an ornery word or two about the competition gives them an importance they may not have enjoyed before the salesperson brought up the subject. Here are the specific reasons why it doesn't work:

1. Prospects discount what a salesperson says in reference to the competition. They simply don't believe it. Salespeople who employ this tactic lose credibility.

2. Salespeople and sales managers get a limited amount of time in front of prospects. Why give up part of it talking about the competition? Wouldn't that time be better spent talking about the company and its products?

3. The prospect who has not considered a competitive company or product may suddenly decide that this alternative is worth investigating.

4. Knowledge about the competitive product line and the competitor's capabilities in general is often incomplete. Any false statement made about the competitor, even though the salesperson is honestly mistaken, brands that salesperson a liar. Everything else that salesperson says is now suspect. The salesperson's status as an "expert" is destroyed.

5. In the effort to get the "bad stuff" about the competition out into the open, the salesperson may neglect to accent some positive aspects of his or her own company's product line.

6. Refraining from engaging in competitive slander elevates the sales manager and salesperson a class above those who do. It's one way to win a reputation for integrity.

7. A good attitude to adopt about the competition is to simply ignore them. Concentrate on finding out what the prospects need and how your company can best fill those needs. Do that and the competition won't exist for you.

What to Do When the Boss Orders the Sales Manager to Engage in Unethical Behavior

Salespeople and managers are sometimes asked by their own management to do something they consider unethical. What to do? It's one thing to assume a posture of high moral indignation when nothing is at stake and quite another to refuse a direct order from a manager when the salesperson's job may be on the line. Here is a practical course of action:

1. Keep the problem within the management level where it originated. Running to senior management usually doesn't work. (It's a sad fact, but whistle blowers are not appreciated.) The most unreasonable boss making the most unreasonable request will appreciate an effort to keep the quarrel in the family.

2. Reason with the superior who made the request. Any decision to misinform a customer or prospect is not in the best long-term interest of the company. Relationships will suffer. Salespeople and sales mangers should be candid about their reluctance to engage in any unethical behavior. Reasons should be offered for why unethical actions are counterproductive.

3. Ask that the superior put the order requesting unethical behavior in writing. This request will often be enough to halt ill-considered acts. The consequences are now squarely on the superior's shoulders. A poor outcome will come back to haunt the boss, not the people who carried out the action.

4. If the order is given in writing, the salesperson should then offer a written rebuttal listing everything that could happen as a result of this action. Both documents are now on file. The superior won't be able to claim that he or she wasn't informed of the possible outcome. This step should handle most situations, unless the superior is most foolhardy.

5. If the superior still insists that the unethical action be taken with an account, the salesperson or manager *should relinquish the account.* Just give it up. Let someone else tell the customer or prospect a pack of lies. (If the situation goes this far, the salesperson should begin looking for a new job. He or she is working for an unscrupulous boss and perhaps an unscrupulous company.)

A Sample Ethics Test

Business conditions and situations change so rapidly that almost every deal today faces an ethical challenge. There is a simple test that sales managers can use to evaluate the ethics of any sales deal. Here it is:

1. Is the deal really in the best interests of the company? (For example, taking an order from a prospect or customer whose ability to pay is questionable may not be in the company's best interests.)
2. Is the deal really in the best interests of the customer? If you were the decision maker in the customer's organization knowing what you know as the salesperson, would you make this deal?
3. Has any information been deliberately concealed or omitted that would change the way the prospect or the company regards the deal?
4. Have any facts been misrepresented to the prospect or the company?
5. Would your anxiety immediately increase if this deal were consummated? If you're worried about what comes after, then something about this deal isn't right.)
6. Will someone, other than a competitor, be a loser because of this deal?

A Final Word on Ethics

Ethical standards should not be adopted because of any strong moral imperative, although that's never a bad beginning, but simply because it's good sales practice. Abiding by the standards is in the company's best interests. Adopting a strong ethical code makes the sales manager's job easier. In fact, it makes every employee's job easier. Ethical standards are not abstract rules printed in the company employee handbook and ignored ever after. In some circumstances there are no written rules covering a situation. That's the reason for the Hemingway quote at the beginning of this chapter. When in a dilemma about the correct ethical action to take, do what will make you feel good after it is over.

INDEX

A

Action plans, 10
    evaluation of, 21
Advertising
    classified ads, 84-88
    cooperative advertising, 355-56
    cost factors, 335-39
    and demand, 334
    direct-mail advertising, 351-55
    local advertising, 333
    magazine advertising, 343-44
    newspaper advertising, 339-42
    on-line, 198, 199
    pre-advertising planing, 334-35
    radio advertising, 346-50
    television advertising, 350-51
    Yellow Pages advertising, 344-46
Allowances, for expenses, 132-33
Answering service, for home office, 190

B

Background investigations, 97-101
    courtesies related to, 97-98
    credit check, 100
    educational history, 101
    necessity of, 97
    questions to ask, 98-100
Budget, 125-32
    expense items, 125-26, 129-30
    field operating budget, 129-32
    and forecasting, 126, 128
    sales staff preparation of, 131
    worksheet for, 127
Burnout, 290, 292-93
    solutions to, 292-93
By-exception method, for expenses, 139

C

Cable TV, advertising on, 351
Call report, 57-65
    benefits of, 67
    design of, 63
    detailed report, 58-60
    information gained from, 64-65
    narrative report, 60, 62-63
    and nonworking salespersons, 68-72, 74
    as reeducation tool, 68
    summary report, 60
    verification of, 72-74
Candor, as sales tool, 405-6
Casual model, sales forecast, 147
Cellular phones, 184
Chain-of-command, 43
Classified ads, 84-88
    cost factors, 85
    example of, 88
    expected responses, 88
    writing of, 85, 86-87
Coaching, sales trainee, 213-15
Commission
    draw against commission, 110-11, 123
    and house accounts, 114-17
    salary plus commission, 111, 123
    salary plus commission plus draw, 111-12, 123
    straight commission, 109-10, 123
Communication, 17-20
    ideal system, steps toward, 19-20
    sales communication system, 18
Communication technology
    beepers/pagers, 184
    cellular phones, 184
    and customer/supplier relationship, 186
    database, 192-96
    effects on sales meetings, 187
    electronic bulletin boards, 198, 199
    E-mail, 185
    fax machine, 196
    fax machines, 183-84
    home shopping networks, 201-2
    Information Superhighway, 201
    Internet, 196-98, 200-201
    on-line information, 183
    phone mail, 184-85

teleconferencing, 185
WorldWide Web, 199
Compensation methods
draw against commission, 110-11, 123
for house accounts, 116-17
salary plus bonus, 111
salary plus commission, 111, 123
salary plus commission plus draw, 111-12, 123
straight commission, 109-10, 123
straight salary, 110, 123
Compensation plans
compensation score sheet, 123
incentive compensation, 108
mistakes related to, 113-14
and motivation, 108-9, 230-31
objectives of, 105-6, 114
and overmanaging, 108
sales contests, 117-20
sales manager compensation, 112-13
and salesperson needs, 107
Competition, knocking, negative aspects of, 408
Computers, types of, 191
Cooperative advertising, 355-56
advantages/disadvantages of, 355-56
Customer asset management, 369
Customer profile sheet, 53-55

D

Database, 192-96
creating custom database, 195-96
sources for, 194-95
types of information in, 193
Dealers, 303-11, 320
activities of, 303-4
attracting dealers, guidelines for, 309-10
dealer agreement, example of, 311
downside of, 305
good dealer, characteristics of, 305-6
locating good dealers, 306-7
price, establishment of, 308-9
and product exclusivity, 304
recruiting dealers, 307-8
sales support for, 305
selling objectives, 304
Delphi method, sales forecast, 158
Direct-mail advertising, 351-55
advantages/disadvantages of, 351
cost factors, 355
effectiveness of, 352
increasing responses, methods for, 354-55
mailing list, 352-53
parts of direct-mail package, 353
response form, 354
writing piece, guidelines for, 353-54
Direct marketing, advantages/disadvantages, 302
Distributors, 312-14, 320, 327-32
activities of, 312
attracting good distributor, 313
mass distribution, working with, 329-31
new power of, 327-28
niches of, 328-29
reactions against giant distributors, 332
services of, 312
Downsizing, warning signs, 48-49

E

Electronic bulletin boards, 198, 199
E-mail, 185
Employment at will, 101
Ethics
benefits of ethical code, 401-2
candor and sales, 405-7
ethical rules for salespeople, 403-4
ethical standards, listing of, 399-400
ethics test, 410
head-on approach to problems, 407
necessity of ethical code, 398
order to perform unethical act, 408-9
personal code of business conduct, 402
sales benefits and ethics, 404-5
training salespeople in, 401
Expense control
bonus plan in, 143-44
and budget, 125-32
expense report form, 134-37
expenses by exception, 139
fixed expenses, 132
guidelines for, 144-45
necessity of, 125
per diem rate, 139
phony expense claims, 139-40, 142-43
sales manager function in, 128
travel expenses, 132-38
verification of expense items, 140-42
warning signs of overspending, 144

F

Fax machine, 183-84, 196
for home office, 190
selling by, 196
Field training, 211-14

Financial incentives, 17
Forecasting, and budget, 126, 128

G

Gap, sales volume, 10, 11-13
Goal-setting, and motivation, 243

H

Hiring
- applicant screening guidelines, 91-92
- background investigations, 97-101
- first impressions, 92
- follow-up interviews, 94-95
- formal offer, 101-4
- hiring mistakes, 80-81, 93
- initial interview, 92-93
- job description, 78
- job hopper, recognition of, 94
- job offer, 97
- needs for more staff, 76-77
- rating job candidates, 95-96
- recruitment methods, 81-88
- and resumes, 88-90
- sales personnel requisition, 77, 79
- sales talent, recognition of, 80
- senior management approval of candidates, 96
- time for, 75-76

Historical data, in sales forecast, 148-50
Historical records, 53
Home office, 188-92
- advantages/disadvantages of, 188-89
- furnishing for, 190-92
- working with, 44-45

Home shopping networks, 201-2, 321
House accounts
- compensation for, 116-17
- negative aspects of, 114-16

I

Indirect marketing, 301
- advantages/disadvantages, 302-3

Information Superhighway, 201
Internet, 196-98, 200-201
- access to, 198
- advertising on, 198
- recruitment on, 83

J

Job description, 78

L

Lead cards, trade shows, 276-78
Leader
- versus boss, 1-2
- leadership methods, 3-4
- traits of potential leader, 17

Lease, office lease, 172-77
Loyalty
- importance of, 43-44, 50
- rewards from, 44

M

Magazine advertising, 343-44
- advantages/disadvantages of, 343
- cost factors, 344

Mail order, 320
Mailroom facilities, 180
Management
- definition of, 2
- by intimidation, 4

Management by exception, 65
Managers. *See* Sales managers
Manufacturers' representatives, 314-16, 321
- advantages/disadvantages to use of, 315-16
- compensation of, 314-15
- locating reps, 316

Marketing
- direct marketing, 302
- indirect marketing, 301, 302-3
- compared to sales, 42

Marketing function, organization of, 41
Mass merchants, 320-21
Meetings
- individual with staff members, 6-9
- to meet new staff members, 6
- *See also* Sales meetings

Motivation
- common motivators, 232-36
- and compensation plan, 108-9, 230-31
- of manager, 121
- manager role in, 232, 236
- and promotion, 240-42
- and sales contests, 236-37
- self-motivation, 242-44
- types of motivators, 8, 16-17

N

Narrative report, 60, 62-63
Newspaper advertising, 339-42
- advantages/disadvantages, 340

cost factors, 340-41
design of ad, 342
design of, 341
position of ad, 341
repetition of ad, importance of, 342

O

Offer letter, for job candidate, 101-4
Office equipment, 178
Office lease, 172-77
general form, 174-77
legal aspects, 173
Office politics, 46-48, 50
effects on sales manager, 47
Office services, 191-92
Office space
cost for, 172
lease for, 172-77
move into, 180-81
necessity of, 167-68, 169-70
preparation for opening office, 177-80
real estate agent, use of, 171-72
selecting location for, 170-71
shared office facilities, 168-69
Organizational structure
examples of, 40
sales manager concerns about, 39
Organization chart, examples of, 37

P

Packagers, 321
Per diem rate, for expenses, 139
Performance
managerial responsibilities in, 284-85
See also Poor performance
Performance reviews, importance of, 14
Phone mail, 184-85
Phone system, 177-78
Poor performance
actions to avoid, 294
and burnout, 290, 292-93
dialog with salesperson about, 287-88
early-warning signs, 281-83
five-step improvement program for, 290
incremental goals, setting of, 288-89
managerial responsibility in, 285, 291
reasons for, 290-92
setting higher expectations for, 285-87
and termination, 295-99
Praise, 8, 17
Probation, 295-96
Promotion, 17, 240-42
assessment of candidates for, 240-41, 378-79, 380-81
giving false hopes about, 242
grooming successors for management, 380
holding back promotion, 241
and motivation, 240-42
new manager, compensation of, 121-22, 387
promotion in place, 391-94
of sales managers, 378-80
Public speaking, 258-59
tips for, 259-60

Q

Qualitative method, sales forecast, 147

R

Radio advertising, 346-50
advantages/disadvantages of, 346, 347-48
buying time, 348-49
decision-making about ads, 347
script, writing of, 349-50
Real estate agent, use of, 171-72
Recognition, 17
Recruitment, 81-88
classified ads, 84-88
of former sales representatives, 83
free sources, 83-84
inside company, 81-82
on Internet, 83
from professional connections, 82
through referrals, 82
Reengineering, 49
applied to sales, 42
Regional summary report, 27
Reimbursement systems, for expenses, 133-34
Resumes, 88-90
example of, 90
important points of, 88-90
Retailers, 320
Review process, 21-35
adjustment of sales targets, 32-33
benefits of, 24, 29
follow-up of, 30-31
importance of, 21-22
points covered in, 22-23
as positive experience, 31
of remote sales personnel, 30

review questions, 29-30
sales force attitude towards, 31
time for, 32

S

Salary. *See* Compensation methods
Sales, compared to marketing, 42
Sales channel
channel in trouble, warning signs, 325-26
failure of, 326-27
importance of, 319
moving products into, 322-23
multiple channels, use of, 319-20
replacing distribution channels, 323-24
types of, 320-21
Sales contests, 117-20, 236-37
guidelines for, 117-18, 119-20
objectives of, 236-37
post-contest sales, 120
postcontest sales, 239-40
posting of results, 238
prizes, 118-19
purpose of, 117
team contests, 238-39
time periods for, 236
types of, 237
Sales drop, actions to take, 159-60
Sales force automation
advantages/disadvantages of, 371-73
advantages of, 361-62
and customer, 369-71
example of application, 360-61
functions of system, 358
implementation of system, 373-75
installation of system, 368
and territory balancing, 362-67
types of programs, 358-59
Sales forecast
adjustment of forecasts, 156-57
blue-sky projections, 154
comparing data, 156
Delphi method, 158
forecasting chart, 153-55
forecasting meetings, 157
historical data, use of, 148-50
importance of, 146-47
methods for, 147
midyear corrections, 160-62
national accounts, use in, 153
objections over quota assignments, 163-66
staff member participation in, 152-53
variable data in, 150-51
worksheet for, 152
Sales function, organization of, 41
Sales itinerary sheet, 56-57
Sales managers
boss as unpopular, 47-48
common mistakes made by, 390-91
communication with employees, guidelines for, 395
dealing with senior management, 396
good manager, characteristics of, 4-5, 381
grooming person for management, 381-85
loyalty of, 43-44, 47, 50
new manager, compensation of, 121-22
promotion of, 378-80
promotion in place, 391-94
responsibilities of, 388-90
running territory, skills required, 388
staff interview of, 8-9
training for, 394
Sales meetings
agenda, 253-54
breaks, 256
cost factors, 246
evening sessions, 256
food/beverage service, 257
guest speakers, 255
hotel accommodations, 250
keeping to schedule, 260-61
office meetings, 247-48
planning for, 248-49
pre-meeting site inspection, 250-51
private meetings, 256-57
purposes of, 245-46
at resorts, 248
seating arrangements, 251
site selection, 249
smoking at, 258
sound systems, 252-53
specialized sessions, 255
teleconferencing, 261-63
travel arrangements, 249-50
Sales objectives
action plans, 10
assistance in meeting objectives, 13
business forecast form, 24, 26
unmet objectives, 34
Sales personnel requisition, 77, 79
Sales projections, charting form, 28

Sales quotas, objections to quota assignments, 163-66
Sales reports, 42-43
call report, 57-65
customer profile sheet, 53-55
deadlines for, 66-67
historical records, 53
narrative report, 60, 62-63
necessity of, 51-52, 53
periodic review of, 52-53
sales itinerary sheet, 56-57
summary report, 60
See also Call report
Sales targets, 32-33
adjusting, 32
off schedule targets, 33
Sales training
with coach, 213-15
college night courses, 227
critique of sales call, 215-16, 218-19
field training, 211-14
formal training program, 206
joint calls approach, 213-14
manager role in, 203-4, 205-6, 211-12, 227-28
multiple training sessions, 210
necessity of continuous training, 204-5
questions as training tool, 214, 216-18
reinforcing good sales habits, 219-21
selling cycles, 221
seminars, 226-27
setting for, 207
in small companies, 225-27
teaching methods, 207-9
topics covered, 209-10
for veteran salespeople, 222-25
Sales volume
gap in, 10, 11-13
last year, analysis of, 10-11
Selling cycles, 221
Seminars, sales training, 226-27
Staff
common purpose, building in, 15-16
dealing with problems of, 14
hiring of, 75-104
management evaluation of, 7-8
meeting new members, 6-7
motivation of, 8, 16-17
Summary report, 60

T

Teamwork
limitations of, 15
sales team, 14-15
Teleconferencing, 185, 261-63
situations for, 262
tips for, 262-63
Telemarketing, 321
Television advertising, 350-51
advantages/disadvantages of, 350-51
cable TV, 351
Termination of employee, 295-99
legal aspects, 295
and probation, 295-96
termination letter, 296-99
Territory balancing, and sales force automation, 362-67
Time-series analysis, sales forecast, 147
Trade shows
cost factors, 266-68, 269
follow-up letter to lead, 278-79
lead cards, 276-78
planning for participation in, 270-73
postshow strategy, 279-80
reasons for participation, 268-69
sales personnel guidelines, 274-76
Training. *See* Sales training
Travel expenses, 132-38
allowances for travel, 132-33
complete reimbursement, 133-34
discretionary payment of, 133
expense control measures, 138
types of expenses, 137-38
Travel schedule, 24, 25
Trust, building of, 399

W

World Wide Web, 199
advertising on, 199

Y

Yellow Pages advertising, 344-46
design of ad, 345-46
goal of, 344
types of ads, 344-45